W9-CIC-364

IAN FLEMING AND SOE'S OPERATION POSTMASTER

By the same author

www.brianlettauthor.com

SAS in Tuscany 1943–45

IAN FLEMING AND SOE'S OPERATION POSTMASTER

The Untold Top Secret Story

Brian Lett

Pen & Sword
MILITARY

First published in Great Britain in 2012
and reprinted in 2013 by
PEN & SWORD MILITARY
an imprint of
Pen and Sword Books Ltd
47 Church Street
Barnsley
South Yorkshire S70 2AS

Copyright © Brian Lett, 2012, 2013

ISBN 978 178159 000 3

The right of Brian Lett to be identified
as the author of this work has been asserted by him in accordance
with the Copyright, Designs and Patents Act 1988.

A CIP record for this book is available from the British Library.

All rights reserved. No part of this book may be reproduced or transmitted
in any form or by any means, electronic or mechanical including
photocopying, recording or by any information storage and retrieval
system, without permission from the Publisher in writing.

Printed and bound by
CPI Group (UK) Ltd, Croydon, CR0 4YY

Typeset in Times New Roman by
Chic Graphics

Pen & Sword Books Ltd incorporates the imprints of
Pen & Sword Aviation, Pen & Sword Family History, Pen & Sword Maritime,
Pen & Sword Military, Pen & Sword Discovery, Wharncliffe Local History,
Wharncliffe True Crime, Wharncliffe Transport, Pen & Sword Select,
Pen & Sword Military Classics, Leo Cooper, Remember When,
The Praetorian Press, Seaforth Publishing and Frontline Publishing

For a complete list of Pen and Sword titles please contact
Pen and Sword Books Limited
47 Church Street, Barnsley, South Yorkshire, S70 2AS, England
E-mail: enquiries@pen-and-sword.co.uk
Website: www.pen-and-sword.co.uk

Author's Note

This is the true story of M's Secret Service, and of his Secret Agents who were 'licensed to kill'. Every event that is described in this book is true. All direct speech is taken from contemporaneous accounts recorded by the participants.

The code names of M and his agents are regularly used throughout this book. They are taken from the written records made at the time. For ease of reference, their real names are listed here:

W.01	Captain Gustavus March-Phillipps
W.02	Lieutenant Geoffrey Appleyard
W.03	Lieutenant Graham Hayes
M	Brigadier Colin McVean Gubbins
Caesar	Lieutenant Colonel Julius Hanau
W	Lieutenant Colonel Louis Franck
W4	Major Victor Laversuch
W10	Lieutenant C.A. Leonard Guise
W25	Captain Richard Lippett
W30	Captain Desmond E. Longe
W39	Major L.H. Dismore
W51	B. Godden
W53	Peter Ivan Lake

For Julian, Robin, Stephanie and Toby

Contents

List of Illustrations

CHAPTER 1

10 January 1942

On the morning of 10 January 1942, M sent a telegram to agent W.01 from his office at 64 Baker Street, the 'large grey building near Regent's Park' as Ian Fleming was later to call it in his James Bond novels. For all M knew, the telegram might be the last communication that he would ever have with agent W.01. It read:

> Good hunting. Am confident you will exercise utmost care to ensure success and obviate repercussions. Best of luck to you and all MH and others. M.

In the early hours of the following day, W.01 and his Maid Honor Force (the MH in the telegram) were due to leave Lagos, Nigeria, to embark upon the most daring wartime operation yet mounted by M's Secret Service, the Special Operations Executive (SOE). It was intended as a totally 'deniable' operation, but in reality if it went wrong, or if any member of Maid Honor Force was captured, the repercussions at international level were likely to be very damaging. Failure and exposure might even persuade Spain and other neutral countries to enter the war alongside the Axis powers, Germany and Italy. M's team, with the assistance of Commander Ian Fleming and Admiralty Intelligence, had of course prepared a cover story against each eventuality, success or failure, but if anything like the truth came out the stories would achieve little.

It was because of this risk, and because of the difficulty of the operation itself, that 'Operation Postmaster' had been so long in the planning. M had been looking at the intended targets of the raid, two enemy ships moored in the neutral port of Santa Isabel in West Africa, for over a year. Maid Honor Force itself had been set up in the late spring of 1941, when M already had the possibility of a raid on Santa Isabel in mind. But it had taken very considerable efforts by M and Louis Franck, his head of station in Lagos, West Africa (known as W), and by Commander Ian Fleming, to persuade the Admiralty and the Foreign Office to give their consent. Indeed, full consent had only finally been forthcoming at the very end of December 1941. Eventually, M had been so short of time that even now, as he sent his final telegram to Agent W.01 and the Maid Honor Force, he still did not know all of those who were to form the complement of men that would take part in Operation Postmaster.

M had complete confidence in the carefully selected secret commando agents who made up the central element that was Maid Honor Force. There were eleven of them. Captain Gus March-Phillipps, their commander (now known as W.01), was an agent whom M had personally selected for his Secret Service a year before. The second-in-command, Lieutenant Geoffrey Appleyard, W.02, had also been personally selected by M. The other nine commando agents on Operation Postmaster had all been hand-picked by their officers.

Other SOE secret agents were to take part in the operation, but only the commando agents with the code prefix '0'were specifically trained in the dark arts of killing, and in particular, silent killing. These were the agents to whom Ian Fleming was later to give the code prefix '00' in his Bond books, coining the phrase that became famous, 'licensed to kill'.

Once M had sent his telegram, there was nothing more he could do but wait. Major Victor Laversuch, Agent W4, who was in command of M's Secret Service unit in Lagos in the absence of W, would pass on the message to March-Phillipps, but once Maid Honor Force had set sail in the early hours of 11 January, they would be out of contact until after Operation Postmaster had been completed five days later. Radio silence was imperative.

M's anxiety showed in his telegram. He had many agents in many parts of the world, but Operation Postmaster might well prove to be a 'make or break' operation for his Secret Service, the SOE. Notwithstanding that SOE had been the brainchild of Prime Minister Winston Churchill himself in the dark summer of 1940, it remained unpopular with all three of the regular Armed Services, and had yet to prove itself. If Operation Postmaster was successful, it would be a tremendous coup for SOE, and their future independence as a Secret Service would be assured. Should it turn out to be a costly and messy failure, however, then SOE's future would be bleak. Even though M was not technically the overall boss of SOE in January 1942 (he was promoted in the following year), he was Director of Operations and Training, and his head would be on the block should things go badly wrong.

Many others who had been involved in the planning of Operation Postmaster but were not going on the operation itself also waited anxiously. In West Africa, SOE's Major Laversuch, Agent W4, was busying himself with last minute arrangements, but he would then remain in Lagos to organize things there, and would not sail with Maid Honor Force. Admiral Willis, the Navy's Commander in Chief, South Atlantic, and General Giffard, the Army's General Officer Commanding, West Africa, both of whom had been opposed to Operation Postmaster, together with the Governor of Nigeria, Sir Bernard Bourdillon, who had been supportive, also waited in Lagos.

Others waited in London. Julius Hanau, code name Caesar, was M's deputy in relation to Operation Postmaster. He waited at Baker Street. Prime Minister Churchill and his War Cabinet had been briefed. In particular, Foreign Minister Anthony Eden waited to see what his own future would hold, and what lies he would have to tell the Spanish Ambassador in due course. Commander Ian Fleming, at the Admiralty, waited to see which cover story it would be necessary to deploy.

Somewhere between London and New York was W, who as the head of SOE's West Africa Section had been a major architect of the plan for Operation Postmaster. He had come to London to help obtain the necessary authority for Postmaster to go ahead, and was now on leave, visiting his family on Long Island, New York. He would later be formally assigned to the United States of America, to aid and advise their embryonic equivalent of the SOE, the Office for Strategic Studies (known as the OSS, and after the war becoming the CIA, in time for Ian Fleming to enlist their cooperation for James Bond). Relations between SOE and the OSS were particularly good in the early days – as they were always shown to be between the CIA and Fleming's Secret Service in the Bond stories. But on the morning of 10 January 1942, what was developing was fact not fiction.

All depended upon the work of Gus March-Phillipps and his men, and upon the support that it was intended they should receive from the Royal Navy after their operation had been carried out. Having sent off his telegram, M had to leave Operation Postmaster entirely in their hands.

CHAPTER 2

The Beginning

It had all started in the early summer of 1940. The war had been going extremely badly for Great Britain and her allies, as the mighty German military machine flexed its muscles and rolled across Europe. In the face of this blitzkrieg, the British Expeditionary Force (BEF) fell back under heavy attack to the beach and harbour of Dunkirk. By late May, there were hundreds of thousands of Allied troops in the area, on the beach, in the sand dunes or wherever they could find cover, hoping for evacuation by sea back to England. One of them was a young Second Lieutenant of the Royal Army Service Corps (RASC), Geoffrey Appleyard.

Appleyard was a handsome fair-haired young man of twenty-three, a Yorkshireman born in Leeds. His family lived in the Manor House at Linton-on-Wharfe near Wetherby, where he had spent most of his life. They were well off, and his father ran what eventually became the largest motor business in Leeds. Geoffrey himself was schooled at a Quaker school, Bootham in York, and later gained a first class Honours degree in Engineering at Caius College, Cambridge. He was also what can best be described as a 'muscular ornithologist', having won the Natural History Exhibition at Bootham School, and later pursued his interest at Cambridge, where he once hunted for the nesting place of a rare black redstart by climbing across the slippery rooftops of houses in that city in the pouring rain. He was not averse to swinging at the end of a rope on the cliffs of Bempton to collect gulls' eggs from the nest. (It was perhaps no coincidence that Ian Fleming would take the name that he wanted to use for his perfect secret agent, James Bond, from a real-life ornithologist.)

Appleyard's good looks, muscled athlete's physique, and deep-set blue eyes made him always popular with the ladies. He was an accomplished oarsman and expert skier, having represented Cambridge in international competition with considerable success, and captaining English ski teams against Norway in 1938 and 39. He was also skilled at ice hockey and water-skiing. But all that counted for little as he crouched low in his sand hole, surrounded by confusion and chaos. The Germans did not care who or what he was, they just wanted to kill him.

The hell that had resulted from the total defeat of the BEF ebbed and flowed around him. Time and again, the beach was strafed by the German Luftwaffe. There was little or nothing that the fugitive soldiers could do in their own defence, save to try to dig themselves deeper into the sand.

The BEF and its allies had been smashed in a few short weeks of violent combat by the overpowering forces of Nazi Germany. Hitler had been steadily building up the strength of his armed forces for a number of years. They were extremely well trained and very well equipped. In contrast, the BEF contained many half-trained soldiers, and much outdated equipment. Hopelessly outmanoeuvred and outfought, thc BEF had fallen back on Dunkirk in the hope of evacuation by sea. For days, many thousands of British soldiers waited on the beach and in the harbour of Dunkirk, pummelled hour after hour from the air by German planes. Many were wounded, most were demoralized. The soldiers found cover wherever they could, digging down into the beach like animals at bay.

Geoffrey Appleyard had been with the BEF in France for a number of months. His comrades in arms described him as combining a flair for organization and planning with superb skill in action, and a unique ability to instil confidence in time of danger. Appleyard's attitude to war, as articulated to a friend, was a simple one: 'It is not enough just to do our duty, we must do more than our duty – everything that we can to the absolute limit.' For the time being, however, he crouched like all the others in his sand dugout, simply praying that he would survive long enough to be evacuated, and that his life would not end uselessly on this beach. Ian Fleming would use the character of Appleyard in some aspects of his James Bond, when he created the spy hero more than ten years later. However, in May 1940 the paths of Fleming and Appleyard had yet to cross, and Appleyard could hardly have felt less heroic as he cowered at Dunkirk.

The strafing continued endlessly, and as he crouched face downwards in his hole Appleyard suddenly felt a powerful blow in the back, sending him sprawling. His mouth was filled with sand, and he genuinely believed that at last he had been hit and his end had come. He waited for the acute pain that would surely follow such a wound and for paralysis to spread through his body. But then a voice spoke in his ear, 'I f-f-feel a b-b-bloody coward, how about you?' That voice belonged to Gus March-Phillipps. Looking round, Appleyard discovered that it was not an enemy bullet or shell fragment that had struck him in the back, but a fellow British officer diving for the cover of the sand hole to avoid enemy fire – Lieutenant Gustavus Henry March-Phillipps.

March-Phillipps' comment captured exactly what Appleyard was feeling. After the confidence and optimism with which the BEF had left Britain in the autumn of the previous year, and after the unease of the phoney war that had lasted until the spring, the German blitzkrieg had brought total defeat and humiliation to the British forces in a sickeningly short time. Appleyard and March-Phillipps were proud men and both detested the situation they now found themselves in. Common sense told them, of course, that it was better to live to fight another day, and that their country sorely needed them to survive, but it felt very 'un-British' to cower thus for hour after hour, unable to fight back, in the hope of rescue. They knew, also, that others of their comrades were still fighting on in a desperate rearguard action to make an evacuation possible.

Gustavus March-Phillipps, at thirty-two years of age, was nine years older than Appleyard, a significant age difference. He was a romantic, and in many ways a very old-fashioned soldier. He looked to the heroes of old like Drake, Raleigh and Robert the Bruce, to inspire the British Army with the spirit to defend itself against the German onslaught. A practising Roman Catholic, he believed fervently in God (as did Geoffrey Appleyard), followed closely by King and Country. He had been commissioned into the Royal Artillery at the age of twenty, and had served for a number of years in India, rising to the rank of lieutenant. He saw action on the North West Frontier, but by January of 1932 he found himself stuck with 23 Field Battery in the garrison town of Meerut, involved in an endless round of ceremonial and social duties.

March-Phillipps had no time for pomp, circumstance and red tape. He became disillusioned with army life and by October 1932 had resigned his commission and returned to Dorset, where the family home was the eighteenth-century Eastway House, in Blandford Forum. Then aged twenty-four, for some years March-Phillipps led the life of a country gentleman. He wrote and had published three novels: *Sporting Print*, *Storm in a Teacup*, and *Ace High*, in which he demonstrated a clear understanding of human nature, and all three were well received.

March-Phillipps was slender and lightly framed, of medium height with dark, slightly receding hair and piercing eyes. He was obsessed by physical fitness, and every ounce of his fighting weight was tight as whipcord. He resembled a greyhound rather than a bulldog. He was described by the ladies as handsome, but had been bitten in the mouth by a horse when a youngster, which had left him with a slight deformation and scarring of his top lip. He covered this with a moustache. He was an accomplished horseman, and had at one time been on the staff of the Dorset Hunt. He had a love of the English countryside and wildlife and, like Appleyard, was an ornithologist. He suffered from a slight stammer, but never allowed it to impede him in anything that he wished to say or do. Indeed, his friends suggested that he turned his stammer into an offensive weapon. He had a fiery but short-lived temper, though in battle he was always calm and in control. He had the inspiration to conceive great enterprises and the skill and daring to carry them out. A natural leader of men, his sense of fairness towards subordinates inspired great loyalty. Many of these qualities Ian Fleming was to take from March-Phillipps, whom he undoubtedly envied, to mould into his James Bond persona.

There was another aspect of Gus March-Phillipps' character that undoubtedly endeared him to Fleming – he loved fine cars. In 1940, March-Phillipps owned and drove a Vauxhall Velox 30/98 Tourer, one of the great sporting cars of its time. It was a huge beast, with a 4,224 cc engine, capable of considerable speed. The Velox 30/98 had first been manufactured in 1913, and the last one was built in 1927. Thus, by 1940, March-Phillipps' Velox 30/98 must have been at least thirteen years old, already something of a vintage machine. The Velox 30/98's natural rival on the British roads was the 4.5 litre Bentley, which had a slightly larger engine and had done well in the celebrated Le Mans races. However, experts claimed that the Velox 30/98 was in fact the faster of the two cars. It is highly likely that at some stage during their acquaintance, Gus March-Phillipps took Ian Fleming for a ride in his Velox, always supposing that between them they found enough petrol for it in war-torn Britain.

When Ian Fleming created Bond in the early 1950s (*Casino Royale*, 1953), he gave him, like Gus March-Phillipps, a vintage sports car. It was not in fact the Velox 30/98, which was by then in very short supply, but one of the last 4.5 litre Bentleys, which Bond had apparently acquired before the war in 1933, when it was 'almost new' (the last 4.5 was built in 1931). Bond drives his Bentley throughout the early novels. It wasn't until the 1960s, when the films began, that Bond's favoured car was updated to the now famous Aston Martin.

The outbreak of hostilities brought March-Phillipps out of country life, back into the army, and off to France in 1939. He served as a staff officer in General Brook's headquarters during the retreat of the BEF from France and the Battle of Dunkirk. He distinguished himself, and was later awarded the MBE. But like Appleyard, on the beach at Dunkirk, he ended up no more than a fugitive, hiding in a sand hole.

Over the hours that followed March-Phillipps' sudden arrival on top of Appleyard, the two men talked. In some ways they found they were very alike, despite the age disparity; in other ways they were very different. But, as sometimes happens in adversity, a bond was forged between them as they sheltered there together. That bond was to become a vital factor in their service as secret agents, and M came eventually to regard them as an indivisible unit, a formidable two-man team.

As they waited for evacuation, both men expressed their determination that if they ever got back to England they would never again allow their homeland to suffer such ignominy and defeat – they would die in their efforts to prevent it. Both desperately wanted the opportunity to fight back in whatever way possible. In due course, under the guidance of M, that desire was to be amply fulfilled.

The accidental meeting of March-Phillipps and Appleyard at Dunkirk was to prove fortuitous, and of undoubted benefit to the England that each loved so much. No doubt both men believed that it was the hand of God that caused March-Phillipps to dive into the particular sand hole that contained Geoffrey Appleyard, thereby bringing the two men together. However, on the beach at Dunkirk, neither could look into the future and foretell that they would live to fight back against the enemy together, halfway round the world, on Operation Postmaster.

Eventually, both March-Phillipps and Appleyard were among the hundreds of thousands of servicemen successfully evacuated from Dunkirk. The destroyer that brought Appleyard safely back to England returned at once to Dunkirk, where it was sunk the next day by enemy action.

A number of others who were to join them in the Maid Honor Force had also suffered on the beach and in the harbour of Dunkirk, before eventual evacuation to England. It gave them all the same strong desire to fight back.

CHAPTER 3

Preparing the Fightback: June to December 1940

Back in England, once the euphoria of rescue from Dunkirk had worn off, the future looked pretty bleak for March-Phillipps, Appleyard and their countrymen. The summer of 1940 was a dark time for Great Britain and her Empire. The BEF had been contemptuously thrown from mainland Europe by the Nazis. Those who had fought with the BEF knew what an awesome military machine the Germans had. Operation Dynamo, as the 'miracle of the little ships' was officially known, had enabled the evacuation of over 300,000 troops from Dunkirk to England, but an enormous amount of equipment had been lost, and many men had been left behind, either dead or as prisoners. Although referred to as a miracle, Dunkirk was in reality a military disaster of epic proportions, with British Forces driven from mainland Europe by far superior German forces, retreating to lick their wounds in Britain. By 4 June, the evacuation from Dunkirk was over. The people and government of Britain and its Empire, and the whole of the rest of the world, waited for Hitler's inevitable assault upon their homeland.

On 10 June 1940, Mussolini's Italy entered the war on Germany's side. Together they became known as the Axis powers.

Things got worse when France capitulated. On 10 July, the French decided there was no future in seeking to further resist German military might, and a vote by their National Assembly installed the World War One hero, Marshal Philippe Petain, as Prime Minister and Chief of the French State. What became known as the Vichy Government of France was set up. The north of the country was already in German hands, but Petain and his Vichy Government sued for peace in the remainder, on the basis that they would collaborate with Nazi Germany. The Germans agreed. The administrative centre of the French Government was then established at Vichy, and it was allowed to run itself as a so-called 'free state', provided that it did what it was told to do by the Germans. Northern France remained occupied by German forces. Happily, there were many French people who disagreed with Petain's approach. Some of those hostile to Vichy France did their best to escape to Britain in order to take up arms against Hitler. They became known as the Free French, and Charles de Gaulle in due course became their leader.

The effect of the French capitulation was not confined to Great Britain and Europe. In West Africa, the situation was also of very real concern. The colonies of French West Africa and French Equatorial Africa were vast, surrounding the British colonies of Sierra Leone, the Gold Coast, the Gambia, Nigeria and British Cameroon. These substantial French colonies nominally fell under Vichy pro-Nazi rule as soon as Petain and his administration came into being, and the British West African colonies therefore immediately found themselves with potentially hostile territories on all sides.

However, as in Europe, many French citizens in the African colonies did not agree with the Petain government. Some of the colonies, including importantly French Equatorial Africa and French Cameroon, became, with British encouragement and support, Free French Territories. From there, at least, the threat was removed. Still, Nigeria, Sierra Leone, the Gambia and the Gold Coast all remained vulnerable. The Gambia, with its capital at Bathhurst, was completely surrounded by Vichy French Senegal and Sudan, and at Dakar, in Senegal, was the seat of Vichy French Government of West Africa under the rabid anti-British General du Bresson. Sierra Leone, with its vital natural harbour at Freetown, was all but completely surrounded by Vichy French Guinea, and neutral Liberia. The Gold Coast (now Ghana and Togoland) was completely surrounded by enemy Vichy French territory, the Ivory Coast, Upper Volta and Dahomey. British Nigeria, with its important capital and seat of government at Lagos, had Vichy French Niger and Chad to its north, and Free French and British Cameroon to its south.

Activity by German submarine U-boats off the coast of West Africa became so bad by early 1941 that convoys from Great Britain had to be re-routed. Rather than travel down the West African coast in what had been an eleven-day voyage, many convoys were now sent across the North Atlantic to Greenland, to Halifax in Canada, then down the coast of the Americas to Pernambuco in Brazil, before heading across the South Atlantic to Freetown or Lagos, turning the voyage into one lasting six weeks. By this time, also, the Mediterranean was a perilous area for Allied shipping. With the North African campaign in full swing, fighter aircraft were needed against the forces of Germany's Field Marshal Rommel. The aircraft frames and parts were shipped to the Gold Coast port of Takoradi, assembled there and then flown up to North Africa. Thus, the threat in West Africa was not just to the colonies themselves, but also to the convoys arriving there, or passing by. These convoys were of the greatest importance to the survival of beleaguered Britain, and were obvious targets for enemy attack. The security of the Gulf of Guinea and the West African convoy routes had to be protected.

Further, the potential threat to the British in West Africa in the summer of 1940 was not limited to the French and Germans. With Italy joining the war on Germany's side, and France capitulating, the question arose as to how the other neutral European countries that held colonies in West Africa would react.

In Spain, General Franco's Falangist Party government was very right wing. During the recent Spanish civil war, Franco had been supported by both the German and the Italian military. Although it was appreciated that Franco did not want to embroil himself in an international war so soon after he had finally gained control of his own country, it was believed that Spain was entirely sympathetic to the Nazi cause.

Neighbouring Portugal, a traditional ally of Great Britain, now laboured under the dictator Salasar, and, although she remained officially neutral, it was feared that Portugal, like Spain, favoured Nazi Germany. Should Spain and Portugal choose to join the war on Germany's side, or should Germany's storm troopers sweep into those countries against token resistance, then the fear was that the Mediterranean could be completely closed to British shipping, causing Britain's position to become truly hopeless, and defeat only a matter of time.

In West Africa, the colony of Spanish Guinea lay in the Gulf of Guinea. The Spanish colony was small, but comprised a number of islands, the biggest of which was Fernando Po, and a mainland territory called Rio Muni. Today, these territories make up the oil-rich state of Equatorial Guinea, but in 1940 the oil had not yet been discovered and they consisted mainly of plantations producing coffee, cocoa and bananas. Fernando Po had a natural harbour at Santa Isabel, only a few miles from the mainland British colonies of Cameroon and Nigeria. The Portuguese owned Portuguese Guinea and Angola, another potential threat should Portugal decided to throw in her lot with Germany.

The capitulation of France to Nazi Germany was therefore a dramatic change not only in Europe, but also in Africa. Until the summer of 1940, British West Africa had relaxed in the knowledge that she had only allied or neutral countries nearby. That now changed. Many of the expatriate European community, who had felt far removed from the European conflict, now realized that the war had potentially arrived on their doorstep and their previously secure border was threatened.

Winston Churchill and his War Cabinet in London were alert to the danger, particularly from Vichy France. However, following the evacuation from Dunkirk, the overriding priority for Britain was obviously its own defence. Hundreds of thousands of men were now back on home ground. They had to be re-equipped and trained to resist the inevitable German invasion. Most importantly, their low morale, always a product of a heavy defeat, had somehow to be boosted.

For the likes of March-Phillipps and Appleyard there was no problem of low morale. However bleak the prospects, for such men the urge to fight back remained overwhelming. As soon as he was back on British soil March-Phillipps, in particular, began to plan for the future. In fact, neither March-Phillipps nor Appleyard would have to wait long before events took an exciting turn. One of the many military problems Britain now faced was that the evacuation from Europe meant day-to-day intelligence on enemy activity had become far harder to obtain. When in regular armed contact with enemy troops the opportunities to obtain intelligence from captured soldiers and documents had been considerable. By retreating to its island fortress, however, Britain had lost that source of intelligence.

Great Britain's recently appointed Prime Minister, Winston Churchill, and his War Cabinet, sought to compensate as best they could. The Dunkirk evacuation officially ended on 4 June and within days Churchill had approved the setting up of special military units for raids on enemy territory. The units were speedily formed, and were named 'Commandos'. Churchill remembered well the effectiveness of the Boer Commandos during the Boer War – mobile units that attacked with speed and surprise and then melted away into the countryside. Apart from the wish to gain valuable intelligence Churchill also wanted to show that Great Britain was not down and out, but could still strike back against its enemy, even if only in a relatively modest way. Such raids would help to restore the morale of the country as a whole, and would show Hitler that Great Britain still had the will to resist.

Thus while the Battle of Britain raged in the air, an increasing number of Commando units trained hard to prepare for a return to Europe. Winston Churchill wanted 'hunter troops' for a 'butcher and bolt' reign of terror on the enemy coast. It was the sort of work that March-Phillipps and Appleyard longed for.

March-Phillipps, having been on the staff of the BEF, was well connected with many officers of influence at Command level. With his burning desire to fight back, he made sure that he was one of those appointed to join the earliest Commando units. In July 1940, within only a few weeks of returning from Dunkirk and now an acting Captain, March-Phillipps became the Troop Commander of B Troop, No. 7 Commando. Once appointed, he lost no time in letting Appleyard know of his new position, and in inviting him too to volunteer for the Commandos. Appleyard immediately did so, and March-Phillipps appointed him as one of his two Section Leaders. With the job came immediate promotion for Appleyard to First Lieutenant. Thus, within a very short time of sharing their sand hole, the two men were officially working together on the formation and training of a force with which they could strike back against the Germans.

Appleyard was delighted with his new unit. He wrote home:

> It is the grandest job in the Army that one could possibly get, and is a job that, if carried out properly, can be of enormous value… No red tabs, no paper work, none of all the things that are so cramping and infuriating and disheartening that there are in the army. Just pure operations, the success of which depends principally on oneself and the men one has oneself picked to do the job with you. It's terrific! It's revolutionary, and one can hardly imagine it happening in this old Army of ours.

James Bond would have agreed with every word. He too hated bureaucracy and red tape. However, unhappily for March-Phillipps and Appleyard, as we shall see some senior officers in Britain's 'old Army' were not to share Appleyard's view.

The first of the Commando raids took place on the night of 23/24 June on a stretch of the Boulogne–Le Touquet coastline. Little was achieved, but at least the counter-offensive action had started. The system adopted by the Commandos was that every unit would be divided into a number of Troops, each of fifty officers and men. A Troop Commander for each would be appointed, and he would be allowed to choose his own two junior officers from amongst any volunteers (as March-Phillipps had done with Appleyard).

The Troop's officers would then choose their other ranks from amongst volunteers throughout the Area Command, providing of course that the commanding officer of the man's unit agreed to release him. They would travel around visiting other military units, interviewing volunteers and selecting their men. Often, the officers would target particular men with whom they had fought in the BEF, whose qualities they rated highly, and would try to persuade their current unit to let them go.

Where Appleyard or March-Phillipps wanted a man that they knew and trusted, they would ask him to volunteer, then select him. Appleyard brought in Corporal Leslie Prout, with whom he had fought in France, and who had been on the beach at Dunkirk. Other men of known quality were recruited in the same way. By the beginning of August, March-Phillipps had his Troop in place. He had used his contacts well. He undoubtedly possessed the valuable knack of getting his own way with his superiors, and of obtaining the men and equipment that he wanted, by regular or irregular means. Like James Bond, Gus March-Phillipps had a contempt for pen-pushers and red tape, and would disregard them with alacrity when he thought he could get away with it. It enabled him then, and again later in his career, to put together a very effective fighting force. As one of his later 'volunteers' Company Sergeant Major Tom Winter commented, 'If Gus wanted a man, then Gus got that man.'

At the start, March-Phillipps' B Troop was no more than a 'normal' commando unit. It was an elite force, but trained initially in the same way as the other recently formed commando troops were training – almost all were new to this form of warfare. By the beginning of August 1940 B Troop was lodged in a large house in Newmarket. There were fifty men all told. Their training began immediately, with a heavy emphasis on physical fitness. They had little transport, although March-Phillipps had brought his Vauxhall Velox 30/98 with him to Newmarket, to the delight of Appleyard, who described it as 'terrific'. Appleyard's father had established the family's car dealing business in 1919, and Appleyard himself was something of an expert on motor cars. His younger brother Ian, who survived the war, became one of Britain's leading rally drivers (he retired in 1953) – a profession that would have suited James Bond had he not joined the Secret Service, judging by the way that he drove his 4.5 litre Bentley. Despite March-Phillipps' fine car, if B Troop had to travel somewhere they walked, officers included.

Appleyard found March-Phillipps to be an inspiring leader, and described the ethos of the Troop in a letter home to his parents dated 1 August 1940: 'It isn't a spirit of safety first, but it's a spirit of adventure, of giving instead of getting, of clean living and physical comradeship and unity, and above all it's God's spirit, of that I am sure.'

Physical fitness was the major part of the Troop's training at every stage. March-Phillipps demanded the highest level of commitment in this regard. Appleyard's description of a typical day's training in Newmarket was as follows:

06.30 Reveille
07.00 Run (about a mile) followed by physical training
08.00 Breakfast
09.00 Parade, inspection, followed by a route march of eight to ten miles in full kit with arms, including cross-country work, map reading, compass work, moving through cover etc
13.00 Lunch
14.30 Swimming parade for swimming, running exercising
16.30 Tea
17.00 Lecture by March-Phillipps
18.00 Free

They also did plenty of work at night – map-reading and compass work in the dark in areas of the country that they did not know. As they achieved greater fitness, so the intensity of the training increased, becoming ever harder.

March-Phillipps continued to recruit men whom he felt could contribute to his objectives with B Troop. His methods were often irregular. One day while out riding in Newmarket he recruited the one-eyed Jan Nasmyth, a graduate of Balliol College Oxford. Nasmyth had lost an eye in a boyhood shooting accident, and had initially been rejected by the army as unfit for service. With the help of the Balliol College careers office, he eventually got into Field Security, who sent him to France with a motorcycle and the rank of sergeant, to search for German saboteurs. He was wounded at Dunkirk whilst awaiting evacuation. When they met, Nasmyth was on foot and March-Phillipps was on horseback in company with a young lady. That did not prevent March-Phillipps from holding an impromptu interview. Nasmyth described it as follows:

> I said that I had only one eye and asked if that mattered. He said: 'Do you ride a horse – and can you judge a distance from a fence when you are going to jump it?' I said that I thought so, and he said: 'That's all right then. You'll do.'

Thus was Jan Nasmyth, once regarded as unfit for military service, recruited into No.7 Commando.

In the autumn of 1940 the Troop moved to a secret commando training centre on the island of Arran, off the west coast of Scotland. There, March-Phillipps continued to put his own individual stamp upon B Troop. The billet for the men was a disused hotel, which had never opened in the winter months and had little by way of the usual comforts. There was no electricity, no hot water, and no furniture other than tables and chairs. In the Scottish winter, the conditions were Spartan in the extreme. The commandos slept on the floor, and the only light they had at night came from candles and small oil lamps they had brought with them. The officers had had billets reserved for them in neighbouring houses, which offered considerably more comfort but, typically, March-Phillipps turned these down and the officers camped in the old hotel with their men. Appleyard described sleeping on the floor with six blankets (of which happily they had an adequate supply) – two blankets beneath him, and four above. Eventually, he had the luxury of a camp bed. The hotel was almost cosy, however, after a day's training. March-Phillipps took his men on lengthy marches in all weathers over the Highland countryside, on occasions sleeping in ditches overnight. It was all a part of a hardening up and bonding process which would stand them in good stead later. Since March-Phillipps and his officers shared everything with their men, there was no resentment in the Troop at what he asked them to do. They were all in it together.

All commando units in training on the Isle of Arran were encouraged to use the boats available, since in due course they would almost inevitably carry out attacks by sea. March-Phillipps saw the potential of a specialist unit skilled in the handling of small raiding craft, and decided to train his men specifically for that purpose. Characteristically acting entirely on his own initiative, March-Phillipps decided that B Troop should acquire its own boat. Rather than going through the lengthy and tiresome process of obtaining permission to requisition such a craft, March-Phillipps simply went out and bought one a few days before Christmas of 1940. (Bond would no doubt have done exactly the same.)

The *I'm Alone* was a 32ft long, 5½ ton, yawl-rigged fishing boat, with a 15hp auxiliary engine. March-Phillipps bought her from a local fisherman, who was then serving with the Royal Navy, for the sum of £35. In order to raise the necessary funds all members of the Troop were levied, contributing between ten shillings (50p) and one pound each. Such was the respect in which March-Phillipps was held by his men that nobody protested, and the money was quickly collected. B Troop was already bonded into a close team, where each man trusted his comrades, and accepted the leadership of March-Phillipps without question. It was the bond that he was able to build between his men and himself that was March-Phillipps' greatest gift.

Once the *I'm Alone* had been purchased, March-Phillipps set his men to work on the boat, adapting her to their needs and giving her a general overhaul, which included a new mast that they made themselves from a pine tree. The boat proved very seaworthy and Appleyard described her in a letter home as 'a magnificent dirty weather craft'. She became an integral part of their training routine. March-Phillipps would work his Troop out at sea in the *I'm Alone* in all weathers, until they came to know her intimately. At the same time, the landbased physical training continued relentlessly – March-Phillipps was deliberately hardening his men up, preparing them for what he hoped was to come.

As 1940 turned into 1941 in the bleak west of Scotland winter, March-Phillipps was laying the foundation for what would become a unique Commando force. His good work was soon to come to the notice of M and 1941 was to bring him a significant change of status.

CHAPTER 4

M and Ian Fleming

M, at the time of Dunkirk, was serving in Norway, fighting a losing guerrilla war against the German occupying forces there. The real M, whose codename Ian Fleming was later to borrow for the controller of his own secret agent, was a short wiry Scottish Highlander, Brigadier (later Major General Sir) Colin McVean Gubbins MC.

In the early Bond books, when the Second World War was still very recent, Fleming was gagged to a significant extent by the Official Secrets Act and gave little clue as to the background of James Bond's spymaster, M, or indeed Bond himself. However, as the years went by, Fleming let it be known that M was a Scot. In *For Your Eyes Only* (1960), Fleming comments, through Bond, upon M's exaggerated faith in Scotsmen. Later still, in *You Only Live Twice*, published in 1964, the year of Fleming's death, Bond is amused by M's use of an old Scottish expression, 'in fief to' ('in thrall to').

Colin Gubbins was born in Japan in 1896, the son of a diplomat and expert linguist, John Harrington Gubbins. John Gubbins was in fact an Englishman of Irish extraction, but his wife, Colin's mother, was a Highland Scot, and to all intents and purposes Gubbins grew up as a Scot. He spent much of his early life living with his grandparents on the Isle of Mull, while his father and mother were still serving in Japan. He was schooled at Cheltenham College, which he did not particularly enjoy, and attended the Royal Military Academy, Woolwich. He was commissioned into the Royal Artillery at the start of the First World War, saw active service throughout that war in the mud of France and Flanders, and took part in the Battle of the Somme. He was awarded a Military Cross for conspicuous gallantry: 'When one of his guns and its detachment were blown up by a heavy shell, he organized a rescue party and personally helped to dig out the wounded while shells were falling all round.' On 7 October 1916, Gubbins suffered a gunshot wound to the neck, and was hospitalized for eleven days. In November 1917, he was gassed by mustard gas near Arras, but happily recovered. In April 1918, he was shipped home, sick with trench fever. Again, Gubbins fought back and survived. He remained a regular soldier after that war, saw service in Northern Russia in 1919, and was serving in Ireland during the insurrection of 1921–22.

Later, Gubbins served on the General Staff at British Army HQ in India during a time of riots and civil disobedience. He was then sent to the Staff College at Camberley, and from there to a Military Intelligence role at the War Office, where he spent a number of years. Between the wars he became an excellent linguist, passing interpreter's exams in French, Russian and Urdu.

In January 1939, with war looming, Gubbins was recuited into a small section in the War Office known as General Staff (Research). His brief there was to study the concept of guerrilla warfare, and he drafted three secret pamphlets designed for fighting a guerrilla war. They were entitled: 'The Art of Guerilla Warfare', 'The Partisan Leader's Handbook' and 'How to Use High Explosives'. When war finally broke out, Gubbins was posted to Warsaw as Head of Intelligence with General de Wiart, but within days of his arrival, the Germans reduced that city to ashes and Gubbins was forced to make a daring escape through Hungary and the Balkans. In 1940, he was sent to the defence of Norway, again under General de Wiart's command. Gubbins was tasked to set up and command the 'Striking Companies', an early version of the Commandos. With these, he fought a guerrilla war delaying the advance of German forces towards Narvik. He blew bridges, mined roads and set fire to forests, often working with local Norwegian civilians, before eventually ex-filtrating, as Norway inevitably fell to the might of Nazi Germany. There, he too had suffered the ignominy of defeat.

When the Special Operations Executive was set up in July 1940 as part of Churchill and the British War Cabinet's response to Dunkirk, Hugh Dalton, the Minister of Economic Warfare, was given control over it. In November 1940, after something of a battle with the War Office, who did not want to let Gubbins go, Dalton secured his services for SOE. Initially Gubbins was appointed SOE's Director of Operations and Training (known as M). Later, in 1943, he became the Executive Head of the whole of SOE (known as CD). Gubbins was still serving as CD when the war came to an end, and remained with SOE until it was dissolved in January 1946. Both of his predecessors as CD wrote to him after they had left the job, Sir Frank Nelson saying in May 1942: 'Thank you for your ever genial, calm and brilliant help and support which you have so freely given me over the last 18 months' and Charles Hambro saying in September 1943 (when Gubbins was appointed as his successor): 'There is no one who has so much right to be where you are today, and if anyone can ensure dividends and success it is you… what a wonderful support you have always been to me… how much I admired your work. You provided all those qualities that I lacked… I would happily come and work under you.'

Gubbins was much loved and admired by his superiors and subordinates alike. He was a man James Bond would have enjoyed working for as much as the men of Maid Honor Force did. A typical comment comes from a young and beautiful actress who was recruited into SOE as a secretary in August 1941, Marjorie Stewart – she described Gubbins as bursting with energy, vitality and strength. Talking of the hard work and achievements of SOE, she said: 'Everytime, you come back to M as the most fantastic activating and motivating spirit, with a fantastic capacity for work, great at galvanising everyone who worked for him.'

After Gubbins' experiences in Norway, where he had seen the power of Hitler's invading armies too often at close quarters, Gubbins was the ideal man to take charge of the operations and training of SOE, Britain's new secret army. He joined them at their headquarters, 64 Baker Street, in mid-November 1940. The real M was forty-five years of age when he arrived at SOE. He had the great gift of being able, in modern parlance, to 'think outside the box'.

SOE, also known by the cover names of the Inter Services Research Bureau, and SO2, had to work closely with the three established services – the Royal Navy, the Royal Air Force and the Army. It was working with the Navy that brought M and and his Secret Service into contact with Ian Fleming. Fleming could not have been more different to M. He was thirty-one when war broke out, almost exactly the same age as Gus March-Phillipps. He was an old Etonian of good family, but since leaving Eton early, after an affair involving a young lady, Fleming had led a varied and not very successful life. He was undoubtedly charming and talented, but lived to a considerable degree in the shadow of his elder brother Peter. Peter, since his school days at Eton, had outshone Ian. Peter had had a successful school and university career, gaining a First at Oxford, and had married a glamorous actress, Celia Johnson. When war broke out, he joined the Grenadier Guards. In the summer of 1940, Peter was recruited to serve under Colin Gubbins in the highly secret Auxiliary Units that were set up to resist and harass the expected German invasion of Britain from behind whatever became the front line. Once appointed as M, Gubbins swiftly recruited Peter Fleming into SOE. In December 1940, now a Captain in the Grenadier

Guards, Peter was sent to command YAK Mission in Cairo. The object of YAK Mission, an idea of Winston Churchill's, was to recruit and train Italians, Yugoslavs, Greeks and Bulgarians to carry out raids against the enemy, particularly on the Italian coast. When that quickly proved to be impractical due to lack of suitable recruits, Peter Fleming was sent in late March 1941 to Greece before it finally fell to the Germans, to train up units there that might be able to operate behind German lines in Greece and Yugoslavia. In May 1941, Fleming was recalled to London, where he was in due course transferred out of SOE to other secret duties.

Peter Fleming's self-confidence and general success in life is perhaps reflected by the form that he, like all other applicants, had to fill in upon applying to join M's Secret Service. The form covered three pages, and comprised forty-three questions (perhaps modest by modern government standards), designed to discover an applicant's strengths and skills, as well as any weaknesses. Peter Fleming dashed off his answers in pencil, treating the form with a marked degree of contempt. By the time he got to Question 9, which asked the question 'Educated?' (meaning which school), Peter simply scribbled 'Yes'. Question 12 'Have you played games and which? With what degree of skill? Do you still play games?' again got a blunt 'Yes'. To Question 19: 'Appearance [Passport description in original language]' Peter replied, 'Medium'. To Question 25: 'Occupation since 3/9/39?', the reply was: 'War'. By Question 38: 'What are your hobbies?' a frustrated Peter replied sarcastically: 'Filling up forms.' He was accepted by M, who of course already wanted him, without delay.

Before the war Ian Fleming had worked for Reuters, later joined a banking firm in London, and then tried stockbroking. Ian's strengths lay on the social side, and he made a number of useful friends in the Foreign Office and in intelligence. He was formally appointed to be Assistant to the Director of Naval Intelligence, Rear Admiral Godfrey, on 3 September 1939, starting out with the rank of Lieutenant, RNVR. Godfrey, a very experienced Naval Officer, born in 1888 and a First World War veteran, could be a very difficult man at times, and the role of his assistant was therefore an important one. By December 1940 Fleming had risen to the rank of Lieutenant Commander, and by May 1941 he was Commander.

Ian Fleming remained with Godfrey until the latter was moved from his job in November 1942. One of Fleming's tasks in 1941 and early 42 was to liaise with SOE. He would meet SOE's Lieutenant Colonel Taylor every week. However, increasingly M began to liaise with Ian Fleming direct. Apart from the reports of Taylor, general planning meetings, and meetings of the

Directors of Intelligence, M would have private meetings with Fleming in order to smooth out difficulties that arose with the Navy. M's desk diaries for 1941 and 42 still exist and record the dates and times of the meetings, beginning with one on 29 January 1941. At critical times for the Maid Honor Force, or Operation Postmaster, a flurry of meetings with Ian Fleming would appear in the diary. Clearly, by the summer of 1941, Godfrey was quite happy to leave much of the liaison work that was necessary with SOE to Ian Fleming, and Fleming had become something of a troubleshooter between Naval Intelligence and M.

Relations between SOE and Naval Intelligence throughout 1941 were often not good. Admiral Godfrey described them as being 'fraught with countless petty troubles', for which he held SOE responsible. Godfrey reported rather patronizingly in December 1941:

> I have been in conflict with them again and again on one subject or another, and have often been exasperated to the point of despair by some folly, but I am satisfied that the period of education is now almost finished and that very shortly SO2 [SOE] will emerge as a fully fledged organization, quite capable of standing up for itself and doing a sound job of work. This is not to say that they have not been doing a sound job of work in the past, but the need for self-advertisement in order to obtain recognition, and a tendency to boast due to their inferiority complex, has tended to obscure the real value of their work.

Thus Ian Fleming's liaison work between the Navy and SOE was important. It was his job to try to iron out the differences between his boss, Admiral Godfrey, and M and his team. For instance, in July 1941, Fleming was instructed to 'clarify' the situation of an SOE agent called Lieutenant A. Glen RN, who had been posted to Lisbon in neutral Portugal after earlier service in Belgrade. His cover in Lisbon was to be that he was attached to the Naval Attaché there. However, the Naval Attaché in Lisbon (a regular Naval Officer) refused to accept him on his staff, under the pretext that he believed him to have been recognized and compromised by a German agent there. In reality, Glen was very unpopular because whilst in Belgrade he had had an affair with the wife of a member of the Belgian Embassy, and had brought her with him to Lisbon. Shortly after Fleming had been tasked to 'clarify' matters, things were made rather worse by Lieutenant Colonel Taylor of SOE writing to Rear Admiral Godfrey, informing him that SOE wanted to recommend Lieutenant Glen for an award for his work in Belgrade. Thus in various ways Lieutenant Glen became rather a 'hot potato' between SOE and

Naval Intelligence. Fleming had to do his best to pour oil on troubled waters, and clearly did so skilfully.

Fleming came up with his own idea for smoothing future relations between the Admiralty and SOE. He entered into discussions with Lieutenant Colonel Taylor, and with Sir Frank Nelson, the head of SOE (a civilian, whose name itself as the head of an upstart organization probably did not make him any more popular with the Admiralty). On 6 October 1941, Nelson wrote to Godfrey, putting forward Fleming's plan for a better working relationship:

> As has been pointed out to us by Fleming, we think it would also be a convenience for the Admiralty if plans in which they were bound to have an interest, and which would therefore have to pass through their hands, could be drawn in a form and in language which would be familiar to and easily understood by them.
>
> Fleming and Taylor have been discussing this question, and I think that they both feel that the ideal solution would be *the transfer to SOE of an officer RN, of about the rank of Commander* [author's italics], who had worked in the Plans Division at the Admiralty. Our idea would be to appoint this officer as a member of our special planning staff which, under Archie Boyle, directs, supervises and checks all plans for our various operations.

Ian Fleming held the rank of Commander, was heavily involved in intelligence planning, and Nelson's letter to Godfrey strongly suggests that Fleming was hoping that he himself might be appointed full time to SOE – and thereby become one of M's secret agents like his brother Peter. Fleming did not get his wish. Godfrey was short of experienced intelligence officers, and clearly valued Fleming's work too highly to give him away to SOE. For the time being, at least, the status quo was preserved. Godfrey wrote back to Nelson agreeing that greater supervision was necessary, but declining the proposal.

Fleming remained a member of Naval Intelligence under Rear Admiral Godfrey's command, and continued to act as their liaison officer with SOE. He clearly got on well with M and his team, and was trusted by them. Thus when the question arose of the cover story to be used for Operation Postmaster, Fleming was the obvious choice to design it. He continued in his liaison role until the spring of 1942, when in fact a naval section within SOE was finally set up. Fleming was not released to take up a job with them. In his mind, however, he retained an in-depth knowledge of M's Secret Service and how it all worked, which he eventually came to use in his novels. By 20 March 1942, Commander Ian Fleming was signing himself off on memos and internal correspondence simply as 'F', an affectation no doubt drawn from his desire to serve as a Secret Agent under M.

After the war, Fleming remained on friendly terms with M (now retired from the defunct SOE and simply known as Major General Sir Colin Gubbins). In the late 1940s, when Gubbins was hoping to write a definitive history of the Secret Service that he had run, Fleming wrote twice to encourage him to do so. However, with the Cold War between the old Allies and the Soviet Union in full swing Gubbins was forbidden from writing the book, an attitude by the British Government that did not substantially change until the 1990s, after the collapse of the Soviet Union.

Ian Fleming had left the Navy after the war and had returned to a previous profession, journalism. As his letters to Gubbins demonstrate, he, like many fellow members of the press, wanted the strictures of the Official Secrets Act to be lifted, so that they could write about many of the secrets of the Second World War. They were not lifted, however, and in 1952 Fleming began to write about M's Secret Service in a way that protected him from prosecution – he turned what he knew into fiction, and created his own secret agent, James Bond. The first book, *Casino Royale*, was published in 1953 and a new Bond adventure appeared every year after that until Fleming's death in 1964.

Fleming created his fictional agent at a time when the Second World War was still very recent history, and when many of the real life figures who lay behind James Bond and M's Secret Service were still very much alive, some of them still on the public stage. Fleming was bound by the Official Secrets Act, forbidden to reveal what had actually happened in the field of intelligence during the Second World War. In writing fiction, as he was later to confess, he knew from his time working in intelligence just how much he would be able to get away with. However, at times, as we shall see, Fleming trod a thin line between what he could and could not say. He loved to leave hints in his books about the real Secret Service. He had lived in the world of intelligence and coding throughout the war, and perhaps was deliberately leaving cryptic clues to enable later historians to unravel the facts behind his James Bond fictions once the official embargo was lifted.

One clue is provided more than once by James Bond himself. SOE was the only British Secret Service to be terminated after the war ended. The others, including the Navy's Intelligence Directorate to which Ian Fleming belonged, carried on. When, as he so often did, Fleming's hero got caught and was challenged with being a British Secret Service Agent, Fleming made Bond reply with words such as: 'I thought the Secret Service packed up at the end of the war' – Bond's riposte to Scaramanga in *The Man with the Golden Gun* (1965), and a similar answer to Blofeld in *On Her Majesty's Secret Service* (1964). Such words are the clearest possible reference to the Special Operations Executive, SOE. It was Ian Fleming's fantasy to keep SOE going into the 1950s and 60s, as the perfect vehicle for the perfect agent, James Bond. SOE, in wartime conditions, would when necessary order its agents to commit murder. Assassination was a legitimate tactic and SOE secretly designed its own weapons for its agents, officially described as murder weapons. This provided Ian Fleming with the basis for his term 'licence to kill'.

Another clue, or perhaps just a tease for those in the know, was Fleming's open use of a 'Special Executive'. The Special Operations Executive can now be clearly seen to be the Secret Service for whom Bond worked, albeit that Fleming had continued its life in fiction for many years after it had in fact closed down. Perhaps it was to tease, or perhaps just to leave a clue for posterity, that Ian Fleming was to create and name a rather different Special Executive in his Bond books. This Special Executive worked in opposition to Bond's Secret Service (the Special Operations Executive), and Fleming called it the Special Executive for Revenge, Terrorism, and Extortion – SPECTRE.

However, in 1941 all of this was in the future. The situation then was that Commander Ian Fleming, as he became in May 1941, was working with the real M, and formed a trusted link between M's Secret Service, with its team of 'James Bonds', and the Admiralty. The Admiralty had ultimate control over all sea-borne operations, and as the plans for Operation Postmaster unfolded Fleming's role was to become a vital one.

CHAPTER 5

Becoming Secret Agents

In January 1941, having heard of their activities with No. 7 Commando, M decided that both March-Phillipps and Appleyard were well suited for recruitment into SOE. He was constantly looking for good men to join his growing force of secret agents. At this stage, M had a training role in mind for March-Phillipps. The first step was to obtain clearance from MI5 (Britain's domestic Secret Service) on March-Phillipps' background. This was a check carried out on all potential SOE recruits. Having received a satisfactory answer from MI5 on 23 January, M invited March-Phillipps to 64, Baker Street for interview. Potential recruits were never informed in advance of the real nature of the SOE. They were invited for an interview at what they believed to be the Inter Services Research Bureau (ISRB), and most were simply told that the work involved research and other activities of interest to the three armed services. They would only learn more after they had been offered a place, accepted and been sworn in. Presumably, this applied to March-Phillipps, although with his network of contacts, he may have already known more. The interview, not surprisingly, went well and on 27 January 1941 M formally notified SOE that he had employed March-Phillipps as an instructor for Allied troops. By 5 March, March-Phillipps was officially on the strength of SOE's HQ staff. He was no longer in the British Army (although he retained his Army rank), he was a secret agent. He would eventually become known as Agent W.01.

Geoffrey Appleyard underwent the same recruitment procedure and also did well in interview. M's diary records that on 25 January 1941, Appleyard reported for duty, and he signed the Official Secrets Act on the following day. He was shortly thereafter assigned to a covert mission to France.

It is not necessary here to recount the full history of SOE, but a summary is appropriate to explain the background to the activities of the Maid Honor Force, and the significance of the change of status of March-Phillipps and Appleyard from Commandos to Secret Agents. SOE was not bound by the Army's rules and red tape, it was a covert organization of irregulars, supported by a sophisticated gadgets and 'dirty tricks' department. Officially SOE did not exist, and it operated on a strict 'need to know' basis, both in its relations with the three Armed Services, and within its own ranks.

On 1 July 1940, in the aftermath of Dunkirk, a secret high-level meeting took place at the Foreign Office, which resulted in the setting up of SOE. Dr Hugh Dalton, the Minister of Economic Warfare, described its purpose in a letter to Lord Halifax:

> We have got to organise movements in enemy-occupied territory comparable to the Sinn Fein movement in Ireland, to the Chinese Guerillas now operating against Japan, to the Spanish irregulars who played a notable part in Wellington's campaign or – and one might as well admit it – to the organisations which the Nazis themselves have developed so remarkably in almost every country in the world. This 'democratic international' must use many different methods, including industrial and military sabotage, labour agitation and strikes, continuous propaganda, terrorist acts against traitors and German leaders, boycotts and riots.
>
> It is quite clear to me that an organisation on this scale and of this character is not something that can be handled by the ordinary departmental machinery of either the British Civil Service or the British military machine. What is needed is a new organisation to co-ordinate, inspire, control and assist the nationals of the oppressed countries who must themselves be the direct participants. We need absolute secrecy, a certain fanatical enthusiasm, willingness to work with people of different nationalities, complete political reliability. Certain of these qualities are certain to be found in some military officers and, if such men are available, they should undoubtedly be used. But the organisation should, in my view, be entirely independent of the War Office machine.

On 16 July, Churchill sent for Dalton, who was a left-wing Labour old Etonian, and invited him to take ministerial charge of the new organization that was to progress and control the subversive warfare that had been proposed. Dalton agreed. Churchill did not like Dalton, but felt that he was well suited to the job. Dalton appointed Sir Frank Nelson, an industrialist, to be the first head of the new department. Nelson was appointed initially to the rank of Wing Commander, and not long after to Air Commodore. Colin Gubbins was recruited as the first 'M' – Director of Operations and Training.

SOE was a genuinely secret service, whose very existence was a secret, and whose activities were always deniable. The ordinary rules were never intended to apply to SOE. Their secret activities would inevitably involve normally unethical and illegal methods. As agents in the field, they would be expected to lie, deceive, bribe, blackmail and, where it furthered their objective, to kill. An SOE agent's conscience would, where necessary, be subjugated to his or her sense of duty. Further the agent would know that his (or her) activities could never be publicly acknowledged by the government, and that if he was found out, he would be disowned, and probably tortured and shot. Every agent sent into the field was given before his mission what was nicknamed 'communion'. This was a suicide pill that the agent could take if he or she feared that they would break under torture. Fleming was later to supply James Bond with a similar pill, which Bond was in the habit of throwing away.

SOE's role in placing agents behind the lines in enemy occupied countries is now well known, but the true ambit of their activities was far wider than that. SOE established a presence in virtually every neutral country, and conducted a huge number of campaigns against enemy interests. They employed anyone who could prove themselves useful, and their recruits came from many different backgrounds. Ewan Butler, a German expert within SOE, listed the occupations of some of those he knew personally: an eminent young actor, a professional burglar, a man who sold rubber goods in Bucharest, two Peers of the Realm, a sprinkling of baronets, a pimp, two or three prostitutes, a jockey, an art expert, a publisher and several journalists. Many women joined SOE and proved extremely successful agents in the field. All recruitment was done by personal contact and recommendation (as one ex-agent later said, you could hardly advertise for employees for a Secret Service that was not meant to exist).

The very nature of the service that March-Phillipps had now joined was bound to make the hackles of 'old school' military officers rise. Another of SOE's own men, Professor G. H. N. Seton-Watson, a Balkans expert, described SOE as 'an upstart organisation, inevitably viewed with suspicion and jealousy by all existing departments. . . the first recruits were a mixture of widely different types from different places, bankers, business men, mining engineers and journalists. . . Nearly all the earlier recruits lacked the habit of subordination to a regular hierarchy, were disciplined by no mandarin ethos and were impatient or even contemptuous of the bureaucratic conventions of the diplomatic service and its auxiliaries'. Such an ethos was certainly welcome to March-Phillipps and Appleyard, and to the men whom they eventually brought into Maid Honor Force.

As the war progressed, SOE grew in numbers and diversity. They utilized many methods of deception, and invented a whole variety of covert devices and gadgets that would have delighted the 'Q' of the James Bond books. Some of the schemes they developed were ambitious and almost grandiose (like Operation Postmaster itself), others had the simplicity of schoolboy pranks. All were designed, however, to disrupt enemy activity and to damage enemy morale. In occupied countries they also had the objective of boosting the morale of the oppressed local population.

Ewan Butler gives examples of minor operations mounted while he was the Head of Mission in neutral Sweden. Neighbouring Norway was in enemy hands. In the cold northern European winter, greatcoats were essential for the comfort of German officers and soldiers. Butler supplied his agents amongst the local population in Norway with capsules of extremely evil smelling fluid, the equivalent of a schoolboy's stinkbomb. An agent would then slip into the cloakroom of a restaurant or bar frequented by Germans, and with two or three capsules, he or she could impregnate every coat in the room. The smell was so terrible that no German could thereafter bear to wear the overcoat until it had been thoroughly cleaned, which would take a matter of weeks. A shortage of wearable coats resulted and in the depth of winter this obviously caused the Germans appreciable discomfort. An added advantage was that for the agents carrying the capsules, the risks were relatively low. Another such trick was to use catapults to break the windows of buildings occupied or used by German troops. There was a shortage of glass to repair windows in Norway, and in the bitter weather this also caused considerable discomfort to the enemy. SOE also despatched from Sweden a large number of dummy packets of German foodstuffs, covertly to German bases in Denmark and Norway. These in fact contained no food, but detailed instructions to ordinary, discontented German soldiers on how to 'pull a sickie', and get themselves into the comfort of a military hospital. The instructions came with little phials of chemicals which, when properly used, could produce false symptoms for a variety of medical complaints varying from a swollen knee to jaundice or tuberculosis.

In early 1941, when March-Phillipps and Appleyard joined, SOE was still in its infancy, and had yet to establish a broad network of agents. Because it was regarded with great suspicion by many within the regular military, it was in need of successes with which to prove its worth. March-Phillipps and Appleyard intended to bring to SOE just such a success.

CHAPTER 6

Operation Savannah

Geoffrey Appleyard, having reported for duty as a Secret Agent on 25 January 1941, did not have to wait long before going into action. M and SOE had an operation ready to go, in which he would take part. Codenamed Operation Savannah, this was to be the first SOE operation in which agents were dropped by air into France. The objective was to attack a bus carrying German pilots to an airfield at Vannes, killing as many of them as possible and thus crippling, for a short time at least, the German ability to utilize the many aircraft at Vannes against British targets. The agents would be in plain clothes. Appleyard's role would be to assist in the pick up of the agents from the French coast after the operation. SOE's plan was a clear example of all-out 'no holds barred' warfare.

A team of Free French SOE agents was to be dropped by No. 419 Squadron from RAF Stradishall. Planning and training had been completed by the beginning of February, but the plan came to the ears of Air Chief Marshall Sir C. F. A. Portal KCB, DSO, MC. Portal fiercely disliked what he felt was a dishonourable and underhand plan, and wrote on 1 February to the Ministry of Economic Warfare (SOE's controlling ministry) to object:

> I think that the dropping of men dressed in civilian clothes for the purpose of attempting to kill members of the opposing forces is not an operation with which the Royal Air Force should be associated. I think you will agree that there is a vast difference in ethics between the time honoured operation of the dropping of a spy from the air and this entirely new scheme for dropping what one can only call assassins…

Gladwyn Jebb, of the Ministry of Economic Warfare, responded the same day saying:

> Our organisation was definitely asked by the Air Ministry to go ahead with the project, and we have, as a result, devoted much time and thought to it during the past few weeks. Certain very brave men have

> volunteered for the job, even though it is unlikely that they will escape with their lives, and they have gone through a course of intensive training…

Faced by approval at the highest level Portal withdrew his objection. In the event the operation was delayed by the weather and did not take place until the night of 15/16 March, when either five or six agents (reports vary) were successfully dropped into France. Captain Georges Berge was in command of the team, which included Adjutant Jean Forman and Sergeant Joel Letac.

Geoffrey Appleyard had volunteered to lead the small team that would recover survivors from the French coast once the operation was completed. He was joined by two Free Frenchmen, one a Chief Petty Officer with ten years service in the French navy, André Desgranges. Desgranges was a married man, born in Baume les Dames, Franche-Comte in eastern France. Not particularly tall, he was immensely strong and appeared constantly cheerful. He had escaped first of all to Canada after France capitulated, and had then journeyed to England to join the fight against the Nazis. He remained officially a member of the Free French Fighting Forces, but was on loan to SOE. His wife was still in France.

Appleyard and his men would be taken by submarine to a point south of the Loire estuary in the Bay of Biscay. Then each would paddle a two-man Folbot canoe to an agreed point on the French coast, pick up any of the agents who had made it to the rendezvous and take them back to the submarine. The Folbot was a low-sided, collapsible wooden canoe. It was still very much an experimental craft, but easy to transport and to conceal. It was, however, strictly limited in its carrying capacity, designed for two men only.

On 17 March, after Berge's team had successfully landed in France, Appleyard's team embarked on the submarine HMS *Tigris*, under Commander H. F. Bone, DSO and Bar, DSC, a most distinguished fighting sailor, and were taken to the Bay of Biscay. Appleyard, very much an outdoors man, found life on a submarine a complete contrast to anything he had previously known. Having experienced the hardships that the crew had to regularly undergo in the cramped space of HMS *Tigris*, Appleyard subsequently became rather less hostile than he had been to the activities of the enemy's submarines.

Appleyard and his men faced a difficult task. In March and April the Bay of Biscay can be very inhospitable and of course the landing and pick up were to take place in the dark of the night. However, the voyage out to the area passed without incident and on 30 March, the night of the appointed landing, when the submarine surfaced a distance of between two and three miles off the coast conditions were a little better than had been expected.

Accounts of what happened next vary. Where there is conflict, the author has relied on M's official account of the operation. No signal was seen from the shore, but the three Folbots were assembled on the deck of the submarine, and an attempt was made to launch them. Sadly, only two were successfully manned and floated off. The third was lost to the sea, thus effectively reducing the expedition to just two men, as the spare seat in each Folbot had to be reserved for whoever they might find on the shore. Appleyard and Desgranges set off across the choppy sea. Paddling as silently as they could towards land, the men peered through the darkness for a signalling light from the agents they hoped would be there, but saw nothing. As they reached shallow water, they could only hope that no hostile reception committee was awaiting them. They landed their canoes successfully on the beach.

Still unable to see any sign of a signalling light, the two men began a detailed reconnaissance of the beach, keeping as low to the ground as possible and moving along the sand noiselessly. Despite a careful search, they found neither friend nor enemy. Time was limited because the *Tigris* had remained exposed on the surface waiting for them, so once their fruitless search was completed the two agents had no option but to return to the submarine. Unknown to them, through a navigational error, they had in fact landed on the wrong stretch of coast. It later became clear that the rendezvous point where Berge and his companions were waiting was about a mile away.

In all types of covert work, timetables are difficult to stick to. Agents may be delayed for innocent or sinister reasons, and may be unable to communicate the delay to those whom they are intending to meet, again for either innocent or sinister reasons. Also, as on this occasion, mistakes can be made by either party in relation to the meeting point. Thus, the plan for this operation allowed for a failed rendezvous on the night of 30/31 March, and an alternative date had been fixed for 4 April. HMS *Tigris* again brought Appleyard and Desgranges to within a couple of miles of the coast, this time at the right spot. However, when Commander Bone surfaced on this occasion he found the weather conditions considerably worse, with a heavy sea running. Nonetheless, as Appleyard scanned the shore he was certain that, albeit only briefly, he saw a signal light. Commander Bone saw nothing and sought to discourage Appleyard and Desgranges from trying to reach the shore. The Folbots were light, flimsy craft, and would be terribly vulnerable to the heavy sea. But Appleyard was sure that this time the agents were there and he insisted that Bone allow them to make their attempt to pick them up.

Eventually the Commander agreed, but he gave Appleyard a deadline to return by 0300 hrs (thereby giving him only a few hours), beyond which he was not prepared to remain and to risk the safety of his submarine and its crew. Bone was a gallant and courageous sub-mariner, and his reluctance to let Appleyard and Desgranges try to reach the shore shows how very difficult the conditions were. Also, the time limit Bone imposed indicates his concern that there might be a trap awaiting them. Neither he nor Appleyard were able to know whether the failed rendezvous a few days earlier had been down to innocent or sinister causes. If the agents had been captured and tortured by the Gestapo then Appleyard and Desgranges might well be about to enter a trap and HMS *Tigris* might be subjected to a planned and sustained attack.

Waves were pounding over the exposed deck of the submarine when the two Folbots were brought up through the hatch to be launched, and a heavy wave swept the Folbot that Appleyard had intended to use into the sea before the crew of HMS *Tigris* could do anything about it. Reduced to one craft, and in the foulest of conditions, a lesser man than Appleyard would have seen sense and given up. Geoffrey Appleyard, however, combined great personal courage with a strong streak of Yorkshire obstinacy. Once he had determined that he was going to do something, like Bond he would do it or die trying, however great the odds against him. Appleyard immediately commandeered the Folbot intended for Desgranges. He would go it alone. He knew that if he managed to find more than one agent on the shore, it would be necessary to make a number of trips back and forth through the violent seas to the submarine.

The first practical problem was to get Appleyard launched. He was able to get into the Folbot on the deck, but then had to be carefully lowered into the sea so that he could paddle away from the submarine's side. On the first attempt the waves immediately capsized the Folbot, throwing Appleyard into the cold black sea. Dragged back on to the deck, Appleyard tried again, and again capsized. A third attempt also failed. So it went on until finally, during a short lull in the weather, Appleyard managed to keep the Folbot upright as he paddled away from HMS *Tigris*. He was very cold and wet, but now at least he could get his circulation going with a good hard paddle over the miles between ship and shore. Despite the high seas Appleyard made the journey without capsizing and successfully grounded his Folbot on the beach. There is no doubt that the winter of hardship and training on the Isle of Arran had improved his powers of endurance.

Once on the beach, with his Folbot intact and hidden, Appleyard did not know at first whether his superhuman effort had merely brought him into the jaws of a trap. The caution that he and Desgranges had exercised on their first landing now had to be doubled. However, Appleyard remained convinced that he had seen a signal from the shore and that the agents would be there – somewhere. He scouted the beach from end to end as quietly and carefully as he could, but found nothing. Aware that time was growing short and that HMS *Tigris* would depart at 0300 hrs with or without him, Appleyard had to take a risk and, using his torch, began signalling towards the land from the beach. When he still got no response he threw all caution to the wind, and began running up and down the beach shouting and flashing his torch at the same time in order to draw attention to himself. This suicidal effort finally brought success and Appleyard saw an answering signal from above the beach. Three surviving agents, Berge, Forman and Letac, were hiding there, and the rendezvous was made a few minutes later.

Operation Savannah had not been a success in its intended form. The intelligence proved to be out of date, the arrangements for the transport of pilots to the airfield had been changed, and no attack on them had been possible. However, Berge and his men had used their time on French soil for a different purpose, meeting with their fellow countrymen, laying the foundations for Resistance organizations in the area and gathering valuable intelligence information, before making their way to the rendezvous point on 30 March.

Appleyard was also informed that the beach had been under observation by the Germans that night, and that the German observers had only recently left. Had Appleyard abandoned caution earlier, he would have been captured or killed.

Appleyard now had three potential passengers and only one available seat in his Folbot. The sea was still running high and time was short. HMS *Tigris* would leave at 0300 hrs and there would probably not now be time to make more than one journey to the submarine. It would be a difficult trip even with one passenger, highly hazardous with two, and simply impossible with three. The Folbot was designed to sit low in the water to aid its camouflage, and with two or three on board (as opposed to Appleyard alone on the voyage to the beach), there would be a very great risk of capsizing. It was decided that Berge and Forman would go with Appleyard, and Letac would stay on the beach and if necessary take his chances thereafter in France.

The first problem was to get the Folbot relaunched through the surf that was crashing onto the beach. Berge and Forman got aboard and Appleyard pushed the little craft out through the waves. Once out of his depth he began to swim behind the Folbot, and when it was far enough out for the sea to be a little calmer he was able to climb in. The return journey was a constant battle against the waves and the swell of the high seas. Time and again it seemed inevitable that the fragile canoe would be swamped, time and again vigorous bailing and hard paddling kept her afloat. Painfully slowly, the Folbot made progress towards where the three men hoped to find HMS *Tigris*, if she was still there. Finally and miraculously, they closed on the rendezvous point at the moment of the submarine's submerging and preparing to leave. Bone was doing his duty to ensure the safety of his ship and crew. He and his officers had finally given up on Appleyard a few minutes earlier, with the words: 'Poor old Apple [as Appleyard was invariably known during his military career], he wasn't such a bad sort for an Army man.' On seeing to his surprise that Appleyard was still in the land of the living, Bone brought HMS *Tigris* fully back to the surface. However, the sea had not quite given up its efforts to foil the mission and, just a few yards short of HMS *Tigris*, the Folbot finally sank. Appleyard, Berge and Forman were left to swim the mercifully short distance that remained to the submarine. They were hauled aboard and climbed down thankfully into the warmth of the ship. Against all odds, Appleyard had got Berge and Forman out of France. Letac later succeeded in making his own way out.

Appleyard was entitled to flop exhausted on his bunk for the rest of the journey back to England. But as in so many of the Bond stories, just when the hero seems to have won through, the action is not quite over. All of a sudden on his way home Appleyard found himself in the midst of a sea battle. HMS *Tigris* was a fighting submarine. She had had the specific task on this voyage of putting Appleyard and his team ashore in the Bay of Biscay, and of picking up the agents that they found there, but Commander Bone reverted, on his way home, to his more familiar role as a scourge of enemy shipping. In the Bay of Biscay he spotted a 10,000 ton enemy tanker. It was too important a target to ignore. HMS *Tigris* was at the end of a tour of duty and was running short of torpedoes. The seas were also still very heavy, which affected accuracy, and after their opening salvo of torpedoes missed its mark Bone decided to surface, to fight it out with the submarine's single gun. The tanker had a surface defence capability – indeed its guns were heavier than that of *Tigris* – but it did not have the benefit of expert naval gunners. When 'all hands to action stations' was sounded, Appleyard found himself allotted the role of ammunition handler, helping to pass the shells to *Tigris*' gun team. The artillery duel raged for an hour and a half before HMS *Tigris* knocked out the tanker's guns and crippled her. Commander Bone then moved within close range and finished off the stricken tanker with a single torpedo. Thus,

Secret Agent Geoffrey Appleyard, one of the models for the future Bond, actually took part in a naval battle.

Ian Fleming, a Naval Commander himself, made James Bond a member of the Royal Navy, perhaps out of loyalty to his own service, perhaps out of vanity, or perhaps to disguise the truth a little. None of those who were to join Maid Honor Force, with the exception of a tall young man called Denis Tottenham, were members of the Royal Navy. However, they became expert sailors and the operations that the Force was to carry out were essentially naval ones. By the time of Operation Postmaster all of them were seasoned in the ways of the sea – they were M's Secret Navy.

Back in England, Appleyard's courageous conduct on Operation Savannah did not go unrecognized. Both M and his ultimate boss, the Minister for Economic Warfare Hugh Dalton, recommended Appleyard for a decoration. M himself signed the citation which included the following: 'It is entirely due to the skill, courage and resource of Captain Appleyard that Captain Berge and another returned to England safely, bringing information of great value. Throughout the voyage, Appleyard's behaviour was worthy of praise in the finest traditions of the service.' Dalton added the comment: 'This officer successfully brought off the two men from the coast under very difficult conditions which taxed to the full both his ingenuity and his endurance.' Geoffrey Appleyard was awarded the Military Cross.

CHAPTER 7

The Birth of Maid Honor Force

M had initially recruited March-Phillipps as a training officer, but March-Phillipps was not satisfied with that. He was happy to train an elite force, but then he wanted to lead it into action. Having joined SOE's HQ staff on 5 March 1941, March-Phillipps immediately proposed to M that he form a specialist force of commando-trained agents for the purpose of small amphibious raids on the German-held coast of Europe. Effectively, that was what he had been planning to do with his original commando troop. M, having had a few weeks to judge March-Phillipps at close quarters, agreed to the request. He granted him authority to form a small special service unit, to be based in Poole, Dorset, for the specific purpose of small-scale sea raiding.

On 7 March 1941, M's diary records that he and March-Phillipps had a meeting with Admiral Godfrey. Although it is not specifically recorded, it seems inevitable that Ian Fleming was also there. March-Phillipps' presence at the meeting indicates that his project for an amphibious SOE raiding force must have been discussed. There are then a number of further private meetings recorded between M and March-Phillipps in March and April. March-Phillipps was given authority to recruit the specialists that he needed either from his old Troop or from other units, and to find a suitable craft to use for the planned raids. It may be that M was already thinking of sending March-Phillipps and his men to West Africa in due course, but initially the chosen target was to be enemy-occupied Europe.

In accepting M's invitation to join SOE, March-Phillipps had taken the significant step from regular army to secret army (or, as it developed, secret navy). He and his chosen men came off the army payroll, and thereafter were funded by SOE, who had their own secret and not ungenerous allocation of funds from the government. So that there should be no easily identifiable record of their existence, SOE personnel were, in the early years, always paid in cash. Further, the moment that he joined SOE, March-Phillipps and those that he chose to form a part of his force became 'deniable' secret agents. SOE itself did not publicly exist, nor therefore did any of its agents. M and his deputy Caesar would both deny any knowledge of the existence of Agent W.01 and his men if they were captured.

Just when March-Phillipps was given the code name 01 is not clear, but by the time he and Maid Honor Force were operating in West Africa he was certainly W.01. SOE used a simple code for most of its geographical sections: West Africa was W, France was F, and so on. When Maid Honor Force was in West Africa, March-Phillipps' code name W.01 thus indicated that he was a commando agent (01: 'licensed' and trained to kill), working in West Africa (W).

Ian Fleming adapted the '0' tag of the Commando agents to '00' for his James Bond and M's other agents who were licensed to kill. When tagging the sections of his M's Secret Service, he was more brazen, using exactly the same simple code as SOE: C is the Caribbean, F is France, J is Japan, S is the Soviet Union, T is Turkey, and so on.

Agent W.01, March-Phillipps, always an adventurer, was no doubt delighted by the concept and codes of SOE, and by the opportunity to form his private force of 'patriotic pirates'. Not surprisingly, Geoffrey Appleyard was the automatic choice to be his second-in-command, once he had returned from his trip to France. Safely back, Appleyard thus became '02' or in due course 'W.02'.

March-Phillipps recruited a number of others who had been with him in B Troop, including Nasmyth and Prout. Leslie Prout was promoted, and given an 'emergency commission' as an Army Lieutenant on 22 April 1941. The *I'm Alone* was left behind on the Isle of Arran, and March-Phillipps' new force came south to Poole in Dorset, not far from his own family home in Blandford Forum. In some ways, the *I'm Alone* was a sad loss, since all had become fond of her and her sea-going qualities were without doubt. In truth, though, she was little more than a plaything and training aid. Appleyard wrote to his family whilst still on the Isle of Arran: 'After the war, Gus and I will probably buy out the men's shares in the boat and have her ourselves. We are already planning our voyages.' In the event, that was not to happen.

Once in Poole, March-Phillipps billeted his force on two houseboats, named *Dormouse* and *Yo'n Jo*, which before the war had been little more than the follies of their rich owners. They provided somewhat improbable accommodation, but at least they were boats. March-Phillipps and Appleyard were tasked by M not just to build and train their force, but to work out schemes for raiding the enemy 'across the water' on the channel coast and as far north as Norway.

The first question was, of course, what craft should they use? March-Phillipps went hunting and found the ship he wanted in Brixham harbour. She was the *Maid Honor*, a one time working Brixham trawler. She had been built in the mid-twenties for fisherman Charlie Howe, and was named after his daughter Honor. She had worked as a fishing boat for ten or eleven years, and was then bought a few years before the war by a Major Bertram Bell, a member of the Royal Yacht Squadron. He had converted her into a trawler yacht. However, she still retained the outward appearance of a classic Brixham trawler. A part of March-Phillipps' reasoning was that since Brixham trawlers were made of wood, not metal, they would not be vulnerable to magnetic mines. This he later tested with the *Maid Honor* on a magnetic range at Portland, and found to be true. Further, since the *Maid Honor* was primarily a sailing vessel, with only an auxiliary engine, she could be used without difficulty for silent approaches to the enemy coast. Importantly, if spotted, a Brixham trawler might well be taken to be just that, a fishing vessel and no threat. Last but not least, the *Maid Honor* under full sail was quite a speedy vessel.

It was just as well for March-Phillipps that M in due course approved the suggested requisition of the *Maid Honor*, because having made up his mind that a Brixham trawler was appropriate March-Phillipps had, not unusually for him, jumped the gun. Leslie Prout described what happened: 'Having obtained agreement in principle to the proposal of small scale raids, Gus pulled off a feat that only he could have got away with. Although having no authority to proceed, he calmly requisitioned a Brixham trawler called the *Maid Honor*. With her, he secured her Skipper, Blake Glanville, and sailed her from Brixham to Poole. . . Berthed in Poole, Gus informed an astonished Navy of the requisition, who in turn informed an astonished Brigadier, who won the everlasting gratitude of the crew by backing us up through thick and thin.'

Requisitioning in wartime could often be a sensitive issue, since not all owners would normally wish to part with or share their homes, vehicles or boats. Furthermore, there was a great shortage of supplies of all kinds, and great competition between the services for the use of anything that was available. SOE, the upstarts of the military, had to fight harder than most to get what they wanted. March-Phillipps, however, once his mind was made up, was very difficult to resist. Having chosen the *Maid Honor*, he simply took her. His greatest coup was perhaps not only to 'steal' the ship, but also to 'steal' its master, Blake Glanville, who happily sailed her to Poole. Glanville was a seasoned sailor beyond military age, who knew the foibles of the *Maid Honor* very well. He was asked by March-Phillipps to stay with her in Poole and to train her crew, which again he was happy to do. Glanville remained an integral part of Maid Honor Force until the *Maid Honor* eventually left Poole for West Africa. He helped to oversee many of the adaptations to her, and became the 'favourite uncle' of all of the youngsters who made up Maid Honor Force.

The 'Brigadier' referred to by Prout was, of course, M. M was clearly an excellent judge of character. He understood and valued March-Phillipps' qualities as a leader and an innovator, and was prepared to support him despite any 'eccentricities'. As Prout says, he overlooked March-Phillipps' brazen impudence in requisitioning the *Maid Honor* (and her skipper) without authority, and backed him up. Wherever possible, M was hugely supportive of his men and the decisions that they made on the ground. Such was the ethos of SOE. Desmond Longe, one of M's agents, said of him later: 'He was very adept at turning a blind eye, and if things blew up, would prolong the correspondence for long enough for the culprits to leave the country.'

The *Maid Honor* was 70ft (21.3m) long, with a draught of 7ft 8ins (2.36m). She was extremely strong, with planks four inches thick on the outside, cement up to the waterline and three skins. She was just under 40 tons in weight, a good sea boat, and speedy. She had been built without an engine of any sort, but her last owner, Major Bertram Bell, had put in a four-cylinder auxiliary engine.

When he came to write his James Bond stories in the 1950s, Fleming did not forget the ship that M's real agents had chosen. In *Goldfinger* (1959), the villain chooses a Brixham trawler as his favoured covert vessel. According to Fleming, Goldfinger had initially built his empire by smuggling gold to India, where the price was much higher than in Europe. In order to do so he had bought a Brixham trawler, and, once a year for ten years after the war, sailed it from England to India and back, with de-constituted gold hidden on board. Those epic voyages were echoes of the voyage that the *Maid Honor* was eventually to make under March-Phillipps' command from Poole to West Africa, though the *Maid Honor*'s secret cargo was not gold but commandos and weaponry.

M had authorized a training base for the Maid Honor Force (as March-Phillipps' unit became known), in a remote part of Poole harbour. The official brief for the Maid Honor Force was now both to carry out raids against enemy-occupied territory and to establish personal contact with local patriots, in order to help create resistance movements. The *Maid Honor*, after a number of experiments, was armed and refitted as a 'Q-ship', an innocent civilian trawler to the casual eye, but in fact armed with a number of hidden weapons. The term Q-ship was inherited from the First World War. (Fleming went on to use the tag 'Q' for the secret gadgets department of his secret service, and for its boss.)

Following the arrival in Poole of the *Maid Honor*, and the official authorization for Maid Honor Force, March-Phillipps and Appleyard continued to recruit. Recruitment remained exclusively by way of personal recommendation, and joining Maid Honor Force had to be a voluntary act – there were no pressed men. If a recruit did not prove up to the job, he would quietly be returned to his previous unit.

One man called for by Appleyard was Graham Hayes, a boyhood friend. Hayes was born on 9 July 1915 and was therefore some seventeen months older than Geoffrey Appleyard. The boys had grown up together in the then small village of Linton-on-Wharfe, Yorkshire. Hayes, like Appleyard, was a keen sportsman, and an enthusiastic member of the local rugby club. Eventually, he trained as a wood sculptor in London and in 1938 set up a studio in Temple Sowerby in Cumberland. Yet another ornithologist, Hayes had tamed a jackdaw, whom he named Grip – the bird was his regular companion going to the local pub and would sit on his shoulder. As a boy he had kept a collection of stuffed birds in his room. He was described by his military colleagues as a quiet, serious minded man of great personal charm, and with an enormous capacity for work. He had the ability to mix with and understand people from all walks of life. According to his mother, in certain company Hayes would refer to himself as John, since he thought that Graham was rather a 'posh' name. He had two brothers, only one of whom was to survive the war.

Graham Hayes was an experienced sailor who had crewed his way around the world on a Finnish sailing ship called the *Pommern* (a 'windjammer' as his mother described it) before the outbreak of the Second World War. The *Pommern* was a four-master, and while Hayes was on board she had taken part in the famous Grain Race from Australia to England. Thus he had knowledge and experience of the exact type that March-Phillipps wanted for the *Maid Honor*. He was also an excellent swimmer and 'underwater man', which was a quality, of course, that Fleming built into his own fictional agent.

Since the *Maid Honor* was to be a Q-ship, and because of the work that Maid Honor Force was later to undertake, there was an additional reason for March-Phillipps and Appleyard to want Hayes. According to his mother, Hayes had been the only Englishman on the *Pommern*, amongst a crew of

Swedes who, naturally, spoke amongst themselves in Swedish. Hayes had very blue eyes and fair skin and could pass for a Swede himself without difficulty. The ruse for the Maid Honor Force on its voyage to Africa was to be that they were Swedish, sailing a neutral ship under a Swedish flag.

Graham Hayes joined the 1st Battalion, the Border Regiment at the outbreak of war, and later joined a forerunner of the Parachute Regiment, officially known as 11 SAS Battalion. When sought out by Appleyard, Hayes jumped at the prospect of action with the Maid Honor Force, and March-Phillipps duly ensured that Hayes' commanding officer was persuaded to let him go. Hayes was transferred for 'special employment' with SOE effective from 1 May 1941, and signed the Official Secrets Act on 21 May 1941. Appleyard witnessed his signature.

Hayes was to become Agent W.03. Thus Agents W.01, 02 and 03 were all amateur ornithologists, as were a surprising number of other SOE agents who feature in the story of Maid Honor Force. So the fact that when Fleming chose a name for his secret agent during the writing of the first book in 1952, it was that of an ornithologist, James Bond, does perhaps offer another clue as to where his real inspiration was coming from.

The fourth and final secret agent from Maid Honor Force who would contribute to the character of Bond was twenty-year-old Anders Lassen. Anders Frederick Emil Victor Schau Lassen, to give him all the names to which he was entitled but rarely used, was born on 22 September 1920, into a wealthy and well-connected upper-class Danish family. Although he never spoke of it, he had an American grandmother on his mother's side. He lived until the age of nine in the fifty-room family mansion at Hovdingsgard, in South Zealand, with an estate that offered plenty of scope for outdoor pursuits. The family then moved to a manor house called Baekkeskov, near one of Denmark's many fjords, Praesto, on the Baltic Sea. As a boy, Lassen became a skilled hunter with bow, knife and gun, and an expert in silent killing. He was very accurate with a throwing knife, a skill that Fleming passed on to James Bond. One of Lassen's greatest gifts was an ability to move speedily without noise, approaching his quarry like a ghost to effect the kill. He was one of those men who, whilst they do not hesitate to hunt and kill wild animals, also love to keep pets and become very fond of them.

Although he had first cousins through marriage who were German, and with whom he was friendly when a boy, once Germany had invaded Denmark Lassen became determined to avenge himself and his country, and wished only to kill as many Germans as possible.

Lassen was tall, slim and broad-shouldered, with the palest blue eyes. When fully mature he was about twelve stone in weight. He was politely described by those who knew him as a boy as 'a little wild'. Prince Georg of Denmark, Lassen's exact contemporary, recounted that he was an uncomfortable house guest: 'He was aggressive and would pick fights at any time, especially when drunk – although that wasn't often . . . the most remarkable aspect of Lassen was the strength of his self-belief; indeed it was rather more than mere belief. At an age when the average boy is uncertain of himself, Anders Lassen was rare in not only knowing his own mind but then in carrying out whatever course of action he had decided on.'

Lassen's quest for adventure led him to leave home as a teenager, and go to sea. In January 1939, at the age of eighteen, he signed on as cabin boy and general dogsbody on the Danish ship *Fionia*. The *Fionia* sailed to Bangkok and back, returning home in June. Lassen then signed on as a cadet on a Danish tanker, the *Eleonora Maersk*, which took him to Bahrain. The tanker was at sea in the Persian Gulf on 9 April 1940, when Germany invaded and took possession of Lassen's homeland.

The crew of the *Eleonora Maersk* voted immediately to make their way to the nearest British port and to offer their services to the British, the nearest port being Bahrain. Many other Danish vessels took the same decision. From that moment on, Lassen fretted to join the action, but it was eight long months before he was able to make his way to Britain, eventually arriving at Oban on Christmas Eve 1940, on board a British tanker, the SS *British Consul*. He wanted to join the Royal Air Force, but was eventually persuaded to sign up for M's SOE instead, in the belief that he would be able to serve Denmark better with them.

Lassen made his way to London where, on 25 January 1941, he and nine other young Danes held a small ceremony, in which each of them swore and signed an oath which they recorded in the soft cover of a pocket bible. The oath read:

> In the year 1941, on the 25th January, the undersigned Free Danes in England swore, sword in hand, to fight with their allies for Denmark's freedom from a foreign yoke.
>
> I hereby swear that I will stay loyal to my king, Christian X. I also swear that I am ready to serve loyally whatever authority is working against the enemy that occupied my Fatherland. I swear that I will never disclose whatever military secrets are entrusted to me.

The gesture was one that would have appealed enormously to Secret Agents

March-Phillipps and Appleyard. The same day, Lassen signed up for training by SOE. Like many of those recruited into SOE, Lassen never did any basic army training – the customary course of nine weeks square-bashing – nor was he assigned to a regiment. He was entered on the 'General List', and the only training he got was with SOE.

Lassen found even the SOE training at Arisaig, their Scottish training camp, difficult to endure. He hated any sort of military foot drill, and was wont to complain: 'I came to fight, not to parade.' He developed a poisoned foot and was hospitalized for a time, but irrespective of that he clearly did not enjoy the SOE course or military authority. By 10 March 1941, he was trying to find a way out of SOE. He had not pleased his training officer, who reported on 11 March 1941: 'He is the weakest character of the party, he is the black sheep of a good family, who has run away from home and become a sailor. He is keen enough on the job, but cannot stand being kept in, he would definitely not be reliable enough for special duties; he might not keep sober when on leave and give away secrets.'

Happily, the Commandant of the Training School had a rather better opinion of him, reporting that Lassen was: 'Determined and keen. Comes of a very good Danish family. Well educated. Failed an exam when studying forestry and, I think, ran away to sea. Considerable experience of hunting and shooting. Should do well as an individual or as a leader of a patrol. Might develop into a good officer later. Has missed much of training owing to a poisoned foot.'

M visited Scotland between 14 and 18 April. He dropped into the SOE training school at Arisaig, hoping to find a suitable recruit for Maid Honor Force. Lassen was recommended and M accepted him. On 15 April 1941, the Commandant reported: 'The brigadier [M] required a man for Patrol-Boat work. I recommended Lassen, who is quite clever and well mannered and speaks English fairly well. He would fit into a job like that better than a regiment as his nature does not like drill and military discipline.' This assessment was undoubtedly influenced by the fact that, shortly before completing the training course, Lassen had stalked a stag on foot in the hills of South Morar, near the SOE Training Camp, and had killed it with his knife – an extraordinary feat, and one that amply demonstrated his suitability for the commando lifestyle. He had absolutely no hesitation about killing with a knife and was able to glide silently across the ground when stalking his prey – animal or human.

Experts in training British agents in the arts of silent killing and hand-to-hand combat had observed a marked reluctance in many recruits to kill with a knife, or to use 'dirty tricks'. Captain W. E. Fairbairn, late Assistant Commissioner of the Shanghai Municipal Police, was the Instructor in Close Combat at the Special Training School. In the introduction to his training manual *All-in Fighting*, he writes:

> It must be realized that, when dealing with an utterly ruthless enemy who has clearly expressed his intention of wiping this nation out of existence, there is no room for any scruple or compunction about the methods to be used in preventing him… (if under personal attack, a recruit's) one, violent desire would be to do the thug the utmost damage – regardless of the rules. In circumstances such as this he is forced back to quite primitive reactions… Killing with the bare hands at close quarters savours too much of pure savagery for most people. They would hesitate to attempt it. But never was the catchword 'He who hesitates is lost' more applicable. When it is a matter of life and death, not only of the individual but of the nation, squeamish scruples are out of place.

Thus, Lassen's ability to creep up on another living creature and kill it with his knife, made him of immediate interest to SOE. M undoubtedly made a good judgement call when recruiting Lassen, and March-Phillipps also took to him as soon as he arrived in Poole to join Maid Honor Force. He spotted the enormous potential in Anders Lassen and became his mentor. Both M and March-Phillipps were proved right. After Operation Postmaster Lassen was commissioned, on March-Phillipps' recommendation, and after leaving SOE in 1943 he went on to become the Special Forces' most decorated soldier, winning the Military Cross and two Bars, and the Victoria Cross. After the war, a fellow member of Maid Honor Force, Leslie Prout, wrote of him: 'Andy Lassen was as great a gentleman as he was a fighter for the cause of justice, and his open and generous nature made him many friends. His personality as well as his great exploits confirmed the admiration that we had for his country.'

Anders Lassen was also a very popular ladies' man. One of his colleagues commented that at the local dances they attended from time to time, his own chance of winning the affections of the 'belle of the ball' on the night in question would go straight out of the window once Appleyard and Lassen arrived. Lassen's hunting instinct and ruthless streak in relation to the ladies would lead him into scrapes and he sometimes had to rely on his athleticism to get him out of an embarrassing situation. He enjoyed the company of women and they enjoyed his, and the fact that a girl was married was no bar to him – like James Bond, if he thought she was desirable he would make his move. His detachment from the deeper emotional aspects of any relationship is illustrated by a remark he liked to make later in the war, when he was living in Dorset. Lassen was having an affair with a woman who had twice been widowed. He jokingly referred to her to his male friends as his 'widow and Bar', in the fashion of a soldier who wins the same medal twice, and therefore wins a Bar to it. It was this aspect of Lassen's character, as well as his considerable skill as a hunter and killer, that Fleming used for his James Bond. In the very first story, *Casino Royale* (1953), Fleming has Bond say: 'Women were for recreation. On a job, they got in the way and fogged things up with sex and hurt feelings and all the emotional baggage they carried around.' Anders Lassen might have agreed.

March-Phillipps and Appleyard continued to build the crew of the *Maid Honor*. They selected each man with considerable care. In such a small and close-knit unit as the Maid Honor Force, a wrong decision could cost them dear. Agent W.02, Geoffrey Appleyard, chose Quartier Maître (the French equivalent of chief petty officer) André Jules Marcel Desgranges, the Free Frenchman who had seen service with him on Operation Savannah earlier that year. Desgranges, like Agent W.03 Graham Hayes, was amongst the first of the new recruits to be secured. Desgranges, apart from his ten years' experience in the French Navy, was a trained diver. According to the now Lieutenant (eventually Major) Leslie Prout, another choice of Appleyard's, Desgranges spoke no English, but became instantly popular with his British comrades.

Frank 'Buzz' Perkins was seventeen, born on 15 December 1923, and seemed even younger than his actual age. His uncle was a major who knew March-Phillipps, and March-Phillipps agreed to accept him, by far the youngest recruit. Perkins was in fact to prove himself eminently suitable during his time with Maid Honor Force, but March-Phillipps was acting in his usual 'irregular' fashion when taking him on. Perkins, apart from his fighting qualities, added weight to the deception that the *Maid Honor* was an innocent civilian vessel. He played the 'cabin boy' role, far too young-looking to be a secret agent licensed to kill.

Another recruit, Denis Frederick Gwynne Tottenham, was just twenty-one and a Lieutenant in the RNVR. He was a well-educated young man who had started sailing at the age of eight. He was happy to abandon his rank in order to join the Maid Honor Force, where he became a Private. At 6 ft 3 ins in height, if he stood barefoot in the cabin of the *Maid Honor*, his head would still touch the ceiling.

Londoner Ernest Evison, of the East Surrey Regiment, joined as the unit's cook, a very important role if they were to be an effective fighting force. Both Appleyard and Hayes were noted for their huge appetites.

The diminutive 'Haggis' Taylor (predictably a Scot) was recruited to become W.01's batman.

Company Sergeant Major Tom Winter proved the most difficult quarry for March-Phillipps. Winter was married with a child, and as his rank suggests he was a very experienced soldier. He was also parachute-trained, having won his wings in October 1940, and like Hayes was a member of the newly formed 11 SAS Battalion. They did not want to part with him. However, Agent W.03, Graham Hayes, strongly recommended him and March-Phillipps was determined to have him. Eventually, after what Winter later described as a 'hell of a battle', March-Phillipps' will prevailed with the War Office and Winter was transferred to the Maid Honor Force.

Thus, March-Phillipps and Appleyard gathered together their chosen men. As always, March-Phillipps put them through intensive physical training and seamanship training. Their levels of fitness became extraordinarily high. Appleyard described in a letter home how one very hot Saturday in Poole, he had had a 'marvellous afternoon'. Despite the heat, he decided to go for a cross-country run, wearing nothing but gym shoes and shorts. From the Arne peninsular, Appleyard ran round Poole harbour to Swanage, Old Harry, Studland, Purbeck, Corfe, Creech Barrow, Wareham and back to Arne, a distance of 32 miles – considerably further than a marathon, and up and down numerous hills. Although his legs felt 'a little stiff' the following day, Appleyard commented in his letter, 'it was glorious, lovely views all over Dorset'.

Appleyard also found time to slip away to Ringway, near Manchester, to undergo a parachute training course at the aerodrome that was later to become Manchester International Airport.

M visited the *Maid Honor* regularly in Poole harbour, and was more than satisfied with the team that March-Phillipps had put together. However, the Admiralty was unimpressed. It remained overtly suspicious of SOE, which it regarded as something of a 'loose cannon' in the naval arena, over which the Royal Navy wished to exert full control. Initially, despite Fleming's efforts, the Admiralty refused permission for Maid Honor Force to operate outside coastal waters unless on a specific operation which they had approved. Ian Fleming continued to liaise with M on Godfrey's behalf, and on Whit Sunday, 1 June, he paid a visit to the Maid Honor Force in Poole.

CHAPTER 8

The Man Who Would Have Written James Bond

It is probable that Ian Fleming, as Godfrey's assistant, had already met Gus March-Phillipps at the formal meeting on 7 March, but in Poole March-Phillipps was able to spend some time with him on the *Maid Honor* and also to introduce him to the rest of the Maid Honor Force. No doubt, Fleming also got a ride in the 'terrific' Vauxhall Velox 30/98.

Fleming and March-Phillipps had a surprising amount in common. They were extremely close in age – March-Phillipps was born on 18 March 1908 and Fleming just over two months later on 28 May. Their fathers had both died in 1917, and each had had to grow up solely under his mother's care. Both were men of considerable charm. Both liked fast cars. However, Fleming had lived all his life in his brother Peter's shadow, and had achieved very little. He left Eton under a cloud, dropped out of Sandhurst, drifted from job to job before the war, and was now a planner and observer, rather than the man of action that he would have liked to become. In contrast, March-Phillipps was everything that Fleming had ever wanted to be. He had also been to public school, the Roman Catholic Ampleforth College, but unlike Fleming had finished his education with credit. He had gone into the Army, completed his officer training and, again unlike Fleming, had been commissioned and served in the Army. As mentioned earlier, in India he eventually became bored by what he regarded as a lack of proper soldiering, and resigned his commission. With the outbreak of the Second World War, March-Phillipps had joined up again, and had been with the British Expeditionary Force in France. He had been decorated with the MBE. Having survived the horrors of Dunkirk and joined the Commandos, he had been transferred to SOE, and had founded and trained the Maid Honor Force. March-Phillipps was the genuine hero and 'action man' that Fleming dreamed of being, but never was.

There was more. Gus March-Phillipps, after leaving the army, had become a successful novelist. His three published books all to a certain extent drew upon his own life and experiences, and in his last book, published just before the war in 1939, March-Phillipps had invented a dashing young man called John Sprake who, like March-Phillipps himself, had served in India but then resigned his commission. Sprake was a sportsman of some renown and an inveterate womanizer. March-Phillipps, with a foretaste of James Bond, described him as a ruthless and driven individual: 'It was not usual for him to be moved by sentiment in others, for it was something that he did not understand. In women he looked upon it as a necessary evil. In men he ignored it.' When Ian Fleming came to create Bond, he adopted John Sprake's character in that and other regards. Further, the book in which Sprake made his first appearance was called *Ace High*, for Sprake was not only a sportsman but a card player and gambler, as James Bond would also be.

There can be little doubt that March-Phillipps' next book would have found Sprake back in the Army following the outbreak of war, becoming a Secret Agent licensed to kill, as March-Phillipps himself had done. The secret war that March-Phillipps was now involved in was dramatic and exciting, and would have provided him with endless material for a new John Sprake novel. No doubt March-Phillipps would have paid the necessary lip service to the Official Secrets Act, as Fleming was to do, but he would have written it nonetheless. It was March-Phillipps, not Fleming, who was leading a 'James Bond' existence, and it was he who was the established and successful novelist. Had March-Phillipps survived the war there is no doubt that in peacetime he would have returned to writing novels and, inevitably, he would have written of secret agents. If March-Phillipps had not lost his life fighting for the country he loved so much, our most famous fictional secret agent might well be 'John Sprake'. As it was, by the time the war ended March-Phillipps was dead, and Sprake died with him. It was not until ten years after Operation Postmaster, seven years after the war, that Ian Fleming finally put pen to paper and wrote his first novel – the story that March-Phillipps could no longer tell. It would be very interesting to know what books Fleming had on his shelf as he began to write *Casino Royale* and whether one of them was *Ace High*.

In fairness, Ian Fleming only wrote the Bond stories himself as something of a last resort. He had remained on friendly terms with M after the war. Fleming was now working for the *Sunday Times*, and wrote twice to M to encourage him to write a history of the Special Operations Executive. In a letter dated 7 July 1949, beginning 'Dear Colin', Fleming wrote, 'I am wondering if you have thought over the idea of writing a popular history of

SOE, both as a tribute to many gallant men and to preserve some of these great adventure stories for posterity… I very much hope you can do this. You are the only person who could… The work of SOE really deserves such a monument.' Fleming indicated that the *Sunday Times* would like to serialize the story, and signed the letter 'yours ever, Ian Fleming'. He wrote again on 17 October of the same year, this time addressing M as 'My Dear Colin', and asking, 'Have you come to a decision? I sincerely hope you have, as I think the story ought to be told.'

By this time quite a lot had been written outside Great Britain about SOE, and others as well as Fleming thought that a true history should be told. Gubbins agreed, but, of course, sought to go through the proper channels, to make sure that whatever he wrote had government approval. Sadly, this was not forthcoming. On 10 December 1949 the Foreign Office embargoed the project. William Strang, who had been one of those responsible for liaison between the Foreign Office and SOE during the war, wrote to M from the Foreign Office, where he still served, on that same day: 'My dear Gubbins, . . . The publication even of such a sober and balanced review as you would write would be undesirable on security grounds . . . The technique of organising resistance movements does not alter greatly with the passage of time and we could not be sure that your book might not give valuable assistance to a future enemy . . . yours sincerely, William Strang.'

Ian Fleming had rightly referred to the activity of SOE as 'these great adventure stories'. He was not the first to think that. An unknown SOE Agent had commented, in one of the reports on Operation Postmaster shortly after it was carried out: 'Some day, perhaps, another Froude or better still, another Robert Louis Stevenson, will delight the public with the story of the operation.' It is perhaps no surprise that in 1952, little more than two years after M had been refused permission for an official history, Fleming began to write his fictional stories about a modern M and a modern Secret Service, and to draw heavily upon the men of Maid Honor Force, whom he had known and clearly admired, and upon the events of Operation Postmaster.

But all this was still in the future when Ian Fleming travelled down to Poole on 1 June 1941. All else aside, he would undoubtedly have been attracted to the daring and sheer romance of Maid Honor Force. His weekend in Poole must have been an interesting one. Apart from March-Phillipps, he would have met and probably dined with the other officers, Geoffrey Appleyard, Graham Hayes and Leslie Prout. The informality of Maid Honor Force and its small size, makes it likely that Fleming met the full team. What he made of the raw young Dane, Anders Lassen, or the even younger Buzz

Perkins, is not on record, but it does seem clear that he came away a firm supporter of the Maid Honor Force, even though his superiors at the Admiralty remained less keen. There is no suggestion that M was at Poole at the same time as Fleming, but his diary does record a visit the following weekend, 8 and 9 June. M stayed at the Antelope Hotel, which the Maid Honor Force used as their headquarters on land, and he went out on the *Maid Honor* itself.

A specific plan was worked out to put the *Maid Honor* to good use, in conjunction with the Dutch section of SOE. No doubt it was discussed by March-Phillipps with both Fleming and M. However, consent still had to be obtained from the Admiralty before the Maid Honor Force could go into action, and when the plan was put to them they turned it down flat. In addition to criticizing specific details, the Admiralty made it clear that they objected to giving information of a secret nature to Army officers who might get captured, and that they were not prepared to restrict the RAF's right to attack shipping generally, even for the purpose of special operations.

Winston Churchill, when he approved the creation of the SOE, did not perhaps realize the resentment it would cause amongst the regular services, or how much they would initially hamper SOE's effectiveness. For M and his Commando Agents, after having created and trained their specialist force, the frustration was overwhelming.

M had a private meeting with Fleming on 2 July, following the rejection of his plans. Rather than have his men remain inactive in Poole harbour, M was now keen to send them off to West Africa. There were worrying developments in Spanish Guinea, and the Maid Honor Force might well be of use there. M talked it over with March-Phillipps and they lunched together on 12 July, after a morning meeting. March-Phillipps was keen to go, welcoming the challenge of the voyage. A decision to send *Maid Honor* to West Africa was of itself controversial. Without copper sheeting to her hull, the ship was unsuited for work in the tropics. However, M felt that the newly constituted Maid Honor Force was just wasting its time at Poole, whereas it might prove a great asset in West Africa, particularly if High Command could be persuaded to approve some action against Santa Isabel harbour, on the Spanish island of Fernando Po. History shows that M was right.

CHAPTER 9

The Problem in West Africa

Lurking in the attractive harbour of Santa Isabel (now Malabo), on the volcanic island of Fernando Po (now Isla de Bioko in Equatorial Guinea), were two enemy ships that M feared were an increasing threat to the security of the British colonies in West Africa, and to the vital South Atlantic convoy routes. One was an Italian liner, the *Duchessa d'Aosta*, the other was a modern German tug, the *Likomba*. M's Secret Service was not confined to Europe; in November 1940 he had obtained sanction for setting up an SOE section based in Lagos, the capital of the British colony of Nigeria. It became W (West Africa) Section.

Controversially, M appointed not a Briton but a Belgian, Louis Franck, to take charge of the new section. Franck was thirty-two years of age, and had been a partner in Montagu's Bank (the bank run by the family of the Naval Intelligence Officer, Ewen Montagu.) He was a good athlete and an excellent linguist, fluent in French, English, Dutch, Flemish and German. He was married, with children. He was recruited by the War Office on 10 May 1940, given the temporary rank of Lieutenant, and immediately sent to France as a special courier to the King of Belgium. After little more than two difficult weeks on the Continent, Franck was evacuated through Dunkirk on 29 May. Back in England, after SOE had been set up, Franck had become an obvious candidate to join them.

M took the view that since, initially at least, the major concerns and priorities of the West African section would be in relation to the French colonies now in the hands of either Vichy France or the Free French, the French-speaking Franck was a suitable choice. Franck also had the advantage of knowing the sometimes rather prickly General de Gaulle, leader of the Free French, personally. And Nigeria was not far, in African terms, from the Belgian Congo. The Belgian government was by now operating from London.

In the general style of M's Secret Service, since the West African section was W Section, Louis Franck, its boss, became 'W'. Leaving England on 6 December 1940, Franck travelled out by flying boat to Lagos in a party of four that would become the foundation of W Section. The most junior member of the party was Lieutenant Victor Laversuch (code name W4), who was later to play a very significant part in the success of Operation Postmaster. Laversuch was an Englishman, born in Tisbury, Wiltshire, in 1902. He was a businessman with a considerable knowledge of Africa, who had signed up for the army in April 1939, and had gone with the British Expeditionary Force to France. He too, like March-Phillipps, Appleyard, Prout, Nasmyth and Franck, had been evacuated from Dunkirk, and was an early recruit into SOE in August of 1940.

SOE had no regard for military rank, except as a means of opening doors. Having arrived in Lagos, W found that he carried insufficient clout with the military bureaucracy there. Accordingly, SOE arranged in April 1941 for W to be given first the rank of Acting Major, then in September 1941, Lieutenant Colonel – much to the displeasure of the military Commander-in-Chief in West Africa, General Giffard. SOE had Churchill's blessing and therefore had to be tolerated, but the military in West Africa did not welcome W's arrival in the first place and SOE's cavalier regard to military rank incensed 'the old general', Giffard.

The terms of reference for the W Section mission were to target the huge area bounded by the northern border of French West Africa where it met Algeria, and the southern border of French Equatorial Africa where that met the Belgian Congo. Working under cover, its task was to provide all possible support for the Free French Government, in an effort to swing the people of the French Colonies from supporting Vichy France to supporting General de Gaulle and the Free French. W and his team were to do this by use of propaganda, by contacting any dissident elements in the Vichy French Colonies, and by carrying out acts of sabotage in those colonies, in what was to become the classic SOE style. The latter, in particular, was unpopular with General Giffard, who did not want anything to happen that might disturb the delicate status quo and provoke an attack on any of Great Britain's West African colonies. He immediately imposed what SOE was to refer to as a 'ban on bangs' – no sabotage or military action was allowed. Obviously, this greatly restricted what SOE was able to do in enemy territory.

As soon as he arrived in Lagos at the end of 1940, W had begun to gather intelligence on Fernando Po. Initially it came from the British Consul in Santa Isabel, Mr C.W. Michie. Great Britain had maintained a small consulate on Fernando Po for many years, staffed by a Vice Consul, due to its significance in the world of trade. The custom until the beginning of the war had been that one of the British trading companies on the island, John Holt and

Company, would provide the candidate for Vice Consul. When war broke out a member of the Colonial Service took over, and that was Mr Michie.

Michie played his hand with skill and became well-liked on the island. As a result, he was able to gather a lot of information about what was going on in Spanish Guinea, to pass on to W. He reported weekly to Lagos. Fernando Po contained a relatively small European community, including a number of Germans and Italians. Although the Spanish Colonial Government was obviously Falangist (the party of the Spanish dictator, General Franco), and answerable to Madrid, there were a number of Spaniards on the island who, perhaps not surprisingly, remained privately anti-Falangist. The Spanish Civil War was for them very recent history.

Michie reported what he knew about the enemy ships in Santa Isabel harbour.The *Duchessa d'Aosta* was an 8,000 ton Italian passenger liner, with the capacity to carry up to fifty-eight passengers, plus a substantial cargo. The harbour was not very big and to enter it with a large vessel required a skilled pilot. The *Duchessa d'Aosta* had arrived at Santa Isabel on 10 June 1940, the very day on which Mussolini had brought Italy into the war on Hitler's side. The Captain had decided to seek refuge in a neutral harbour, for fear that his ship and her valuable cargo might be captured by their new enemy, the British. On this voyage the *Duchessa d'Aosta* was carrying wool, copra, hides, copper and coffee, which she had picked up at various ports in southern Africa and was hoping to take back to Europe. She had an Italian crew of significant size, somewhere between forty and fifty men.

Following her arrival the *Duchessa d'Aosta* sat at her mooring less than fifty metres from the quayside, in the centre of the bay, with her cargo still on board. Michie had a grandstand view of her from the dining room of the British Consulate building, which stood just beside the cathedral in Santa Isabel, and overlooked part of the bay. Through contacts and friends Michie obtained the ship's manifest, listing in detail what cargo the *Duchessa d'Aosta* was carrying. The manifest was not quite complete, one page was apparently missing, but the cargo was clearly of considerable value. Michie wrote a despatch on 27 January 1941, which W forwarded by diplomatic bag to London, enclosing the manifest. Michie wrote:

> I have the honour to forward one copy of the Manifest of the Italian cargo vessel 'Duchessa d'Aosta', which has been sheltering in the harbour of Santa Isabel, in Fernando Po, since 10 June 1940. The manifest was handed by the Manager of the Spanish stevedoring firm, Messrs Agencia Fortuny Ltd to the English firm of Messrs Ambas Bay and Company Limited, who in turn gave this Consulate a copy . . .

> The Manifest contains six pages. It is understood however that a seventh page is missing. The Manager of Messrs Agencia Fortuny informed me that the Spanish port authority requested a copy of the missing sheet from the Ship's Master, who declined to produce it but offered no explanation. The port authority then repeated the request through the Spanish Guinea Government, which replied to the effect that it had been agreed that the contents of the missing sheet need not be divulged.
>
> It is understood that certain lorry chassis are on board and are manifested on this sheet. It is also rumoured, but not very credibly, that armaments form part of the cargo. Certain small items in the cargo have already been sold here, some clandestinely by the crew and others openly by the Master. Paint and a small quantity of copper are known to have been disposed of. The Spanish authorities are aware of this but have made no attempt to claim custom due.

The value put on the cargo that did appear on the manifest was £220,000, a substantial sum in 1941. That valuation did not include the copra that was listed, since it was believed this might have rotted during the *Duchessa d'Aosta*'s time at Santa Isabel. Nor, of course, could it include whatever was listed on the missing seventh sheet of the manifest.

There was an obvious suspicion that the ship was carrying armaments. Why else should the Spanish Guinea Government allow the Italian Master of the *Duchessa d'Aosta* to keep one page of the manifest secret? Also, might that not explain why she so rapidly took refuge in the port of Santa Isabel once Italy joined the war? Furthermore, the radio on board was still thought to be active, and might be used to report British shipping movements to the enemy. It was thought she could become a supply ship for the German U-Boat submarines that were hunting passing British convoys and preying on British shipping out of Lagos and Freetown, Sierra Leone.

Mr Michie further reported on the other Axis ship to have taken refuge at Santa Isabel, at the very start of the war in 1939, a 200 ton German tug, the *Likomba*. With her was a smaller diesel-driven barge, the *Bibundi*. The latter had been used as a means of escape by German personnel from the Tiko plantation in the nearby British Cameroons, when war had been declared. Well over a year later the *Likomba* and the *Bibundi* still remained at anchor in the harbour, moored not far from the *Duchessa d'Aosta*. The *Likomba* posed a different threat to British interests – a modern sea-going tug, she could be of considerable use to the Germans if they could get her back into action.

The *Duchessa d'Aosta* and the *Likomba* became the subject of careful consideration by SOE. It is clear that as early as January 1941, M, Caesar his deputy and W were looking for ways to neutralize the threats that they posed. W began reporting back to M and Caesar regularly, hoping some action against them might be authorized.

There were also increasing concerns about Spanish Guinea's neutrality. On 28 January 1941, the day after Michie's letter about the *Duchessa d'Aosta* and the *Likomba*, W passed on the intelligence that he had gathered regarding the character of the present Spanish Governor on Fernando Po:

> The Governor, Captain Victor Sanchez-Diaz, is said to be violently pro-Nazi, and anxiously awaiting Spanish accession to the Axis; German and Italian National anthems are played at Government receptions, and officials are expected to display portraits of Hitler and Mussolini in their offices . . . Public opinion is veering round to the view that Spain will be forced into the war, willy nilly, but the thought is not a welcome one. A Spaniard reported recently that plans were laid to seize the Canary Islands from the Falangists if Spain was dragged into the war. The planting community appear to be entirely disinterested. There are some thousands of Nigerian labourers on the island who will be liable to make trouble for the authorities in the event of war.

The Nigerian labourers were from a British Colony, and were pro-British. They were entitled to British protection even while working in neutral Spanish Guinea. W's reference to 'in the event of war' emphasizes concerns that Spanish Guinea might enter the war on the side of the Germans. Consul Michie had reported that an increasing number of armaments and troops were reaching Fernando Po. The Spanish garrison on the island now comprised 40 European officers and men, 500 native soldiers and police and 100 European reservists. There were machine-gun detachments around the coastline and 12 four-inch guns on the island. Machine guns had been mounted on the barracks, customs house and public works buildings in Santa Isabel, overlooking the harbour.

W's report added weight to the suspicion that the *Duchessa d'Aosta* might be carrying a secret cargo of munitions, and might therefore be under the protection of the pro-Nazi Spanish Governor. It also, obviously, heightened concerns about future activities on Fernando Po. The overtly hostile stance of the Governor made life much more difficult for Consul Michie in his attempts to gather intelligence of value to Britain.

The early months of 1941 passed and the *Duchessa d'Aosta* and the *Likomba* remained where they were. A further report from W to Caesar and M, dated 2 May 1941, emphasized a need to counteract what W described as an increasing German infiltration of Spanish Guinea. He described Fernando Po as an important island 'in which we should certainly ensure that no surprises will be in store for us.' The reference to 'surprises' must be taken to include W's concerns about the continuing presence of the two enemy vessels at Santa Isabel, so close to British waters.

While M worried about the general situation on Fernando Po, he was helping W to build his team in West Africa. M recruited Major Leonard Henry 'Dizzy' Dismore, thirty-five years of age, and sent him out in the spring of 1941. Before the war, Dismore had been a journalist and for a number of years the news editor for Kent County Newspapers. He was married with a young family, but had joined the Territorial Army in 1937, as the storm clouds gathered over Europe. He had been commissioned into the Buffs, and was yet another who had served with the BEF and been evacuated through Dunkirk. He spoke French, German and Portuguese. He had joined SOE in March 1941, and was sent almost at once far from home, to set up an SOE Training School for black African agents at Lokumeje, in up-country Nigeria. He was later to take part in Operation Postmaster.

In May 1941, four more SOE officers were shipped out to West Africa, three of whom were to play significant parts in Operation Postmaster. They were the 26-year-old Captain (later Major) John Eyre (who like M had seen service in Norway), Lieutenant Desmond Longe, also 26, and the much older Captain Richard Lippett, aged 44, a First World War veteran.

Desmond Evelyn Longe had served as a private in the Territorial Army before the war. He was a banker, and had found himself on Ian Fleming's favourite island of Jamaica when the war broke out. He had made his way home and was commissioned into the Royal Norfolk Regiment, but by early 1941 was bored with regular soldiering within the confines of Great Britain. Through a personal friend, his name was passed to M at SOE, and Longe was recruited, trained and posted as Chief Instructor to SOE's guerrilla and sabotage schools at Lochailort and Arisaig in Scotland, training mainly Norwegians and Danes, although he does not seem to have met Lassen at this stage. In May 1941 Longe was sent to West Africa, for the purpose of training black Africans to operate against the Vichy French. He was a fully trained explosives expert, as was John Eyre, who had a similar brief.

Richard Lippett was a Welshman. He served in the Royal Engineers until 1924, when he was placed on the reserve list. He had been recruited by SOE in December 1940, and given the rank of Captain. Lippett spoke fluent Spanish.

Because of the need for the convoy to go via Greenland, Canada and the Americas, it took six weeks to reach Lagos. Longe later paid tribute to the US Navy, who, although the United States had not yet entered the war, shadowed the convoy for much of its route to ensure that no harm came to it. Nonetheless, the voyage took its toll on the SOE men. The tension was never-ending, since they were always vulnerable to U-Boat attack, and as the weather became hotter, tempers began to fray. A casual and rather unnecessary remark by John Eyre querying Lippett's patriotism led to the two men falling out badly. Lippett was furious and the damage was never adequately repaired. Happily, in West Africa the two men were to have little to do with each other, although both eventually played important parts in Operation Postmaster.

On arrival in Lagos, Eyre and Longe were provided with offices in Lagos Police Station. The colonial police were happy to cooperate with SOE, though the military were not. In due course Eyre was sent to Accra on the Gold Coast, to help train black African agents there, and Longe was sent up-country in Nigeria to the training school at Olokumeji, to join Major 'Dizzy'Dismore doing the same thing. The Africans that Dismore and Longe trained were valuable agents, enjoying far greater freedom of movement over the borders into Vichy French territory than any European, and able to bring back intelligence about troop movements and defence posts there. Longe even claimed to be privy to the contents of the Vichy French Governor's wastepaper basket, through a female agent who worked as a cleaner in his office. His only reservation was that, if the money was right, he believed his own cleaners might sell what was in his wastepaper basket to the Vichy French. In the days before shredders, obtaining the contents of enemy wastepaper baskets was a regular SOE trick. Scraps of torn-up documents would be reconstructed, and were often sent back to London in a diplomatic bag for further inspection in Baker Street.

Olokumeji was a very remote but beautiful spot, where no Europeans lived apart from Dismore and Longe. However, some of the indigenous Africans were extremely affluent and well educated. One invited Longe to his home in order to show off the trophies he had won playing polo in England.

Richard Lippett's value to SOE was different to that of Eyre and Longe. His ability to speak fluent Spanish was important, and M's reason for sending him out there must have been against the eventuality that he would have to send an agent undercover into Spanish Guinea. Lippett, a mature and resourceful man, proved later to be an excellent choice for that role.

A number of other agents were recruited locally. Charles Alexander Leonard Guise, aged thirty-three, is an example. He was recruited into SOE from the Nigerian Government service. While working up-country in Obudu, he received a telegram from the Chief Secretary in Lagos in February 1941, asking him whether he spoke Spanish. Since he had spoken it as a boy, Guise replied 'yes', even though little of his Spanish had stayed with him. He was summoned to Lagos, interviewed by W in March, and signed up, with the rank of Lieutenant.

SOE's concerns continued to grow. In June and July 1941, it was observed that the German tug *Likomba* had taken a lot of fuel on board, and appeared to be getting ready to go to sea. There were fears that she (like the *Duchessa d'Aosta*) might act as a supply ship to German U-Boats or surface raiders, a task to which she was apparently physically well suited. However, for the time being at least the *Likomba* stayed in Santa Isabel harbour.

During the same period, on 16 June 1941, it was observed that the *Duchessa d'Aosta* was taking on drinking water, and that the top of the funnel had been painted red, both signs that she might be getting ready to go to sea again. There was further information to confirm that the *Duchessa d'Aosta*'s wireless had been left unsecured by the Spanish authorities, and she was therefore in a position to make reports contrary to British interests. Listeners discovered that the *Duchessa* was sending radio messages to a German Swiss shipping company in Las Palmas.

The activity on both ships in June and July 1941 led SOE increasingly to the view that together they formed a 'supply fleet in being', ready to venture out and assist German craft. Although the ships were nominally impounded by the 'neutral' Spanish, it seemed clear to W, and to M, that no action would be taken to stop them sailing if they wanted to. Additionally, there remained the ever present fear that Germany might take over Fernando Po, with or without the consent of Spain, and put the ships to good use.

By early July 1941, specific planning for action against the ships in Santa Isabel harbour had begun. W made arrangements to improve and increase the flow of intelligence, ordering the ex-Government Service officer Guise (now Agent W10), to commute to Santa Isabel regularly, under cover as a diplomatic courier to the Consulate, to gather information about the island's coast and waterways, plus any other local information he could get. This appears to have been his first job with SOE. As his codename W10 suggests, he was not commando trained or 'licensed to kill', but he was to prove a very effective agent, and his work was of vital importance to the eventual success of Operation Postmaster.

The first thing Guise had to do was to get himself a boat, so that he could make his way to and from Fernando Po without relying on local steamers like the Spanish MV *Domine*, which visited the island regularly. He therefore travelled to Victoria, in British Cameroon, to visit the boatyard of the 'Custodian of Enemy Property' there, where he found and requisitioned a small German river tug with diesel engines called *Bamenda*. Although Guise was to describe her as most unsuitable for the high seas (she didn't even have a compass), he later estimated that he had successfully travelled 8,000 miles in her. In *Bamenda*, Guise was able to travel back and forth between the ports of Douala, in Free French Cameroon, and Santa Isabel on Fernando Po at will. He was instructed to find out everything he could and to look for a way, by bribery or strong action, to seize the *Duchessa d'Aosta*, about whom M and W were most concerned. He was, however, told to avoid compromising Vice Consul Michie at all costs.

Despite initial Spanish suspicions, Guise was gradually able to settle into life in Santa Isabel as an accepted face, coming and going to the harbour and the consulate under his cover as courier. He gained valuable additional intelligence about conditions on the island, and about the navigation of its coast and its difficult harbour. W began to rely heavily upon the accuracy of the intelligence that Guise supplied, as the Maid Honor Force would do much later on. Guise however tells one story against himself which might have worried W had he known about it. On one of his voyages to Fernando Po, without a compass, Guise managed to lose his way on the ocean to the south of the island, and remained literally 'all at sea' for more than two days, until he was luckily found by a passing British warship, HMS *Rochester*. The captain kindly 'lent' him a small prismatic compass, with which he was subsequently able to navigate rather more successfully.

By 8 July 1941, M had made up his mind to act. In his view, the most dangerous (and valuable) ship at Santa Isabel was the *Duchessa d'Aosta*. On that day, he and Caesar cabled W, telling him that SOE was anxious to secure the immediate immobilization of the *Duchessa d'Aosta*, and ordering him to inform them of the action that he proposed to take.

But in a cable back to London on 12 July, W replied: 'Action almost impossible.' He stressed the lack of real British presence on the island, and despatched a report the same day, explaining the up-to-date position in detail:

> We have a very excellent representative in the consul, Michie, who is popular, industrious and has given detailed and carefully prepared reports. He is assisted by the Courier Guise (running between Fernando Po and Douala) who is likewise very capable and keen. They

> report on an active organized German community of some forty on the mainland and island. The community have large commercial interests. They have a great deal of influence with the Spanish officials, whose Falangist ideology is akin to their own. They are active in propaganda work and they have an organized system of espionage, working into AEF [French Equatorial Africa], and the British Colonies on the mainland. The position of the courier is extremely delicate. He has only recently been appointed and is regarded with the greatest suspicion by the Spanish authorities. Although he has done a great deal in a short time to establish satisfactory relations, the slightest mischance or false step might easily lead to a request for his recall and we should be left without contact with the island, and through the island with Spanish Guinea. The number of Italians is above fifty. The Duchessa d'Aosta is known to be in port and to have wireless communication with Europe.

M was not deterred. On the same day that he received W's cable, he had a morning meeting with March-Phillipps and also lunched with him. M knew that he was in possession of a secret weapon that might crack the problem of the ships in Santa Isabel harbour – the Maid Honor Force. By early July of 1941, the Force was fully established, equipped and trained. Furthermore, because of the difficulties caused by the Admiralty, Maid Honor Force was sitting frustratedly at Poole, with nothing to do. Faced with the growing problem in Santa Isabel, it was a logical step to send March-Phillipps, Appleyard and the rest of the Force to West Africa. M made the decision that they were to go, but he could not send his Q-ship to West Africa without the consent of the Admiralty.

M met with March-Phillipps again on 14 July, and then went into a series of meetings with Ian Fleming. On 22 July M saw Fleming at 1730 hrs, and on the same day Fleming obtained Admiral Godfrey's consent in principle to the transfer of the Maid Honor Force to West Africa. M saw Fleming again at 1100 hrs the following morning, 23 July, and yet again at 1330 hrs on 24 July. A memorandum for Godfrey to present to his bosses at the Admiralty seeking formal approval for the transfer of the *Maid Honor* to Freetown, Sierra Leone, was drafted and perfected. The proposal was put forward in Godfrey's name and gained the Admiralty's endorsement on 26 July. It may well be that the Admiralty simply wanted to send the *Maid Honor* as far away as possible. But whatever their lordships' motivation, the 'James Bonds' of Maid Honor Force were finally to be launched.

M had not taken this decision lightly. Apart from the apparent unsuitability of a wooden-hulled ship for tropical waters, the long voyage to the Gulf of Guinea was a perilous one for a small sailing vessel like the *Maid Honor* even in peacetime. In time of war, as now, she would also be vulnerable to enemy action and, by her very nature, impossible to protect from a serious predator of any size.

Maid Honor Force would be on what was described as a 'deniable' mission. The *Maid Honor* was a Q-ship, and the men would travel and work in civilian clothes. The *Maid Honor* would fly the Swedish flag when necessary. If Maid Honor Force, or any of its men, were captured, His Majesty's Government would deny all knowledge of them. They would be abandoned to whatever fate their captors might decree.

Godfrey's memorandum to the Admiralty contains a detailed description of the *Maid Honor* as she was at that time: 'A converted Brixham trawler of the larger type, about 65 tons [an over-estimate, even allowing for the added weight of her new armaments]. Her maximum speed under sail is 11 knots, with auxiliary motor – six knots, and with both motor and sail running – twelve knots.' She was to have a crew of seven, and would be armed with a variety of concealed weapons. She had a two-pounder gun concealed in the dummy wheelhouse, and carried 100 rounds for it. She was to carry 4 five-pounder spigot mortars, 4 Bren light machine guns, 4 Tommy guns, 6 rifles, and 36 hand grenades. To help in her operations, six additional men were to be sent to Freetown by a different route, to bring the total complement of Maid Honor Force to thirteen. All were experienced in sabotage and were expert seamen, thanks to the training they had received in Poole. So far as the Admiralty was concerned, the objective of Maid Honor Force was to provide a means of communication between West Africa and the Cape Verde Islands, and to undertake 'subversive operations' on both land and sea. In a memorandum drafted for him dated 31 July, addressed to the Naval Commander in Chief, Portsmouth, Godfrey described the sending of *Maid Honor* to the South Atlantic as being 'to carry out such sabotage operations as may be ordered by SOE'. He said: 'No definite project is yet in view, but plans are at present being drawn up for her.'

M, astute tactician that he was, seems to have made no mention to Fleming or Godfrey of his clear intention that Maid Honor Force was to be used for a raid on Fernando Po. The Admiralty almost certainly would not have approved the project had they known about it at that time. M knew, of course, that eventually he would have to obtain specific approval for whatever operation he decided to mount on Fernando Po from both the Admiralty and the Foreign Office. Much red tape would inevitably have to be cut before an attack of any sort could be launched against two enemy ships in a neutral harbour. But it would obviously help to have the necessary commando force already in position in West Africa. In effect, M was smuggling out to W the weapon that he needed for such an operation. The Maid Honor Force was intended to become a truly secret weapon for SOE West Africa, based in Freetown and operating from a quasi-civilian fishing boat. Hence the need for the cloak of secrecy under which the Maid Honor Force was to travel, the deniable nature of their mission to West Africa, and the fact that their initial destination was to be Freetown, Sierra Leone, rather than the local SOE headquarters at Lagos, Nigeria. The real objective, of course, was intended to be Fernando Po.

The voyage of the *Maid Honor* over 3,000 miles from Poole to Freetown was an adventure in itself, but how much did M tell Maid Honor force of the real purpose of their voyage? From anecdotal evidence it is clear that Agents W.01, March-Phillipps and W.02, Appleyard, knew at least in outline the real reason why they were being sent to West Africa. They undoubtedly welcomed the challenge, and all the members of Maid Honor Force had had enough of training. They were ready.

CHAPTER 10

The Voyage to West Africa

Although the *Maid Honor* retained the outward appearance of a fishing boat, a lot of modification had in fact been done, as Godfrey's memorandum to the Admiralty made clear. The equivalent of Ian Fleming's future Q Branch had been hard at work. A dummy deckhouse of plywood had been built to conceal the Vickers Mark 8 two-pounder cannon now mounted on the deck. The deckhouse could only be entered from below, and was instantly collapsible by the pulling of a lever. The gun would then be ready for action at all angles, but care had to be taken not to damage the ship's rigging, sails or masts when it was fired. A part of the deck had been lowered to allow twin machine guns to fire through the scuppers. Fake crow's nests were fitted to the masts to act as firing platforms. In bizarre contrast to the ship's varied secret weaponry, within the *Maid Honor*'s main cabin there were still a series of painted panels, depicting her victory in a 1936 Torbay regatta. These had been commissioned by her last owner, Major Bertram Bell, when he first bought her and had converted her from a working fishing boat to a pleasure yacht.

The *Maid Honor* had also been provided with a new type of mortar, the spigot mortar, for use against submarines on the surface (if they ever found any) or any other ships. This was a recently developed weapon. It was easily transportable and easily concealed, and the *Maid Honor* was one of the first 'guinea pigs' chosen to try it out. When fired accurately the spigot mortar had considerable destructive power. It is recorded that SOE sent down Lieutenant Commander Nevil Shute Norway (better known as the novelist Nevil Shute, but also a top pre-war engineer with Vickers) to examine the suitability of the *Maid Honor* to be fitted with the new mortar. He gave the go-ahead, and a trial firing from on board was duly arranged in Poole harbour. 'Q Branch' sent down one of the real Q's assistants from the SOE Research and Development Station at Brickendonbury House in Hertfordshire, Major C. V. Clarke MC, who filmed the spigot mortar being test fired from the *Maid Honor*. The test was successful, but not without incident. When the firing began, Graham Hayes, who had been sitting on the side of the *Maid Honor* relaxing with his pipe, was hurled into the water by the violent recoil, losing both his pipe and his shorts in the process. To March-Phillipps' concern, red-hot particles from the charge burned a number of small holes in the mainsail. Nonetheless, it was considered that the spigot mortar was a suitable weapon with which to arm the Q-ship *Maid Honor*, and she was supplied with four.

Major Clarke's film of the *Maid Honor* and her crew still exists. As so often when a camera is nearby, there was a certain amount of fooling about by the crew. March-Phillipps and Appleyard climbed the rigging to the top of the main mast, and March-Phillipps then swung himself back down again to the deck, hand over hand. In a time long before today's gym-toned and heavily muscled bodies, the super-fit men of the Maid Honor Force seem relatively slim of build, and only Geoffrey Appleyard (the rowing man) comes anywhere near the muscular physique of the current James Bond, Daniel Craig. The test firing appears to have been treated as something of a party event and a number of visitors came on board, including a young lady who was probably the very popular daughter of the landlord of the Antelope Hotel in Poole.

Perhaps as a result of his heightened awareness of the possibility of damage to the sails, March-Phillipps arranged just before the *Maid Honor* left Poole for her to have a spare set to take with her. According to Lieutenant Prout, these were 'borrowed' on March-Phillipps' explicit orders from another Brixham trawler in the dead of night, shortly before the *Maid Honor* sailed, and were only discovered missing after she had gone. Leslie Prout, one of the culprits who was staying behind in Poole to travel out later, was hauled over the coals by M as a result. But Prout had only been obeying orders, and March-Phillipps by then was on the high seas, heading for West Africa.

The *Maid Honor*'s disguises and secret weapons undoubtedly appealed strongly to Ian Fleming. As mentioned, SOE's large and inventive department dedicated to covert weapons and disguise were a model for his 'Q Branch', the department of 'special gadgets' in the Bond stories. SOE's real special gadgets department was formally known as the Scientific Research Department, and came under the overall command of the Director of Scientific Research, Dr (later Professor) Dudley M. Newitt, the model for Fleming's boffin-like 'Q'.

Dudley Newitt was forty-six years of age when recruited into SOE. He had fought in the First World War, on the North West Frontier of India, and in Mesopotamia and Palestine, and had won the Military Cross. After the war he took a degree in Chemistry at the Royal College of Science (later Imperial College, London), became a chemical engineer and later an academic. He controlled a large and enormously inventive department in SOE. Newitt understood military matters, and was an energetic and inspiring leader. However, his appearance was deceptive, and he was sometimes described as 'a typical absent-minded professor' or 'absent-minded boffin' (in the style of Fleming's Q). In fact, Newitt's vagueness concealed a high level of organization, energy and drive.

Fleming built up the role of Q gradually in his books. Q, and Q Branch, get brief mentions in the second Bond book, *Live and Let Die* (1954), in which they provided Bond with a rubber frogman's suit, which fitted perfectly. In *From Russia with Love* (1957), Q Branch produces a refined secret agent's attaché case containing spare ammunition for Bond's beloved Beretta (a favourite weapon of Anders Lassen), two throwing knives (again, favoured by Lassen), a cyanide pill (which Bond threw away), a silencer for the Beretta, and fifty gold sovereigns (which were commonly carried by SOE agents).

Three of the Bond films were made during Fleming's lifetime and with his approval. Q himself first makes an appearance in 1963 in the second, *From Russia with Love*, where he is referred to by M simply as, 'the Equipment Officer, Q Branch'. In the next film, *Goldfinger*, made during Fleming's lifetime, but premiered a month after his death in September 1964, 'the Equipment Officer' is named by Bond as 'Q', and Bond visits the Q Branch laboratory. After Fleming's death, Q's role grew film by film until he and his gadgets became an essential part of the Bond culture.

The *Maid Honor* was a Q-ship, which is no doubt where Fleming got the name of his 'Q Branch' from. The letter 'Q' epitomized disguise and deceit, often in breach of the rules of war. The *Maid Honor* masqueraded as a Swedish civilian ship and flew, when necessary, the Swedish flag. On the surface, she remained a fishing vessel, but within minutes she could collapse her innocent-looking deckhouse and bring her armaments to bear on any target. Her plain-clothed crew were in fact all trained Commandos who carried military rank.

Newitt's department within SOE even produced a catalogue of special devices from which their agents could choose their equipment for a mission, called the *Descriptive Catalogue of Special Devices and Supplies*. This included a frogman's outfit (described as an Amphibian Breathing Apparatus), an incendiary attaché case, briefcase and suitcase, a variety of unpleasant covert knives and guns, including a Thumb Knife and a Sleeve Gun. The latter was described in the catalogue as, 'a short length, silent, murder weapon, firing 0.32 ammunition. It is a single shot weapon designed for carriage in the sleeve with the trigger near the muzzle to aid unobtrusive firing when the gun is slid from the sleeve into the hand. The gun is intended for use in contact with the target, but may be used at ranges of up to about three yards'. The stock on offer included other deadly weapons, but also items such as tyre busters (concealed explosive charges designed to explode when driven over) and secret ink. It was exactly the sort of catalogue that Fleming's James Bond might browse through when visiting Q's laboratory.

Other weapons invented by Newitt's department over the years for use by SOE's agents included the Welpen, Welpipe, Welwoodbine and Welcheroot. These were all disguised, single shot .22 pistols designed to be used either as a last resort weapon by SOE agents, or for the purposes of assasination. As the names suggest, the Welpen was a pistol disguised as a pen, the Welwoodbine a pistol disguised as a Woodbine cigarette (although the agent could change the paper around the gun to suit the local brand of cigarette where he was operating) and so on. Newitt's team also designed incendiary cigarettes, of which agents were supplied with many thousands. The emphasis was always on the disguise. Newitt and his research department were always striving to create devices that would make a secret agent's life easier.

In early August the *Maid Honor*, newly converted to her Q-ship role, was fully prepared to depart from Poole. March-Phillipps had driven her crew hard in training and all had become as familiar as they could be in British waters with the skills necessary to handle her. But before she sailed, the twenty-year-old Anders Lassen wanted to ensure that the Q-ship *Maid Honor* was a lucky ship. He had been given what he swore was a sailor's lucky charm – a piece of a dried dolphin's tail (although his comrades believed from its appearance that it could have come from almost anywhere), and he decided that he should attach it to the *Maid Honor*. Not satisfied with a more accessible part of the ship, Lassen made a dangerous ascent to the truck of the topmast, a height of about 60 feet, where he nailed the dolphin's tail into place to bring the *Maid Honor* good fortune on her perilous voyage.

Careful planning had been undertaken. Sea-going clothes suitable for a civilian crew had been purchased in London and, once the voyage to Sierra Leone had been confirmed, a visit to the Board of Trade had provided Maid Honor Force with access to all relevant charts, and details of the lights and markers that they would encounter on their visit to Funchal on the Portuguese island of Madeira, the point at which they were to break their voyage to Freetown in order to re-stock with fresh water and supplies.

Jan Nasmyth, one of the planners of the expedition, was entirely realistic about the danger of a voyage to West Africa:

> The theory was that a sailing ship without an escort would not be worth a torpedo. But if a U-Boat surfaced to attack with a gun, the Maid could give an account of herself with the machine guns and cannon. The Royal Navy, it was presumed, kept German surface raiders out of the Atlantic, and so the main danger lay in attack by air patrols. That danger seemed very considerable and the Vickers cannon, although a dual purpose weapon, might have been ineffective as an ack-ack gun through being hemmed in by masts and rigging. I should say that the Maid was entirely vulnerable to attack by air. One just had to hope that the Germans wouldn't notice her.

Nasmyth missed the actual operation, since he went on compassionate leave to be with his dying father.

On a long journey, the *Maid Honor* could carry only a small crew. The plan was that there should be a crew of seven: March-Phillipps, Graham Hayes, Anders Lassen, Buzz Perkins, Denis Tottenham and two other Danes who had been recruited into the Maid Honor Force along with Lassen – one was a navigator, the other could cook. One of the purposes of having the three Danes on board was to give the appearance, when necessary, that the *Maid Honor* was a neutral Swedish ship. Graham Hayes could also pass as a Swede and Buzz Perkins, who was blond, looked too young to be in the military. Maid Honor Force also had their Swedish flag, which they would fly when necessary to complete the deception. Tottenham later described himself (accurately) as the only 'proper Navy' member of the *Maid Honor*'s crew on the voyage to Africa.

The ebullient young Anders Lassen, who albeit not 'proper' Navy was a professional seaman, appears to have been the sole member of the crew to have made a realistic assessment of the *Maid Honor*'s chances of success. He was well aware of the hazards that the voyage would bring, and being the sort of outspoken young man that he was, announced to his shipmates that the voyage was doomed and he was going to his death. The others laughed off his concerns and Lassen, having made his prophecy, carried on with his job. The voyage to Freetown, and the action that followed, caused Anders Lassen to grow out of the angry young man that he undoubtedly was in early 1941 into a very effective and reliable commando. March-Phillipps, a much older man, became his hero and icon and Lassen learned an enormous amount from him.

There is a minor dispute as to the exact day when *Maid Honor* finally sailed from Poole. The recollection of a number of Maid Honor Force was that it was 10 August 1941, but M's diary suggests it was the 9th. His diary reads: '10.30 onwards, arrive Antelope, Poole. Maid Honor to sail by 3.00.' There was a farewell lunch at the Antelope Hotel for the whole Force and their friends, before March-Phillipps and his six fellow crew members sailed the *Maid Honor* out of Poole harbour. There was something of a festive atmosphere both amongst the crew and the small party who saw them off. March-Phillipps' aunt apparently waved from the shore at Sandbanks. As his diary suggests, M had abandoned Baker Street for the day, and came on board with the rest of the party as the *Maid Honor* was piloted out to Old Harry Rock, outside the confines of the harbour. A rare wartime bottle of champagne had been acquired with which to toast the voyage. The *Maid Honor* parted company from the pilot and her well-wishers at Poole Bar buoy and set off under full sail and with her engine running, in what was intended to be a speedy and stylish departure. In fact, she nearly came to grief as she met the full force of a sea whipped up by a strong west wind, and the high spirits of her crew were quickly dampened.

The bad weather continued on the sail to Dartmouth. The other two Danes failed to match up to March-Phillipps' exacting standards during the seventy-mile voyage, one being chronically seasick and the other proving an inadequate navigator. March-Phillipps, who never tolerated anyone he regarded as not up to the job, put them both ashore at Dartmouth. That left him under strength with a total crew of five (the *Maid Honor* would normally carry a crew of at least six.) More significantly, it left him without a trained navigator, which for a voyage of the length they were facing was a very significant handicap. One of the crew, perhaps March-Phillipps himself, went ashore in Dartmouth to buy a ship's log. The log was designed for weekend yachtsmen, entitled 'Log Book for Yachts'. It contained handy hints on how to keep a log and related matters. Although the completed logbook provides a useful record of the *Maid Honor*'s journeys, it clearly demonstrates how amateur at navigation and record keeping the entire crew was. They were about to attempt a momentous voyage, with only the most basic knowledge of navigation between the five of them. However, on the positive side, the departure of the two Danes removed doubts as to whether they were carrying enough fresh water for everyone. Further, for what was bound to be a difficult journey, March-Phillipps was now satisfied that he had a reliable and well bonded crew, small though it was.

Agent W.02, Geoffrey Appleyard, had received orders that he (together with Lieutenant Leslie Prout), should travel as an advance guard to Freetown, separately from March-Phillipps, so that in the case of mishap to either, the other could command the operation in West Africa. Appleyard was there to see the *Maid Honor*'s departure, then left England on 15 August, travelling in civilian clothes on a civilian liner. As it happened, it was the P and O's *Strathmore*. Appleyard had visited her in Dubrovnik in August 1937, when she had been cruising in the Adriatic. Typically (as no doubt James Bond would have done) Appleyard had swum out from the shore to board her. Furthermore, the *Strathmore* was almost identical to her sister ship the *Strathallen*, on which Appleyard had travelled with members of his family in 1938. He felt very comfortable aboard and enjoyed his voyage. The convoy in which he travelled was fortunate and was troubled only once by a possible threat from U-boats, which in the event came to nothing.

The remainder of Maid Honor Force travelled out together on a separate ship a bit later, arriving in early October 1941. Before they left, they were sent up to Scotland for further sabotage training. Like Appleyard they travelled in civilian clothes, as befitted secret agents. All travelled to Freetown, Sierra Leone, deliberately chosen as being some distance away from Fernando Po and from the main SOE base in Lagos, where they would have been more conspicuous. Since their real objective was to attack ships in a neutral harbour, contrary to international law, secrecy was paramount. So far as M and SOE were concerned, nobody apart from their own small inner circle should ever know that Maid Honor Force existed.

It had been impressed upon all the men of the expedition, both on board the *Maid Honor* and travelling by civilian liner, that once they had left England they would be on a 'deniable mission' and therefore, in effect, on their own. Each man had been required to sign a declaration acknowledging that he understood this. The contrast with normal military work was stark. All now carried civilian passports supplied by SOE, and if questioned would declare that they worked for a variety of civilian government bodies. Never a force much impressed by uniform, all the men of Maid Honor Force were now to remain in civilian clothes at all times. What had to be avoided was any news of the arrival of a specialized British commando force in West Africa. If anything went wrong, they would be disowned by the British Government, and if captured there would be no easy transition to a prisoner of war camp. They might well be shot as spies. One of March-Phillipps' pencilled standing orders to his crew reads: 'Avoid a fight if humanly possible, but resist capture to the last.'

The *Maid Honor* left Dartmouth on 12 August. Once out of territorial waters, the ship was at risk of attack by air or sea throughout every daylight hour, while at night the danger of attack from the sea remained. The watch had to be alert at all times. On the second day out from Dartmouth, the weather turned against them and March-Phillipps recorded in the log, 'Strong winds, little visibility'. The crew were understandably nervous as to how the *Maid Honor* would perform in really heavy weather after all the modifications that had been necessary to turn her into a Q-ship. Additionally, her previous owner, Major Bertram Bell, had partly replaced the original ballast of pig iron with lead ingots, in order to increase the headroom of the cabin. Brixham trawlers have the reputation of being amongst the world's soundest small sailing craft, but the *Maid Honor* was no longer quite the same ship that she had been when first launched.

Fighting the high seas and foul weather, the first five days of the voyage were extremely rough and performing the simplest of tasks was hazardous. The small crew worked tirelessly. March-Phillipps drew heavily on the knowledge of his most experienced sailors, Graham Hayes and Denis Tottenham, and on the professional seamanship of Anders Lassen. The *Maid Honor* survived, despite all her modifications.

Day Six was a Sunday, and the *Maid Honor* came upon a fishing fleet somewhere southwest of Brest. March-Phillipps recorded in the log: 'Sailed right through a tunny fishing fleet, no markings, no flags. Two of them sailed with us for the afternoon, remaining a few miles to the windward and then went about. Bright sun, great sailing weather but ship still very wet.'

Lassen, who was the only one of the crew with wartime long voyage experience, found that his very considerable doubts about the feasibility of the voyage began to diminish. Even though their small ship had only limited protection, no wireless contact with the outside world, and no specialist navigator, they were gradually eating up the many miles that they had to cover. As the *Maid Honor* progressed day after day without interference from the enemy, it began to look as if M and March-Phillipps had been right to gamble as they had. Lassen no doubt believed that the dolphin's tail he had nailed to the mast was contributing to their good fortune.

The tenth day of the voyage found them halfway between the Azores and Cape St Vincent in the far southwest of Portugal. On 25 August, the thirteenth day after leaving Dartmouth, the *Maid Honor* sighted Madeira and later in the day, flying the Swedish flag, the trawler dropped anchor off Funchal. It was a nervous moment. Maid Honor Force was now in Portuguese territorial waters, and although Portugal remained neutral, the crew did not know how the authorities would react to their presence. They suspected that the island carried its quota of German spies. Certainly, if their true identity was discovered, they would be likely to be arrested and the *Maid Honor* impounded. A heavily armed British commando vessel would not be welcome in neutral Portugal. They knew, of course, that if they were arrested and flung into some Portuguese prison, M would not be able to come to their rescue. However, it was necessary to take on fresh provisions for the next lengthy and demanding stage of their voyage and March-Phillipps had no option but to stop.

Maid Honor Force had its cover story prepared. Along with their false civilian passports, the men carried fake seamen's paypackets. The story was that they were a neutral Swedish crew on a neutral Swedish yacht. They were not allowed to go ashore, or stay for longer than was necessary to re-provision, because they had been delayed by a storm and their owner-captain was insisting on making up that time as fast as possible. Lassen spoke Swedish, Hayes after his many months on the Swedish windjammer could improvise, Perkins was blessed with Scandinavian looks and his very youth suggested that the *Maid Honor* was a civilian, not a military ship. March-Phillipps nonetheless prayed that no one amongst the Portuguese port officials spoke any Swedish.

Having dropped anchor, they could only wait for the harbour authorities to come and investigate. Happily, the wait was not a long one. Their approach had no doubt been observed with interest from the island. It was a very tense moment when the Portuguese coastguard launch came alongside, followed by a small squadron of bumboats bringing fresh water, fruit and eggs. For the secret agents of the Maid Honor Force, this was the first test of the effectiveness of their 'cover'.

Happily, the coastguard officials were relaxed and friendly. Lassen and his fellow 'Swedes' carried the day, and the ship itself received only the most casual inspection. Its hidden weaponry and false deckhouse remained unsuspected. The *Maid Honor* also successfully passed the inspection of the many curious eyes on the bumboats, some of whom were undoubtedly in the pay of the enemy. Fresh water was taken on board, and fruit and eggs purchased to supplement their dwindling rations. When the little mercantile flotilla duly departed, the five men felt an enormous sense of relief and satisfaction. Their lies and deception had worked.

Good fortune continued with them when they left Madeira. The weather was fine, and they picked up the benefit of the trade winds, making good speed over the next few days. The log records speeds of 7, 8 and even 10 knots per hour between 25 and 28 August.

Sadly, their luck then changed. The ship began to labour and make water, and March-Phillipps discovered that they had an engine problem. At first it was thought to be due to a leak in the exhaust gland, but after that was repaired the problem got no better. A leak to the store gland was then diagnosed and March-Phillipps ordered that they stop to fix it. This time the repair worked and eventually the *Maid Honor* got under way again, still enjoying the benefit of the trade winds. A log entry for 29 August reads, 'Fish meal of flying fish'.

The wind dropped again after a further five days. Now the *Maid Honor* found herself in acute danger. She was in the 'doldrums', stuck off the coast of French West Africa, which was in Vichy hands. Intelligence suggested that the Vichy French at the naval base of Dakar were actively pro-German. When France had capitulated in the summer of 1940, the Royal Navy had attacked and sunk a number of French warships in the Mediterranean to prevent them falling into German hands, and resentment against the British in the Vichy French Navy remained strong. A joint British and Free French attack on Dakar in September 1940 had failed. Therefore, if the *Maid Honor* was identified as a British warship, however modest, whilst off French West Africa, she could expect no mercy.

March-Phillipps had intended to steer a course that would take them safely to the west of the Cape Verde islands, far off the coast of French West Africa, as speedily as possible. He obviously wanted to get this potentially hazardous part of the voyage out of the way. However the fates were against him, and after their fine sail from Madeira, the Maid Honor Force now found themselves virtually becalmed off the enemy coast, still hundreds of miles north of the Cape Verde Islands.

The crew were tired; they were maintaining six-hour watches, one on, one off, and there were only five of them. All five men shared the watches, March-Phillipps as well as his men. Aware of the dangers of being spotted either from the air, or from the sea by the Vichy French, the lookout on each watch was on full alert. On the afternoon of the second day without wind, a warning cry came from the lookout. Two ships had been sighted, one a merchantman but the other a battle cruiser. In the distance, the nationality of the two ships could not be made out. The likelihood was that they were Vichy French.

March-Phillipps feared the worst. He clearly believed there was no chance of a deception such as that used in Funchal succeeding now. Once boarded it would be only a matter of minutes before it became clear who they were. On the huge and empty ocean, there was nowhere to run and nowhere to hide. Thus there was no point in trying to preserve the pretence of being a neutral fishing boat. March-Phillipps ordered the guns to be manned. The deckhouse was collapsed, and the two-inch cannon was made ready to fire. If it came to a fight, they would resist to the last, however hopeless it might be. To take on a battle cruiser with their two-inch cannon would be a task far harder than that of David against Goliath, but March-Phillipps, like the James Bond of the future books, would never give up, however hopeless the odds seemed. He was determined, if necessary, that they would go down fighting.

It was very soon clear that the battle cruiser had seen them. The small crew waited anxiously at battle stations as the unidentified warship gradually shortened the distance between them. The closer that the mighty ship approached, the more awe-inspiring the sight of its great guns became. A suppressed feeling of utter inadequacy pervaded the Maid Honor Force. All their preparation and training was now to be wasted. A single shell from one of the battle cruiser's guns would blow the *Maid Honor* and its crew to pieces. But fight they would. At least their own gun would have a large target to shoot at. Such luck as Lassen's dolphin's tail could bring them was now very sorely needed.

The coin of fortune turned lazily in the air as the minutes passed. Which way would it fall? Was it a death sentence or a reprieve? Five pairs of eyes, some with binoculars, strained across the ocean. Finally there came a loud cry of relief. The battle cruiser was a British one, HMS *Barham*.

March-Phillipps stood his men down and, once again reverting to the role of civilian sailing yacht, the *Maid Honor* hove to and waited to be boarded. It was soon covered by the battle cruiser's guns, as a boat brought a boarding party across to investigate. Despite the confidential nature of their mission, March-Phillipps was able to answer enough of the ensuing questions to satisfy the British boarding party as to their identity. HMS *Barham* then extended their hospitality to the crew of the *Maid Honor*, offering them hot baths on board the battle cruiser, and supplying them with fresh fruit. The *Maid Honor* and its crew in due course proceeded on its way, much heartened and refreshed.

The winds did not pick up for another four days and March-Phillipps became increasingly worried as to whether the fresh water would last. He ordered that seawater be used for all tasks; fresh water was to be used for drinking only. Clothes and bodies could be washed in sea water. Food was not a problem. Lassen introduced the rest of the crew to a trick he had learned in his days travelling the world on commercial tankers. He would knock a few small holes in a tin, place a piece of carbide from the lamps inside it, and toss it over the side. Inevitably the shiny tin would be swallowed quickly, often by a following barracuda shark, and would explode once it mixed with the contents of the shark's stomach. Fresh fish steaks, lots of them, would result.

The wind finally rose again for a short time on 6 September, but almost immediately the engine packed up. Water had got into it and it needed to be thoroughly dried out. By the time it had dried, the wind had dropped again. The engine continued to give trouble. On 8 September, with the *Maid Honor* becalmed, the engine failed to start at all. For six days, the ship lay motionless on the ocean, with its engine silent. Examination of the engine by the older members of the crew pronounced it well and truly dead, but seventeen-year-old Buzz Perkins refused to accept defeat. He started working on it and would not give up. March-Phillipps in his official report to M of the voyage later said:

> I should like to commend young Perkins as an engineer. On outskirts of doldrums we found that our engine had taken on seawater and was apparently impossible to start. The case of the engine seemed hopeless but he removed the cylinder heads, fitted new gaskets, reground the valves with home made valve paste, unstuck the pistons, which had rusted solid, in twenty-four hours by removing the big end bearings, and reassembled the engine again, all in a heavy swell and a temperature of one hundred and twenty in the engine room. Graham Hayes was a great help to him. I think this was a great piece of work, and I would like to mention it in particular with all the other work he has done which has been excellent. He has proved the most reliable man on the ship, even although he is the youngest by several years.

Thanks to Perkins, on 15 September, seven days after the breakdown, the *Maid Honor*'s log records: 'Engine miraculously started, and pulled Maid away at four and a half knots.' A lot of time had been lost, however, and over the first sixteen days of September the average speed of the *Maid Honor* was less than two and a half knots. Much of that time was spent in dangerous waters and progress was painfully slow. But Lassen's dolphin tail continued to work its charms, and no enemy vessel interfered with such progress as they were making.

The concern over whether the fresh water would last was increasing. As March-Phillipps' report of Perkins work on the engine makes clear, it was at times extremely hot. According to the thermometer, the temperature in the ship's galley at one point reached 135 degrees Farenheit (57 Celsius), which was only a degree below the world shade record of the time. The men had to drink substantial quantities of fresh water simply to survive, something between one and one and a half gallons, per man per day. Relief came finally on 18 September 1941, when the monsoon arrived and the fresh water problem was almost instantaneously resolved. With the engine fixed and a decent wind blowing, the *Maid Honor* started to pick up speed, reaching a maximum of 10 knots an hour.

Three days later, on Sunday 21 September, the Maid Honor Force reached Freetown, Sierra Leone. They had been at sea for forty-one days and had covered 3,185 miles. Despite their many difficulties during the voyage, their lack of a properly trained navigator, and their time in the doldrums, they had made the journey in near record time for a sailing craft of the *Maid Honor*'s size. The 'James Bonds' had arrived. On the following day, Anders Lassen enjoyed his twenty-first birthday. He had matured a lot during the voyage, but had lost nothing of his independent spirit, which March-Phillipps nurtured with care. Lassen had been happy to be back at sea, away from the rules and regulations of the Regular Army. He was a youngster very much in March-Phillipps's own mould and was happy to learn as much as he could from the older man. The youngest member of the crew, Perkins, was still only seventeen but he too was growing up fast.

Even in peacetime, the voyage of the *Maid Honor* would have been a remarkable achievement. To do it in wartime and with the battle of the Atlantic raging, was remarkable. M's confidence in March-Phillipps and Maid Honor Force was entirely justified. The five men on board had demonstrated just how resourceful and durable they were.

Meanwhile, Appleyard and Prout, in civilian clothes and travelling separately from the rest of their men, had left Britain on 15 August, and predictably had had a much speedier journey than the *Maid Honor*. Travelling the direct route they arrived in Freetown before the end of August, and set up an appropriate camp for the Maid Honor Force at Lumley Beach, at the end of Cape Sierra Leone and about nine miles from Freetown. It was a discreet spot, away from the prying eyes of Freetown itself. The Royal Navy assisted by erecting a number of huts for them, although the sleeping accommodation was in tents. The camp was out of the way, and there was plenty of space nearby for training, including the beach itself. Appleyard was a far better nuts and bolts man than March-Phillipps, and Prout had already taken on the role of 'quartermaster general' for the Maid Honor Force, a role which he continued with considerable success throughout their time in West Africa.

Although Appleyard was dismissive about Freetown, describing it as a very one-eyed, ramshackle outpost of the Empire, the campsite that he found for Maid Honor Force was very beautiful, with views over the tropical bay and clumps of banana and coconut trees nearby. In a part of the world traditionally described as a 'white man's graveyard', Appleyard hoped the campsite would be healthy and would benefit from sea breezes. They would sleep beneath mosquito nets at night, in the hope of fending off the malaria-carrying mosquitos.

On about 18 September, with the *Maid Honor* overdue and still somewhere on the high seas, Appleyard was called to Lagos for consultations with W and W4. Until the *Maid Honor* arrived, Appleyard (now officially Agent W.02 since he was attached to W Section) was in command of Maid Honor Force, and was its representative in West Africa. Even if the *Maid Honor* with its crew of five failed to arrive, six more agents would reach Freetown in due course, and SOE Lagos would have to hand a small but highly trained new team of eight secret agents, all licensed to kill. W was experiencing the same difficulties with the local high command in West Africa that M's Secret Service was experiencing everywhere at this stage in its history, but no doubt he hoped to put the Maid Honor Force to good use, in particular against the ships in Santa Isabel harbour. Despite the Admiralty approving the despatch of the Force to Freetown, the ban on bangs was still for the time being in place for the SOE in West Africa (as imposed by General Giffard), preventing them from using explosives, or attacking targets. Still, even if that order was not revoked and sabotage was ruled out, there was much that Maid Honor Force might achieve with the use of its Q-ship. W continued to press for approval of the Fernando Po project, in the hope that the presence of a commando team in Freetown might help to persuade the 'old men' (Giffard and Admiral Willis) to give their approval. Santa Isabel was not the only potential target for a raid. Two German ships, the *Wamaru* and the *Wagogo*, were lying at anchor in the port of Lobito, in Portuguese Angola, another neutral colony. W's plan was that there should be two operations, one against Lobito, the other against Santa Isabel.

Appleyard's description of wartime Lagos is interesting, and may explain to some extent why General Giffard and Admiral Willis proved to be rather out of touch with the way that the modern war had to be fought. Appleyard wrote home that: 'There are wonderful facilities here for Europeans, including riding, polo, racing, tennis, squash, sailing etc. Lovely houses and gardens.' From another point of view, a report to the Admiralty, also in August 1941, complained: 'Ships lying at anchor during the night are silhouetted against the brightness of a blaze of light on shore. . . Lagos is quoted as a place in which the black-out regulations appear to receive scant attention from officials.' It was obviously a very different atmosphere and lifestyle to war-torn Britain.

Whilst in Lagos Appleyard received the news that the *Maid Honor* had finally reached Freetown, and when he returned there a few days later he was delighted to be re-united with his friends and colleagues. March-Phillipps and the other four crew of the *Maid Honor* were understandably ebullient at what they had achieved. They had overcome everything the elements could throw at them and had managed to stay out of the enemy's way. Now, after a short rest, they were raring to prove what their Q-ship could do against the enemy.

When shortly thereafter the final contingent arrived in Freetown, the full Maid Honor Force of thirteen men was re-assembled, and all was finally in place. Their seaside camp at Lumley Beach worked well and they became the guests of a nearby Royal Artillery mess that served an Anti-Aircraft battery. Since this unit had formerly been the Leeds Territorial Army Battery it was full of Yorkshiremen, one of whom, to the delight of Appleyard and Hayes, came from their home village of Linton-on-Wharfe.

Whilst they awaited orders, Maid Honor Force concentrated on physical training and acclimatization. The five who had sailed the *Maid Honor* out from England were fit and hardened to the hot sun. Those who had come by liner, however, had inevitably lost fitness on the voyage and now found themselves in a totally different environment. The hot and steamy climate of equatorial West Africa meant that training was far harder than it had been in either Poole or in Scotland. It was for good reason that West Africa had become known as the white man's graveyard. Because of the difficulties of the local climate it was the custom that members of the military and of the colonial service would be sent home on leave every fifteen months. The main problem was malaria. March-Phillipps and his men soon discovered that the healthiest place to sleep was on the deck of the *Maid Honor* herself, where the mosquitos apparently feared to tread. Because of the oppressive heat, it was constantly necessary for the men to take on fluids. Further, the local climate did not encourage even the smallest of infections to clear up. Appleyard wrote home in October, reassuring his family that he remained perfectly well, but stating that their party had already suffered two cases of malarial fever. He commented that the first dose of malaria seemed to knock a man out for about a fortnight.

It was not until about three weeks after the arrival of the *Maid Honor* that

March-Phillipps' men were given any work to do by the local High Command, and for that period of time they remained hanging around at Lumley Beach. Illness and inactivity are never good for a unit's morale and the men of Maid Honor Force were frustrated by their period of enforced idleness. However, it is an indication of March-Phillipps' leadership qualities, and the way that Maid Honor Force had bonded together, that morale at all times remained high. They spent three or four hours a day in the sea, swimming and diving, and fishing with long spears. In the early mornings and the evenings, their campsite was particularly beautiful, and at night there were hosts of fireflies surrounding them, lighting up the darkened beach.

CHAPTER 11

Preparations and Frustrations

As Maid Honor Force had been travelling, in its various ways, to West Africa, the planning and arguing continued over what action SOE would be allowed to take in the area. One of the reasons behind M's decision to send Maid Honor Force was that SOE West Africa needed to prove its worth. They were still regarded as an upstart organization and needed to chalk up a good victory. Also, in West Africa everyone knew how badly Britain was suffering back home and many yearned to get involved in the real action of the war, rather than simply to stand guard on an outpost of the Empire. A decisive local action by SOE would boost everybody's morale.

Unfortunately, the military supremos in West Africa and the South Atlantic took a very different view. General Giffard and Admiral Willis both had plenty to keep them occupied. Giffard, amongst other duties, had the responsibility of guarding the extensive borders of this part of the British Empire from attack, in particular from the territories held by the Vichy French. Willis had the vital convoys to guard. To neither man did the presence of the *Duchessa d'Aosta* and the *Likomba* in Santa Isabel seem of primary importance. M and W continued to argue that the manoeuvrable German tug, *Likomba*, was a positive threat to British shipping in the South Atlantic and, further, that if she were to be captured she could be usefully employed by the British against her former owners. They also argued that the *Duchessa d'Aosta* was a valuable ship (the estimate for the ship alone was between £125,000 and £150,000), and carried a valuable cargo. There was also the problem of the *Duchessa*'s radio, believed to be still broadcasting. It was clearly desirable that the radio should be closed down, and whatever intelligence it was sending should be cut off. However, neither Willis nor Giffard was persuaded. General Giffard in particular was keen that SOE, of whom as a very traditional soldier he strongly disapproved, should do nothing in West Africa that might 'rock the boat'.

Happily for M and W, the Governor of Nigeria, Sir Bernard Bourdillon, took an entirely different view. He and his senior staff were strongly supportive of SOE's West African mission. As things later turned out, without his help, Operation Postmaster would never have been possible.

While the argument ground on, SOE's W Section got on with the job of gathering detailed information about Santa Isabel and Fernando Po. SOE were specialists in sabotage, and one option (providing that the ban on bangs was lifted) was to blow up both of the enemy ships moored there. However, if this was done in a neutral harbour it would be likely to cause a diplomatic storm and considerable embarrassment for His Majesty's Government – unless it were done in such a way that the Spanish would never be able to prove the British had carried out the attack. Thus very detailed intelligence and planning was required. All aspects of the coastal and harbour defences had to be studied, as did the danger of pursuit after the attack had been carried out. All of this fell within the remit of W's new agent on Fernando Po, W10, Leonard Guise.

The harbour of Santa Isabel was something of a goldfish bowl, easily observed by many pairs of hostile eyes. Agent Guise's regular visits to Fernando Po as the new 'diplomatic courier' had aroused many initial suspicions, but he was working to establish the sort of routine that would allay these, so he would be less conspicuous. Each time he made one of his weekly journeys by boat to Santa Isabel, W10 would take careful note of the shoals, currents and buoys in the harbour approaches. As time went by, while on shore in the heat of the little colonial port, Guise was able talk more freely with the locals on the island and, without appearing to probe, gather additional intelligence from them.

By the end of August, working persistently and in all weathers, Guise had collected a lot of valuable intelligence, which he duly reprted to W. He had learned that morale amongst the crew of the *Duchessa d'Aosta* was, not surprisingly, low after their long period of inactivity in the harbour of Santa Isabel. They had nothing to do and were generally unwelcome to the local residents. Some had managed to leave the island, but there remained on board at least six officers, and thirty-four crew. The original Captain of the liner had been allowed to return to Europe, and the Chief Officer was now in command. He was an efficient enough officer, who maintained control over his crew on board. However, the two junior officers of the *Duchessa d'Aosta*, and other members of its crew, were apt to make a nuisance of themselves when on shore, which contributed to their unpopularity with the local Spaniards. According to rumour, many of the Italian crew were anti-Fascist. At least four of the crew had been sent to Spain because they were ill and a large number of those who remained were suffering from venereal disease.

The *Duchessa d'Aosta* was not ready for sea. With the knowledge he had gained of the harbour, Guise estimated that she would only clear the bottom of the harbour by a narrow margin. Her wireless was apparently still operative. Her cargo was said to be worth £250,000. No guard appeared to be placed upon either the *Duchessa d'Aosta* or the *Likomba* by the Spanish garrison. The quay was patrolled adequately, but by non-European troops, who did not appear to be very efficient.

So far as the defences of Santa Isabel were concerned, the barracks overlooked the harbour from the east side of the bay, and there was a twenty-four hour guard posted there. It was known that there were four-inch guns at the barracks, which probably covered the harbour. Nobody went bathing in the harbour due to a fear of sharks. In his report for W and London, Guise drew an outline plan of the harbour, showing the positions of the *Duchessa d'Aosta* and the *Likomba*.

With the benefit of the intelligence produced by all Guise's hard work, W began to prepare a plan of action for a raid on Santa Isabel. Guise's careful studies, soundings and assessments had confirmed that the harbour was too shallow for a ship the size of the *Duchessa d'Aosta* to sink properly. The bottom of the harbour was rock, which would assist the force of the explosion, but nonetheless the ship might only be disabled. It might be possible to repair and re-float her. The alternative was to attempt a 'cutting out' operation, and to steal one or both ships from under the noses of the Spaniards. Such a project would be extremely difficult to execute successfully, but with Maid Honor Force based in Freetown it might be possible to find a way. All the planning had to be done against the background that the operation, whatever it was, must be completely deniable by the British Government, and no concrete evidence of British involvement could be left behind.

To improve the flow of intelligence still further, and with an eye to the future needs of any operation, W decided that another SOE agent, the Welshman Captain Richard Lippett, code name W25, should now be sent to Santa Isabel. His role woud be different to that of Guise, the diplomatic courier, and he would be far more vulnerable to Spanish repercussions should SOE's activities be exposed. Lippett's orders were to embed himself into the small local community, to make as many local Spanish friends as possible, to find out as much as he could about what was really going on on Fernando Po, and to build up useful contacts for the future. He would be provided with such funds as he needed, both for his own needs and, more importantly, to buy information. Lippett was now forty-five years old, and ex-Royal Engineers.

He was a large man, once a heavyweight boxing champion. His cover would be that he was employed as an engineer for the shipping company, John Holt's of Liverpool, which had interests and premises in Santa Isabel. The major disadvantage for Lippett would be that he would not have the benefit of any diplomatic immunity, unlike Guise, the 'diplomatic courier', or Michie, the Vice Consul. If caught, he would be in very serious trouble. International law would provide him with no protection, and spies, if captured, were routinely executed. The decision would have to be taken later whether Lippett was to be left on the island while the operation actually took place.

On 30 August, with the Maid Honor Force now on its way, Consul Michie arrived in Lagos from Santa Isabel on a visit, and W took the opportunity to discuss matters with him face to face. On the same day, following their meeting, W cabled M in London updating him on developments in Santa Isabel and putting forward, for the first time, a positive proposal for action against the enemy ships.

W's cable began with the only good news. The vehemently pro-Nazi Governor of Spanish Guinea, Sanches-Diaz, had been recalled to Madrid to take up the post of Director of Colonies there. Consul Michie was on friendly personal terms with his successor, Acting Governor F. L. Soraluce. However, even that good news was limited, since Michie expected that Soraluce would be under orders from Madrid to remain officially hostile to British interests.

The bad news was more extensive. On the basis of the intelligence that he had received from Michie and Guise, W informed London that forty-four of the crew of the *Duchessa d'Aosta* were believed to remain in Santa Isabel. This was significant, since it meant that any attempt to board that ship might be resisted by a substantial number of men. Also, it was thought that the *Duchessa d'Aosta* was officially interned, therefore not allowed in normal circumstances to leave the harbour. This would make it impossible for her to be taken out under her own power, since it would take some time to get up steam and the preparations were bound to be noticed. Further, it was considered that the Captain of the *Duchessa d'Aosta* could not be bribed (a tactic that SOE was quite prepared to use), while the crew members were thought to be too unreliable to be worth trying to suborn into acts of sabotage. Guise's observations suggested, however, that the propellers of the *Duchessa* could possibly be sabotaged if approached by canoe. The German tug *Likomba* was reported to be fuelled and ready for sea. It had been noted that recently there had been an increase in the number of Spanish personnel and material arriving on the island. It looked as if the local garrison was being reinforced.

W recommended an outline plan of action: (a) to send a Maid Honor party by canoe to immobilize by delayed action explosives the propellers of the *Duchessa d'Aosta*, (b) simultaneously to the blowing of the propellers, to capture and bring out the *Likomba*, and (c) to arrange by rumour to put the blame on anti-Axis Spaniards (the anti-Falangists). W asked for approval for the plan and notified London that, once approved, he needed a minimum of six weeks to put it into effect.

M and W now had a plan in place and following the arrival of Maid Honor Force they would have the weapon to carry it out. The problem that remained, however, was to persuade the Admiralty and the Foreign Office to give their approval for an attack on neutral Spanish territory. W in Lagos could only wait and hope that M and his team in London succeeded in getting the go-ahead. But W was not idle. He continued to gather as much intelligence out of Santa Isabel as possible.

In addition to the efforts of Michie and Guise, help came from an unlikely source. By sheer good fortune, in early September the ship's officers of the *Duchessa d'Aosta* decided to throw a party on board for the locals, but got into a muddle with their guest list and by mistake invited a member of the exceedingly small British community on the island. This was the British chaplain, Reverend Markham, whom the Italians apparently thought was Spanish. The Reverend Markham's chapel in Santa Isabel served not only the British European community on the island, but also the large Nigerian African workforce.

Secondary though it was to his duty to God, the Reverend Markham possessed a strong sense of duty to his country. He accepted the invitation to the enemy ship and duly attended the party. Once on board, feeling far more conspicuous than he actually was amongst the relaxed party-goers, Markham did his best to observe all that he could about the state of the ship and its crew. He was able to chat amiably to a number of the officers and crew, and to wander through various parts of the ship. He discovered that morale was indeed low amongst the crew, of whom he counted eight officers and thirty-five men. Markham observed that the vessel was in a poor state, and that necessary maintenance had been neglected. The ship showed no signs of being got ready for sea. Regular watches were being kept, but the general impression was one of indiscipline. Markham, doing a thorough job as SOE's unofficial spy, managed to remain for about an hour before the Italians realized that they had in fact invited an enemy on board, and he had to withdraw rather hurriedly to the shore. However, by then his job was done, and he was able to pass on valuable information to the SOE team.

The picture that the Reverand Markham's intelligence confirmed was that the *Duchessa d'Aosta*'s crew, although numerous, were demoralized and their discipline was poor. They were, of course, civilians who lacked any military training. They had now been stranded in Santa Isabel harbour, far from home, for over a year. Most were in their thirties and forties, and all were no doubt missing their families. There was one stewardess on board, a woman of fifty-three years of age. There was evidence that members of the crew had been stealing the brass fittings from the ship to sell in Santa Isabel. The cargo had also been broached for consumption on board by the crew. All in all, they should be a soft target for a commando raid, particularly if it could somehow be arranged that the officers were not on board to organize any resistance when the raid took place.

As time went by, the courier Guise was increasing his knowledge of the Fernando Po coastline and local conditions whilst he went about his official work as diplomatic courier. M was later to write of him: 'He travelled to and from the island of Fernando Po… in all weathers, sometimes in considerable personal danger. In the course of his visits to the island he made a series of extremely valuable personal reconnaissances, whose complete accuracy was confirmed subsequently.'

There were various ways of reaching Santa Isabel by sea. The most obvious was from the port of Doula in French Cameroon, which was in the hands of the Free French. However, it was also possible to reach the Nigerian mainland by native canoe – a journey which, depending on conditions, could take as much as fifteen hours. The South Atlantic and the Bay of Guinea could prove exceedingly rough and were prone to tornadoes. The approach to the harbour at Santa Isabel, an old volcanic crater, was not easy, and one of Guise's tasks was to become as familiar as possible with the hazards of navigating the entrance to the bay. He began to painstakingly map all of the significant lights and buoys in the harbour. Using his own boat, the *Bamenda*, he could vary his route into the harbour on each visit without giving rise to suspicion, and study the advantages and disadvantages of the different approaches.

Agent W25, Captain Richard Lippett, had arrived at the end of August under his cover of working as a consulting engineer for the shipping company of John Holt's of Liverpool, and was carefully embedding himself in the local community. He put himself about as a man who enjoyed the company of Spaniards and all things Spanish, and quickly began to make friends. The European community in Santa Isabel was a small one, and it was not long before Lippett knew who everybody was, and began to count many of them as his friends.

SOE endeavoured to increase their strength on Fernando Po still further. The invaluable Vice Consul Michie was due to go on extended leave in December, and the Government of Nigeria, whose responsibility it was, did not have an appropriate substitute for him without weakening their representation in Spanish Guinea. Michie, although he had supplied very useful information to SOE, was not one of M's agents. The fact that he would be leaving now gave SOE an opportunity to introduce one of their agents in his place. The serving deputy Consul on mainland Rio Muni was one of M's men, Agent B. Godden (W51). He was available to stand in for Michie on Fernando Po, but that would leave Rio Muni itself uncovered. The opportunity to introduce an extra agent was too good to miss. M had his eye on a young man called Peter Ivan Lake, late of Clifton College and London and Oxford Universities. Lake was the son of the serving British Consul in Palma, Majorca, Walter Lake. Thus it could be said of him that he had some sort of consular background, which would hopefully satisfy the Spanish as to Lake's bona fides.

Peter Lake was twenty-six, married, and (yet again) a banker by profession. He had joined the Bank of West Africa in 1937, and between 1938 and 1940 worked for them at Accra, on the Gold Coast. He returned to England in 1940, and was called up to join the Royal Corps of Signals. Then he transferred to the Intelligence Corps and by September 1941 was a Lance Corporal in the Field Security Section, H.Q. Eastern Command. One significant reason why SOE wanted him was that he was fluent in Spanish and French, and had a working knowledge of Portuguese and Italian. Interestingly, he also stated in his 'job interview' with SOE that he was an expert ornithologist – a recurrent theme in Operation Postmaster. Lake officially signed up with SOE on 1 October 1941. He became Agent W53, and was appointed as Assistant Consul to Fernando Po. Because of Spanish red tape, Lake did not actually arrive in Santa Isabel until 6 January 1942. In the interim, when Michie left at the beginning of December, Vice Consul B. Godden, Agent W51, was in place to provide temporary cover in Santa Isabel.

However, Michie's departure was still a long time off when the *Maid Honor* arrived in Freetown on 21 September. At that time, W had still not heard back from M or Caesar as to whether permission for the Santa Isabel raid had been granted. So W cabled to London asking what he should now do with Maid Honor Force. The response suggested various types of operation that Maid Honor Force might undertake while permission was awaited, including using the *Maid Honor* to search for suspected submarine bases. W's frustration was evident – on 29 September he cabled back to

London rubbishing their suggestions, and complaining about having to wait for a reply to his Fernando Po plan. He emphasized that his scheme was being endangered by delay, and that it would still require several weeks of preparation once approval was granted. He stressed that if the plan was successful it would secure great advantages for the British war effort, especially the use of the *Likomba*, a vessel admirably suited to sabotage or any other work in West Africa. On 30 September W backed this up, cabling London to the effect that Guise had reported that the *Likomba* was to all intents and purposes ready to sail, and that the German Government was showing an increased interest in the affairs of Fernando Po.

Caesar, on M's behalf, cabled back on 30 September, giving the bad news that the plan was not approved. On 1 October, he cabled W again to explain, expressing his and M's own disappointment. Caesar told W that the Admiralty had been indifferent with regard to the *Duchessa d'Aosta* (which W wanted blown up), feeling that the ship was unlikely to be of much practical value as a result of long disuse. With regard to the *Likomba* (which W wanted to steal), they had not even approached the Foreign Office, since they felt sure to have been met with a refusal. Caesar added: 'I hope you are not regretting having directed us to go ahead with the Maid Honor. We feel ourselves that even if the ship does not prove entirely suited for operational purposes, and this has yet to be confirmed, you will find her crew of value to you for training agents and land operations. She was, of course, approved by the Admiralty who had full knowledge of her destination and the type of work she was to undertake, and moreover when we consulted you by telegram in the first instance, you telegraphed describing it as a good idea.' Caesar also promised W that SOE London was still working hard to remove the 'ban on bangs', and that M would support W and his team if there was any trouble with the Foreign Office over what they got up to in neutral territories.

M and Caesar continued to do their best. On 9 October W was informed that action against the *Likomba* would be acceptable, but only outside territorial waters – in other words, if she sailed, then she could be attacked. As she was an enemy vessel, that hardly needed to be said and did nothing to ease W's frustration. M had a private meeting with one of Godfrey's deputies, Admiral Holbrook, on 13 October, but the meeting resulted in no further progress on the Fernando Po project.

CHAPTER 12

Interlude in Freetown

As mid-October approached the men of the Maid Honor Force were becoming frustrated with the lack of action. They had all arrived safely in West Africa, were now rested and acclimatized, and well settled in their camp at Lumley Beach. However, they obviously could not start on Operation Postmaster until and unless approval came through from London. They waited impatiently for something to do. In the meantime, they trained and kept fit. W arranged for both Longe and Eyre to fly to Freetown to meet the Maid Honor Force. Longe and Eyre were both explosives experts, equally frustrated by the ban on bangs. Longe later described March-Phillipps, Appleyard and the rest of their men as 'a party of such delightful, enthusiastic and courageous men, prepared to face any task allotted to them, no matter what the odds'. In West Africa, the Maid Honor Force was a breath of fresh air.

However, their presence was still not approved of by either of the local commanders, Major General Giffard or Rear Admiral Willis. Both had had to accept the arrival of Maid Honor Force, but only because, on orders from London, they had no choice in the matter. Giffard in particular did not want them doing anything exciting that might upset the status quo, the neutrals, or get in his way.

Admiral Willis suggested bluntly that the *Maid Honor* should turn round and go home. He cabled the Admiralty to that effect in early October, saying that he could see no useful employment for the ship in the South Atlantic: 'She has no status and if boarded her disguise would be discovered. Her offensive value against enemy submarines is doubtful and she is unsuitable for reconnaissance in either neutral or Vichy French waters.' Further, he doubted whether there were any suitable targets for Maid Honor Force in his command, and thought they would be better employed in the Northern Hemisphere.

Ian Fleming wrote to M on 14 October 1941, thanking him for a copy of March-Phillipps' report on the *Maid Honor*'s voyage to Freetown and commenting: 'He certainly seems to have put up a very good show, and it was bad luck that he didn't break the record.' However, Fleming offered no comfort in relation to Admiral Willis's view that the *Maid Honor* was of little obvious value in West Africa, saying, 'on the face of it, we [the Admiralty] are inclined to agree'.

Nonetheless, Admiral Godfrey, head of the Naval Intelligence Directorate and Fleming's boss, had in fact issued orders on 17 September for the use of the Maid Honor Force when it arrived in West Africa, and these orders still stood. Their duties were: (a) to transport agents to and from the scene of their activities, (b) to transport sabotage devices and explosives as requisite, (c) to cooperate with such captains of neutral merchantmen as might be persuaded to hand over or scuttle their ships, (d) to act as a Q-ship against enemy submarines, and (e) to carry out any other subversive activities that might be selected for them. Those orders had been cabled to Willis in September and also sent by mail. Willis, however, claimed that he had never received them, so they were sent again and Willis found himself, for the time being at least, stuck with the Maid Honor Force whether he wanted them or not. Therefore, whilst the struggle continued between SOE and the powers in London over authorization for a raid on Santa Isabel, something had to be found for the Maid Honor Force to do. Willis finally agreed to the use of the *Maid Honor* as a spy ship for reconnaissance purposes.

The high level of German submarine activity in the area was still a cause of concern, particularly off Freetown. British ships were being lost. It was felt by the Merchant Navy that the British authorities in Freetown were only 'playing at war'. The British shipping company Elder Dempster had been reduced to offering a reward of £50 to any ship's gun crew that fired at an enemy plane, £100 if the plane was destroyed or disabled, and £250 if the latter was achieved without any damage to the ship. Submarines were a more difficult problem, and there was much discussion as to where they might be refuelling.

Willis therefore decided that the *Maid Honor* should go scouting for U-Boat bases along the West African coast, relying on intelligence from a variety of sources. Working out of Freetown, under cover of their anonymous fishing boat, the Maid Honor Force was ordered to follow up intelligence leads, sailing to a suspected area and, where appropriate, making closer reconnaissance by dinghy or by Folbot canoe. The Maid Honor Force was to go where regular Royal Navy or Army forces could not. They were to creep in, spy out an area, gather as much information as possible, creep out and report back.

With his usual combination of enthusiasm and optimism, Agent W.01, March-Phillipps, acquired a number of depth charges, in the hope that the *Maid Honor* might encounter a submarine at sea. Nominally, the depth charges would be defensive, in case any German U-Boat thought the *Maid Honor* was worth a torpedo, but in truth March-Phillipps was dying to find a submarine to use them against. He was still on tenterhooks to strike back, to actually do something to discomfort the enemy. The reality was that if the *Maid Honor* had used a depth charge she would have been more likely to blow herself out of the water than do serious damage to a U-Boat. Even Gus March-Phillipps realized his plan was wildly optimistic, saying to Geoffrey Appleyard about the depth charges: 'If we can't knock a sub out any other way, we shall heave these into the ocean. The sub will then proceed to perdition, closely followed by ourselves.'

The *Maid Honor*'s reconnaissance work began in mid-October 1941 and continued until mid-November. Her log records three missions. The first began on 10 October when, after a delay in Freetown of nineteen days, she finally left Lumley Beach at 1600 hrs, on what her log describes as 'Submarine Patrol'. The need for security did not prevent the Maid Honor Force from keeping a log on board, containing a record of the ship's travels since it had left England on 12 August. Either the log had a very careful hiding place, or else it would have been rapidly dumped overboard if the need arose. During its reconnaissance work, the *Maid Honor* carried a radio to report any relevant sightings.

The first voyage lasted five days, as the *Maid Honor* sailed north along the coast of Sierra Leone, and French and Portuguese Guinea. She sailed, as always, under her disguise as an innocent fishing boat, but remained vulnerable to attack by air or sea. March-Phillipps hoped that she would excite no attention amongst the cosmopolitan small craft that plied their trade up and down the coast. By now, the men of Maid Honor Force were all bronzed and fit, and looked the part they were playing. They enjoyed the warm sea breezes (when they blew) as a pleasant contrast to the unrelenting heat of the mainland, but always the sense of danger remained. On Sunday, 12 October there was much excitement. The Maid Honor Force believed that they had sighted their first submarine, a distant shape on the sea's surface, which then suddenly disappeared from their view. It did not appear again and they were too far away to do anything about it other than to radio in a report of what they had seen. If it was a submarine, then happily the *Maid Honor*'s disguise must have worked, since no torpedo came running in her direction. There were no other noteworthy incidents on her first voyage, and the *Maid Honor* returned to Freetown on 14 October.

After a week's break, during which necessary maintenance was done to the ship, Maid Honor Force's next expedition was to carry out reconnaissance to the south of Freetown, along the Liberian coast. Liberia was another of the British West African Empire's neutral neighbours. Its sympathies were uncertain and its coastline something of an unknown quantity. SOE and the Admiralty wanted better intelligence on what was going on there. After Liberia, Maid Honor Force was to sail further south again, along the Ivory Coast. The *Maid Honor*, with a crew of nine on board, left Freetown on 23 October and this time was at sea for eight days. On 28 October she sailed into what the log, in its casual and often inaccurate style describes only as 'Baffer Bay', dropping anchor at about noon. The plan was to send a landing party ashore for a good look round. Unlike Vichy France, which was known to be openly hostile to the British, there was no particular reason to expect hostility to their ship or its crew from the Liberians – provided, of course, that it did not emerge that the *Maid Honor* was in truth a military vessel. The landing party went ashore (the log does not make clear their identities), and later returned safely to the ship, which sailed again at 1800 hrs.

One of the Maid Honor Force's specific tasks on this voyage was to reconnoitre an apparently sleepy river port on the Liberian coast called Sinoe (also known as Greenville), which lies by a lagoon where the River Sinoe meets the Atlantic Ocean. March-Phillipps decided that Agents W.02 and W.03, Appleyard and Hayes, should carry out a close reconnaissance, using the *Maid Honor*'s dinghy. As on the previous day no trouble was anticipated, and Appleyard and Hayes were to use the pretext of needing to purchase fresh fruit and vegetables to justify their trip into the harbour.

Leaving the *Maid Honor* anchored off shore, Appleyard and Hayes, in plain clothes as always, rowed openly across the lagoon and into the port in the dinghy. They did not expect to be challenged. However, as they entered the harbour, they rapidly discovered that Sinoe was not as sleepy as they had hoped. They saw a large rowing boat heading straight for them, and were speedily intercepted by a local official, accompanied by eight oarsmen. This gentleman challenged them as to who they were and what they were doing. Appleyard and Hayes were clearly caught off guard by this. They had rehearsed no cover story other than that they were looking for fresh fruit and vegetables. They did not have Lassen, the 'Swede', with them and Appleyard, who answered the questions, did not seek to persuade the official that they were Swedish. As Appleyard was to admit later, his answers to the questions were far from convincing (or would have been to a fellow Englishman.)

Question: 'What is the name of your ship?'
Appleyard: ' B.M.60.'
Question: 'What is the master's name?'
Appleyard: 'Johnson.'
Question: 'What is your name?'
Appleyard: 'Jones.'
Question: 'What is your companion's name?'
Appleyard: 'Brown.'

The official also found these answers unconvincing and was very reluctant to let them land. Appleyard, determined to carry out the reconnaissance, insisted that they must land, as they had a sick man on board who needed fresh fruit. Asked for the name of the sick man, Appleyard replied that he was called 'Green'. On humanitarian grounds, the official finally allowed them to land and purchase provisions. He imposed a condition, however, that after they had done so they should allow the sick man, and their ship, to be inspected. Appleyard ('Jones') felt that he had no choice but to agree, knowing even as he did so the problems that an inspection would cause. The men kept their nerve. The reconnaissance must come first; after that they would sort out what to do about the inspection.

The pair took their time to select and purchase a suitable quantity of fruit and vegetables. As they did so, they took a good look at their surroundings. Then, having delayed as long as they could, they made their way back towards the dinghy, loaded with their purchases. A uniformed colonel now appeared, and they were informed that this officer would accompany them back to the *Maid Honor* in order to carry out the inspection of the ship and its crew.

Appleyard and Hayes knew that anything more than the most casual search of the *Maid Honor* would reveal her armaments and expose her true character. Then, no doubt, the colonel would seek to arrest them. If he succeeded, since its mission was 'deniable', the Maid Honor Force would be regarded as little more than pirates who had brought their heavily armed and carefully disguised vessel illegally into Liberian waters. 'Jones' (Appleyard) and 'Brown' (Hayes) had no way of communicating with the *Maid Honor* to let the others know what was about to happen. Somehow, word had to be got to March-Phillipps ('Johnson') and the rest of the crew to warn them that there must be a sick man called Green on board for the colonel to inspect, and that all their names had changed for the day. Happily, it was the habit of all the Maid Honor Force to refer to each other by nickname or Christian name (regardless of rank), so the change of surnames should not be the greatest problem.

Appleyard and Hayes solved the problem with a very simple strategy. They knew, of course, that their return in the dinghy would be carefully watched from the *Maid Honor*, and that the significance of the Liberian colonel would be immediately appreciated. The biggest problem was to arrange for a sick man called Green to be lying in a bunk when the colonel boarded their ship. On arrival at the *Maid Honor*, Appleyard deliberately botched the first attempt to make fast, allowing Hayes to leap aboard and warn March-Phillipps of what was going on. Appleyard then took as much time as possible on his second approach and by the time that the colonel was able to board, a suitable 'Green' was ready for him to inspect.

The colonel was received aboard with much ceremony. 'Johnson' (March-Phillipps) greeted him with a double measure of navy rum from the gallon jar that the Maid Honor Force always kept on board, and the visit quickly became convivial. The ailing 'Green' was duly inspected lying on his bunk, to the colonel's satisfaction. The inspection of the *Maid Honor* herself was deflected by more rum and a series of lies. At one point, worryingly, the colonel expressed interest in the deck house, which in fact housed the *Maid Honor*'s cannon. However, he was quickly informed that it would be quite impossible to open the deck house for him to inspect, since it contained mails for South Africa and was sealed until arrival there. With his suspicions now calmed in large part by the rum, the colonel did not press his request, nor did he trouble to make any detailed inspection of the rest of the ship. Had he done so, he would of course have found many other hidden armaments, including four depth charges concealed beneath fishing nets in the stern. There is no record to say whether he asked to see the ship's log. If he did, no doubt he was fobbed off with another excuse.

The crew of the *Maid Honor* parted company from the colonel on genial terms and breathed a deep sigh of relief as he was rowed back towards the shore. Time for them had passed extremely slowly while he had been on board, and they appreciated how close they had been to discovery. It was the ability to keep their nerve and to carry out this form of 'man on man' deception so effectively that made the Commando Secret Agents of the Maid Honor Force special – and which later led Commander Ian Fleming to adopt them for his James Bond adventures. Many commandos were trained to kill in 'Bond' fashion, but very few indeed had the ability so expertly to deceive. The *Maid Honor* sailed without further interference, and was able to continue on her mission. Upon eventual return to Freetown, March-Phillipps was able to add significantly to the available intelligence regarding the Liberian coast.

Although the Maid Honor Force was simply marking time until approval arrived for the Fernando Po raid, the work they were doing was exacting and dangerous. On the high seas the *Maid Honor* was always open to challenge and discovery for what she was. If confronted by an enemy warship, the little craft's only real chance lay in surprise and a lucky shot with her cannon, or one of her spigot mortars, supposing there was time to bring them into action. If any of her men were caught inshore in her dinghy or in a Folbot canoe, they would be easy prey.

For all that, the *Maid Honor* was a happy and confident ship. Her crew had faith in her and, more importantly, in her Captain, Gus March-Phillipps. He had brought the *Maid Honor* successfully all the way to Freetown, and he and his crew now handled the ship expertly and knew her quirks intimately. She required very regular maintenance on her returns to Freetown, but was an enjoyable vessel to sail. All of Maid Honor Force preferred to be aboard and at sea than to be at Lumley Beach. Usually, even when she was at anchor at Lumley Beach the crew would sleep on deck to avoid the mosquitoes, rather than in their tents. They had brought a gramophone on board, and all enjoyed listening to music in the evenings.

During the operations, as well as the breaks at Lumley Beach, Appleyard found time to pursue his interest in ornithology, sending 'ornithological notes' home to his brother Ian in Linton-on-Wharfe. He noted the arrival of two swallows, of the kind seen in England (and Europe), on board the *Maid Honor* at dusk one evening, when the ship was twenty miles out to sea. He had climbed up to their perch on the topmast truck, noticed that neither of them was ringed, and said they were 'birds of the year'. Another time he reported seeing what he thought was a grey wagtail. He recounted an occasion when, thirty miles out to sea from the mouth of a large river, they sighted a huge mass of floating reeds and discovered to their astonishment that the floating island was covered with nesting 'tern-like' seabirds. However, Appleyard was essentially an English ornithologist, and commented: 'I can still take no real interest in these African birds – the storks, flamingoes, herons, eagles, buzzards, vultures, cranes, terns, frigate birds etc., they all seem travesties of some English bird and almost repellent!'

In his letters home Appleyard described a very busy life, in which virtually every day was spent on board the *Maid Honor*. The regular crew on the spying missions was nine. With little regard for censorship, he later described them in a letter to his sister on Christmas Eve 1941:

> We are three officers on board – Gus (Captain), Graham and I. Then there is Tom Winter, who was a sergeant in Graham's parachute battalion. He is a special protégé of Graham's and the two always work together. Next comes André Desgranges, who is my special protégé, works with me, and is one of the finest chaps with whom I have ever had anything to do. . . He was a deep sea diver in the French Navy before the war, and is also a good engineer. He is big, strong as a horse and has black curly hair and a perpetual grin! He speaks no English, even after six months with us, but is the most un-French-like Frenchman, in an emergency he is absolutely cool, unexcitable and collected. . . He really is a wizard and I feel tremendously fortunate to have such a stalwart with me as my right hand man. He is well educated. Age 30. He is the second man on my watch.
>
> Also we have Andy Lassen – a Dane – who is a crack shot with any kind of weapon and a splendid seaman. Denis Tottenham, aged twenty-four, is a good seaman. He has done a great deal of sailing, is 6'4" in height and is in charge of the third watch. Then there is Buzz Perkins, the youngest of the party, who is a very sound lad, very keen and willing and tough. Finally, there is Ernest Evison, the cook (whole time job when we are at sea), who in his job is invaluable and unbeatable. Scrupulously clean, he is an excellent cook, trained in France and Switzerland, and so speaks good French and German. He comes of a long line of cooks, is only twenty-four, and was secured for us by Prout, who has known him personally for some time. We are very lucky there. And so you see we are a very well fitted crowd and really get on extremely well together, a very important thing in so small a ship and under such conditions.

Leslie Prout was now acting as quartermaster, and 'Haggis' Taylor, March-Phillipps' batman apparently did not merit a mention.

To the considerable regret of March-Phillipps and his men, the intelligence with which the Maid Honor Force was supplied on her expeditions up and down the coast never proved to be productive, and they never actually found a submarine base. Their life was none the less full of danger and excitement, particularly when they took their dinghy, or a Folbot, into the shark-infested waters along the coast, and into the numerous vermin-infested estuaries.

On 7 November 1941, a credible report of submarine activity took the *Maid Honor* from Freetown to the delta and mouths of the Pongo River, at Boffa in neighbouring French Guinea, about forty miles north-west of Conaky, a deep sea port used by the Vichy French Navy. It was believed that a German submarine supply base must have been established there, since all of French Guinea was in Vichy hands, and there had been regular enemy submarine activity in the area.

The *Maid Honor* sailed down from Freetown and approached as close to the large Pongo delta as March-Phillipps felt that they safely could. Because of the number and confusion of the waterways in the delta, March-Phillipps decided that an extended close reconnaissance would be necessary by Folbot canoe (the small wooden folding boat that Appleyard and Desgranges had used in France). He and Appleyard would undertake the survey over three days and two nights, leaving Agent W.03, Hayes, in command of the *Maid Honor*. March-Phillipps launched the Folbot at a point still some ten miles from the shore. Hayes' orders were to return with the *Maid Honor* to the same spot on the third day to pick them up.

The *Maid Honor* hove to at 1830 hrs, and the Folbot canoe was successfully launched. March-Phillipps and Appleyard accomplished the ten-mile paddle to the delta mouth without great difficulty, but then found themselves faced by heavy surf where the waters of the delta converged with the sea. The surf threatened to swamp their tiny low-lying craft, but eventually, more by luck than judgement, they managed to find a way through the turbulent waters and were able to enter the mangrove swamps of the delta. Conditions were hot and unhealthy, and malaria-carrying mosquitoes abounded.

Having negotiated their way successfully into the swamps, March-Phillipps and Appleyard could not risk carrying out their reconnaissance in daylight, but had to await the night-time cloak of darkness. After dark they set out, steering their canoe through the swamps and exploring the river mouths. They paddled as silently as possible, always aware that the enemy might be close by, never knowing what or who they might meet. The night was exhausting, as March-Phillipps and Appleyard worked their way doggedly through the waterways of the delta, always alert to any strange sound or movement. The daytime was unpleasant in a different way. The two men lay hidden in the mangrove swamps, under heavy attack from mosquitoes, passing their waking time by playing improvised games of chess, with the mudbank as their chess board and twigs for the pieces.

On this expedition, the enemy was not only a human one. Apart from the endless mosquitoes, another danger was crocodiles. These infested the mangrove swamps and were no doubt not averse to human prey. If attacked, Agents W.01 and W.02 could not afford the luxury of firing a shot, lest it be heard by the human enemy. On one of the pitch-dark nights, March-Phillipps and Appleyard were paddling their Folbot up yet another river entrance when the canoe seemed to lose a lot of its speed. March-Phillipps, in the stern, told Appleyard, in the bow, to stop slacking and paddle harder. Appleyard retorted that he was already paddling hard. It became obvious something was impeding their progress. Appleyard peered forward through the darkness to inspect the bow of the Folbot and the water ahead, to find out what the problem was. He suddenly saw two massive rows of shining white teeth resting across the bow within two feet of where he was sitting. A huge crocodile had come on board. Reacting in true James Bond fashion, Appleyard immediately struck at the crocodile with his paddle as hard as he could, and succeeded in knocking the creature off the bow of the canoe. Happily, the force of the blow deterred the crocodile from further action and it retreated. March-Phillipps and Appleyard breathed a sigh of huge relief and paddled as rapidly as they could on their way.

For two nights they searched, but found no sign of any submarine base. When they had completed their second night, March-Phillipps and Appleyard duly returned to the mouth of the delta. They successfully renegotiated the heavy surf and paddled out to their rendezvous point. Now, however, the tactical design of the Folbot which had helped them to remain unobserved in the delta over the previous two days, went against them. The canoe was so low in the water that it was very difficult to spot from the *Maid Honor*. Twice the ship cruised by the agreed rendezvous point without spotting them. Fortunately, on their third pass, at about 1030 hrs, Hayes spotted their frantic signals and picked them up. Had he not done so, they would have been in very real difficulty. The weather was very unsettled at that time of year and the South Atlantic prone to tornadoes, or 'bullums' as they were called locally. Throughout the time that the Maid Honor Force were based in Freetown, these would occur every two or three days. Had the *Maid Honor* not picked them up March-Phillipps and Appleyard would have had no alternative but to attempt a return to land, since once a 'bullum' came along they would not have been able to keep the Folbot afloat. On land, they would have faced almost certain capture. As it happened all was well and the *Maid Honor*, with her full complement aboard, duly returned to Freetown.

Unfortunately, following the return to Lumley Beach on 11 November they received orders to cease the reconnaissance work. The Naval Commander, Admiral Willis, had become nervous and had decided that Maid Honor Force's activities, even at their current level, were too risky. He feared political repercussions from their visits to neutral territory, and refused to authorize any further expeditions. As a result, for the next three weeks the Maid Honor Force sat at Lumley Beach doing nothing.

While High Command dithered and prevaricated as to what to do with the Maid Honor Force in West Africa, the *Maid Honor*'s crew involved themselves in necessary maintenance work on their ship. Her condition was beginning to cause some concern. The *Maid Honor* was not well suited to the tropics and the longer she remained in West Africa, the less fit for pupose she became. The main difficulty was her wooden bottom. She was unprotected from the predators that thrive in the climate and conditions of the South Atlantic. Since her arrival in September, regular maintenance had been necessary to clear her bottom of sea worms, which otherwise would bore holes right through the wooden hull. The Maid Honor Force worked on her hull after each voyage, whilst 'resting' back at their camp on Lumley Beach. They would beach the ship so that her hull was exposed as the tide receded, and endeavour to carry out the necessary work before the sea returned.

On one occasion, because of the extent of the damage to her hull, it was necessary to carry out a repair by riveting on a copper plate. Graham Hayes, the wood sculptor, was in charge of this. Unfortunately it took longer than expected, and the *Maid Honor* was threatened by the returning tide before the work was finished. Hayes was entirely fearless in water, and as the tide began to submerge the ship he continued to work on the copper plate beneath the surface, without oxygen, holding his breath for as long as he could. It soon became clear however, that he was fighting a losing battle. He simply could not stay below the water level for long enough at any one stretch. Hayes' solution was a simple one. He instructed the others working with him to hold him forcibly beneath the water until he signalled that he was in extreme distress. This they duly did a number of times until the job was completed. Hayes had a young black African servant at the time, who apparently rejoiced in the name of 'Liverpool Blackout'. The youngster watched what was going on with increasing concern, and eventually called out a number of times in distress: 'Please, don't drown him!' It was a considerable feat by Hayes. He was to demonstrate that endurance and fearlessness of the sea again before the end of Maid Honor Force's time in West Africa.

Hayes was not the only one prepared to work on the *Maid Honor* under water. On another occasion, one night whilst at sea, the ship's propeller became fouled by a rope. The propeller was eight feet below the level of the water, and under the stern of the ship. Two volunteers were required to dive down, holding their breath, to cut it free. The volunteers were Appleyard and Hayes. The job proved a tricky one, particularly in the dark, and it took them two hours of repeated dives to finally free the propeller. Happily, the local sharks did not interfere, but both men suffered for some time afterwards with their ears, as a result of the sustained periods under the water. Appleyard described this incident in a letter home as 'rather a frightening job'. Successful agents like Appleyard and the men of Maid Honor Force recognised fear, but never let it get in their way, or prevent them from doing what needed to be done – an ability Ian Fleming understood and bestowed on his own super-successful agent, Bond.

The Maid Honor Force's time based in Freetown was difficult. At sea, on their reconnaissance expeditions, it was not so bad. They utilized the cover of their fishing boat extremely well and carried out their reconnaissance missions thoroughly. When necessary, they lied with nerve and skill. They were at least doing something. But a strong sense of frustration remained, because this was not what they had trained to do. They were an elite commando force, trained to attack enemy targets, to sabotage and to kill. Their true desire was to hit back against the enemy and, for many of them, to settle old scores dating from the horrors of defeat at Dunkirk. Anders Lassen and André Desgranges, whose countries were occupied by the enemy, sought revenge for the suffering of their families and countrymen. While the 'ban on bangs' remained in West Africa, they were not allowed to carry out commando missions. Their 'licence to kill' had been suspended. They longed for an incident at sea that would justify them in using some of the armaments on the *Maid Honor*. Tom Winter was later to say that throughout their many voyages along the West African coast, March-Phillipps longed for a U-Boat to surface and, fooled by their appearance, to ask them for fresh fish. Then, with the advantage of surprise, the Maid Honor Force could use its two-inch gun and the spigot mortars to blow the U-Boat out of the water – or so March-Phillipps hoped.

March-Phillipps hated the inactivity, and his feelings are illustrated by a poem he wrote while in Freetown. It was nominally about the *Maid Honor* herself, who was moored at that time to a buoy in midstream, with the ebb tide flowing out of the river mouth at a speed of five or six knots, but it undoubtedly reflected his own underlying frustration.

The ebb tide dashing out to sea
Sighs and surges under me
Sets the captive vessel dancing
Like a restless pony prancing,
Fretting to be free;
Sidling, edging, plunging, shearing,
Like a maddened pony rearing,
Frantic to be free.

Hear the tide call 'follow follow',
West towards the sun,
Sure as hawk and swift as swallow,
See the ebb tide run;
Over shoal and shallow thrashing,
Through the deeps and channels dashing,
See the main ebb run!

All can hear but few may answer
When the ebb tide calls,
Strong as lion, light as lancer,
Still the ebb tide calls;
Follow where the sun is sinking,
Where the first pole star is winking
As the darkness falls.

The ebb tide dashing to the sea
Slackens, slackens under me
And the restless vessel steadies
In the current's dying eddies,
Draining to the sea.
Through the darkness falling, falling,
Hear the echo faintly calling,
'Follow and be Free!

March-Phillipps longed to be free of the restrictions placed on the *Maid Honor*'s activities – to be free of the ban on bangs and be able to take real action against the enemy, rather than skulking through the deltas and swamps of the West African coast, hunting for submarine bases that were never in fact there. Even that activity was now banned. Appleyard, in one of his regular letters home, told his family that they would soon be leaving West Africa.

The sense of frustration brought on by a lack of proper action and employment is depicted strongly in one of Fleming's novels. In *On Her Majesty's Secret Service* (1963) Bond, who has been shifted away from his usual secret agent duties, drafts a resignation letter, complaining of the misuse of qualities that have previously fitted him for his role as '007'. In the second half of November 1941, stranded on the beach at Lumley Point, March-Phillipps and the men of Maid Honor Force were experiencing exactly the same feelings.

At last, when they had all but given up hope, word came from Lagos that authority had finally been granted for the Fernando Po attack, and that Maid Honor Force was to proceed to Lagos with all possible speed. Somehow, M and W had done it. While Maid Honor Force had been cruising the coast of West Africa, SOE had doggedly continued to seek clearance for the project that had brought the *Maid Honor* to West Africa in the first place, and finally they had won.

Appleyard wrote home: 'Now it doesn't look as though we will be pointing our "sprit" home quite as soon as I thought we should be doing as bright new prospects are opening up. However, don't worry, we shall be home in the spring as was originally promised. Actually, they can't keep the ship out in these waters longer than that because of the danger of worm.'

CHAPTER 13

Gaining Approval for Postmaster

M and W had been working away on the plan for Operation Postmaster, so as best to gain the necessary authority, throughout the Maid Honor Force's time at Lumley Beach. Things in Santa Isabel were unchanged; the two enemy ships were still in the harbour. During October 1941 a report had come in that yet more arms were being brought to Fernando Po and that there were indications the island was being fortified. One dangerous possibility was that the island might be about to go over to the Germans, and might then be used for offensive purposes against the Allies. However, General Giffard remained firmly opposed to SOE, the ban on bangs was still in place, and the plan for action against Santa Isabel was certainly not supported by him.

W and his team in Lagos, and M and Caesar in London, did not give up. M had been wise not to put the August proposal before the Foreign Office. At the time that proposal was sent to London the *Maid Honor* had not even arrived in Freetown – indeed, it was not known whether she had perished somewhere on the high seas. Having received an unfavourable response from the Admiralty in relation to sabotaging the *Duchessa d'Aosta*, M had held his fire. He no doubt hoped that once the Maid Honor Force had arrived and demonstrated its competence and expertise, the plan for an attack on the ships in Santa Isabel might be more favourably received.

In Lagos, after the initial rejection there followed a long period of suspense and it seemed the Santa Isabel plan would progress no further. There was absolutely no support in local official military circles, and only if authority was obtained from the Foreign Office and the Admiralty in London could the objections of the West Africa commanders, General Giffard and Admiral Willis, be overridden. Ordered by the Admiralty to find work for the Maid Honor Force, Willis had been obliged, for a while, to comply, but only with the greatest reluctance.

Happily, W was due for some home leave that October. It gave him the opportunity that he wanted to present the case for the Santa Isabel raid personally. He left Lagos on 15 October and arrived in London in early November. W's detailed knowledge of the situation and his persuasive powers were invaluable. M and W met and discussed tactics. The value of M's decision not to approach the Foreign Office with the first plan in September now became obvious. Because no previous adverse decision had been made by them then, the field was clear. If M and W could persuade the Foreign Office to give their approval, it would be very difficult for the Admiralty not to do the same.

The plan had undergone some modification. March-Phillipps and Appleyard had known of the Fernando Po project before leaving Poole, but when they arrived in Freetown they were brought into full consultation with W and his team. At some stage during the period of waiting, March-Phillipps decided it would be feasible to take both ships out of Santa Isabel harbour – there was no need to blow the *Duchessa d'Aosta* up. It was a very ambitious view, but typical of March-Phillipps. He convinced W that this was possible, and W convinced M. A significant advantage to the change of plan was that it offered a valuable prize to the Foreign Office (the *Duchessa d'Aosta* and her cargo), which would help to justify the risk involved in violating neutral waters. That, together with the presence of W in London, the performance of the Maid Honor Force in October and November, and the presence of their special unit with its particular expertise in the right place at the right time, all strengthened M's hand.

M and W in fact intended, if they could, to obtain a far broader authority for action than just the Santa Isabel raid. They hoped to revitalize SOE activities in West Africa and to get rid of the ban on bangs completely. There was a similar operation planned on the port Lobito, in Portuguese Angola, two German ships moored there being the target. Furthermore, SOE sought a general authority permitting attacks on enemy-controlled shipping in certain specified territories, including the Spanish West African Colonies, subject to the agreement of the local British diplomatic representatives. M and W knew that Governor Bourdillon of Nigeria, the senior British diplomat in the area, was on their side.

M put the proposal to the Foreign Office on 12 November 1941. Armed with detailed intelligence and carefully worked-out plans, his arguments prevailed. The Foreign Office granted its full approval for the attack on Santa Isabel. M notified Lagos immediately.

The Admiralty was the next target. M called for Ian Fleming, and the two men met at 1230 hrs on 14 November and again at the same time three days later. Fully briefed, Fleming reported back to Godfrey and the Admiralty duly granted their approval on 20 November. The ban on bangs in West Africa was well and truly gone.

The Santa Isabel raid was now assigned its operational name of Operation Postmaster. Since W was on leave, and was going on from London to visit his family in Long Island, New York, his second-in-command in Lagos, Major Victor Laversuch, W4, took command of the planning and administration of Postmaster at the West African end. Laversuch had already been very much involved in the efforts to obtain authorization for the operation. He had shared the early frustration and was now no doubt triumphant. March-Phillipps and the Maid Honor Force were notified at Lumley Beach, and ordered to make haste to Lagos.

The change of plan, and the intended capture and towing out of the *Duchessa d'Aosta* as well as the *Likomba*, would mean that there would be no place for the *Maid Honor* herself on Operation Postmaster. She was ideal for use on a covert sabotage raid (she might sail silently under cover of darkness into Santa Isabel harbour), but she was obviously incapable of towing either of the two enemy ships out to sea.

There remained some dispute in London as to who should be in command of the Postmaster expedition. March-Phillipps was not the most senior SOE officer in West Africa. On 21 November there was a meeting at M's office in London. M himself, Caesar, and W were amongst those present. A memorandum of the meeting is marked, 'For our own records, but not for circulation'. It reads:

> After preliminary discussion in which W explained the local details, the question of the leadership of the organisation and organisation (staff work) as regards Fernando Po was specifically discussed. W felt that although the personnel at his disposal in West Africa in general, and the 'Maid Honor' in particular, were admirable in their own way, it did perhaps not have the necessary qualifications of leadership for the successful conduct of an operation of this kind, which required a good deal of planning and special leadership. W although recognising that March-Phillipps has qualities of courage and enterprise, considered him lacking in commonsense and therefore not a suitable leader for this job.
>
> M, on the other hand, thought that March-Phillipps, with the assistance of Appleyard to work out a detailed operation, was quite capable of handling this operation successfully.

M's view for the time being prevailed. Operation Postmaster was on, and March-Phillipps was to command it. There was now a lot to be done in a very short time.

CHAPTER 14

Blackmail on Fernando Po

The overarching principle of the planned raid on Santa Isabel was that it should not be positively identifiable as a British operation – no concrete evidence could be left behind. If all turned to disaster, British responsibility and involvement had to be deniable. As it now worked out, shortly after consent was finally granted Vice Consul Michie, who had played a major part in the gathering of intelligence and planning so far, was due to go home on extended leave. He would not be on Fernando Po when the operation took place. Since his imminent leave was already known about and was part of accepted practice, and his substitute had been notified to the Spanish authorities, it was felt it would look too suspicious if Michie stayed on unexpectedly and then the ships disappeared.

Therefore, it was agreed that Michie should depart as planned. He would then be temporarily replaced by the Deputy Consul, Agent W51 Godden from Rio Muni, and after that by Assistant Consul Lake. The bonus was that Peter Lake was also an SOE agent, the newly recruited Agent W53. In the event, because of delays, they were both in Santa Isabel when the raid eventually took place.

The raid was inevitably a very high risk affair. The *Maid Honor* no longer being considered a suitable craft for the operation, the plan was that two civilian tugs, one very powerful, should be employed. The powerful tug would face the task of removing the *Duchessa d'Aosta* from its mooring in the Santa Isabel harbour, while the smaller tug took the *Likomba*. The raid would take place during a moonless period, after the lights of Santa Isabel had been turned off for the night, which was normally at 2300 or 2400 hrs. There could be no off-shore support from the Royal Navy. It would be necessary to navigate the two tugs into the harbour and alongside their target ships, and for them to tow out their prizes, all in the dark of the night.

The *Duchessa d'Aosta*, being a substantial liner, would have only a narrow channel available to her out of the harbour. It would not be difficult for the enemy to block that channel should the alarm be raised early. The raiders would not attempt to start the engines of the two captive ships, which might well not be in working order through neglect or for a variety of other reasons. The two tugs would do all the work necessary to pull their prizes straight out of the harbour and away to the open sea.

One thing that had to be done before the ships could even begin to be towed from the harbour was the severing of their mooring and anchor chains. This meant the use of explosives, so the type and thickness of those chains was very important. The resourceful and reliable Agent W10, Guise, was given the task of measuring each and every chain. It was far from straightforward. The ships were moored close to the shore, within easy view of the local population as they went about their daily lives. Both ships always had some crew members aboard. For the anchor chains, a reconnaissance by dinghy at night might work, but would be an all-or-nothing affair – if Guise were to be caught, he would be hard pressed to provide any plausible explanation as to why he was rowing around in the dark measuring anchor chains. Therefore, Guise decided to use the local climate to his advantage, and to row across the harbour in the heat of the day. Having dropped anchor from the *Bamenda* in the harbour of Santa Isabel, he would then row ashore in a dinghy. This was hard and sweaty work.

Guise moored the *Bamenda* in a position which meant that the anchor cables of the *Duchessa d'Aosta* and the *Likomba* would provide natural resting points on his uncomfortable journey to and from the quay. In order to keep his rowing boat steady it would then be perfectly natural for him to hang on to the anchor cable with one hand, whilst mopping the sweat from his brow with the other and catching his breath. Of course, Guise could not produce or use any formal instrument to measure the thickness of the chain, in case he was being watched. He could, however, measure it by his handspan and examine it visually. To any watching eyes he would appear to be behaving perfectly naturally – a sweating European taking a few moments' respite from the effort of rowing across the bay in unaccustomed heat. Back on land, Guise made a careful record of the thickness of each chain. Little by little, he managed to compile a list of the specifications of each and every 'stay' that held the *Duchessa d'Aosta* and the *Likomba* in place. Then he supplied the list to Laversuch for the use of the Maid Honor Force.

The explosives that severed the anchor chains had to work first time. Even if they managed to escape notice boarding the two vessels, once the explosive charges went off, all secrecy was lost. There were obvious dangers from the shore once this happened and the alarm was raised. Santa Isabel contained the government of Spanish Guinea and a garrison of Spanish Colonial troops. There were a number of four-inch guns on the island, of which some were believed to be with the garrison. There were also machine guns said to be mounted around the harbour, and there were anti-aircraft guns. The two tugs chosen for the raid would carry no heavier armament than Bren light machine guns.

In addition, there were the crews of the two target ships to consider. *The Duchessa d'Aosta* had an Italian crew of about forty-four, including eight officers; the *Likomba* had two German officers and a native crew. The *Duchessa* was a large ship with a number of decks. There was ample room for a running battle or firefight. *Likomba* was much smaller, but its geography and design was such that armed resistance from within would be difficult to quell.

An enduring concern was the size of the crew remaining on the *Duchessa d'Aosta*. There were enough Italians on board potentially to put up a significant defence, even in their apparently demoralized state. M and his team therefore looked for a way to ensure that no senior officers would be on board at the time of the attack, so there would be less chance of anyone rousing and organizing the crew to defend the ship. The obvious solution was to create a diversion that would take the officers away from both target ships on the night of the raid. That was more easily said than done, however, since it could not be anything that might be connected with the British Consulate, or with any British agent on the island. Without their officers, it was hoped that neither crew would put up any organized or armed resistance. The Maid Honor Force would rely on silence, stealth, professionalism and speed to carry out the attacks and free the ships.

Ian Fleming must have loved the whole idea of Operation Postmaster. A force of British Secret Agents, licensed to kill, were to creep under cover of darkness into a small harbour on a volcanic tropical island and, after setting off a number of explosions, to steal away two enemy ships from under the very noses of an unsympathetic foreign power. Ian Fleming, in real life, was to write the cover story.

When Operation Postmaster took place, of the British Secret Service agents present on the island, two of them (Godden and Lake) would be staff attached to the British Consulate and therefore would have the protection of diplomatic immunity. Only one agent would be entirely exposed to any repercussions and that was Captain Richard A. J. Lippett, Royal Engineers, Agent W25. Unlike Agent W.01, Gus March-Phillipps, and the rest of the Maid Honor Force, Lippett was not 'licensed to kill', but like them, if it all went wrong he was deniable, and if he was implicated in the raid Lippett could claim no protection from the diplomatic service. He would be dealt with as what he was – a foreign spy. His cover as an employee of John Holt's would afford him as little protection as James Bond's 'Universal Exports' did for him when times were difficult. Though his role was a vital one Lippett was thus completely unprotected, except that as a British citizen he could call on the British Consulate for such limited help as it could give. He was one of many secret agents run by M during the Second World War who, if captured, could expect to be tortured and shot.

Working on a need-to-know basis, particularly since he was so vulnerable, Lippett was never informed of the full details of the intended operation in Santa Isabel harbour. He was given his own clearly defined brief, nothing more. He obviously would have guessed that the ships were to be taken or destroyed and in due course knew to the minute when it was going to happen, but he was never told how it was to be done, or by whom. It is certain that before the raid he never met any of the Maid Honor Force. If he had, they would have wanted to shake his hand and thank him for the excellent work he was doing.

Lippett was obviously a courteous and charming man. When in Santa Isabel, he stayed at what seems to have been the only hotel, the Montilla. He put himself out to meet as many of the local Spanish community as possible and quickly became popular, regarded as a sympathetic man and a friend to Spain. Lippett became particularly friendly with the owners of the hotel, Señor and Señora Montilla. He was also on good terms with the bank manager, Señor Ruiz, with whom he would regularly play Piloto, a Spanish card game, at the local club. As the target date for the raid came closer, Lippett got into the habit of going for a stroll across the front of the bay with Ruiz after dinner, on the pretext of aiding digestion, but in reality to check on activity in the harbour. He would play badminton regularly with a group of Spaniards on a piece of waste ground behind the British Consulate. He was on cordial terms with the chief of police, Miguel Llompert. A local physician, Doctor Sola, became his friend, as did the Governor's pilot, Señor Alacon. Thanks to all this socializing there were few Spaniards in Santa Isabel whom Lippett did not get to know and to call friends.

Whilst Lippett was so successfully embedding himself in the local Spanish community, he was at the same time identifying the anti-Falangist Spaniards on the island, and also paying cash sums to some of the black Africans for useful titbits of information. One of the anti-Falangists with whom he became friendly was the assistant manager of the hardware store,

Abelino Zorilla, who spoke fluent French and English. Lippett identified Zorilla as one of those who might be particularly useful in the future.

However, a continuing problem for the Secret Service on Fernando Po was the persistent surveillance of the British Consulate and resident British nationals by the Spanish authorities. This duty had been inherited by the new Governor from his pro-Nazi predecessor, and as a part of his official anti-British position, he had continued it. As the date for Operation Postmaster approached, the surveillance became increasingly irksome. It restricted the ability of Lippett, Guise, Michie and Godden to obtain good quality intelligence. It also got in the way of Lippett's seduction of those whom he believed could assist his operation.

The problem was eventually solved by a very traditional means.

Governor Soraluce had a black African mistress. To have such an affair was not suited to his official position. The Governor of Spanish Guinea should be above repute. Knowledge of his affair reached M's team, most probably through the Governor's erstwhile friend, Vice Consul Michie (although possibly from some other local informant). One way or another, it became known to the Secret Service where and when Soraluce would meet, and relax in the company of, the lady in question. It was decided that such information might be used to the benefit of Operation Postmaster.

The surviving SOE reports do not identify by name the person who was deputed to carry out the necessary surveillance on the Governor. The 'spy' is simply referred to in the report as the Vice Consul, which seems clearly to indicate Michie. However, there is an element of doubt, since the title was loosely used: Michie was officially a Vice Consul, but more generally referred to as the Consul or Consul General; Agent W51, Godden was the Deputy Consul, who was based on the Rio Muni mainland at Bata, but came to Santa Isabel full time when Michie went on leave in December 1941; Agent W53, Lake was the Assistant Consul, who did not arrive in Santa Isabel until early January 1942, probably too late to be a genuine candidate. There are two clues that suggest that the 'spy' was indeed Michie. The first is that, after Operation Postmaster had been carried out, Michie was awarded the OBE for his contribution to it. That contribution was not specified in the 'coded' format of the citation, but it included the words: 'He was responsible for much careful and thorough preparatory work.' The second clue is that after Operation Postmaster had been completed, M's Secret Service tried very hard to recruit Michie into the ranks of their secret agents (they failed because the Nigerian Civil Service flatly refused to release him). Both clues suggest that Michie was responsible for much more than the mere passing on of information to W in Lagos. Also, of course, Michie was officially the Vice Consul. The author's conclusion is that the spy was indeed C. W. Michie, His Britannic Majesty's Vice Consul.

On an appointed day, the spy concealed himself in a suitable position, with a good view of the place where the Governor and his mistress were likely to disport themselves. It was, as so often, a hot and sultry afternoon in Santa Isabel and the Governor, stark naked, was soon observed using watering cans to shower his equally naked mistress as she lay in a bath. The spy is described in the SOE report as enjoying the hobby of amateur photography, so the presumption must be that photographs were taken, although none apparently survive. Sometime later, the Governor was privately confronted with the facts of what had been observed, presumably by his erstwhile friend Vice Consul Michie. No doubt embarrassed and horrified, the Governor agreed that publicity for his affair was the last thing he wanted. In return for discretion, he agreed to relax the heavy surveillance on the small British community on Fernando Po. Thereafter, official Spanish relations with the British community on the island improved considerably, and M's Secret Service agents found themselves with far more room for manoeuvre. It was not the first, or the only time, that blackmail was used by SOE to achieve its objectives. As the saying goes, 'All's fair in love and war.'

The only surviving SOE record of this 'honeytrap' incident is to be found in an unfortunately anonymous and undated report on the W Section, contained in a file at the National Archives in Kew. Because of the droll style, it is tempting to think that it may have been written by Guise, Agent W10, whose sense of humour rings through from his own report of Operation Postmaster. The relevant passage reads:

> The Spanish Governor of Fernando Po had his suspicions, and kept our Vice-Consulate at Santa Isabel under a strict surveillance, which was difficult to circumvent and definitely irksome. His Excellency himself suggested, quite unknowingly, a means of ending it. One sultry afternoon, our Vice Consul emulated the Elders. From a post of vantage, he beheld not only an unchaste Susannah in her bath, but also the Governor, clad in his natal suit, emptying watering cans over the head of his inamorata. His Excellency appreciated the inconvenience which publicity might entail. The surveillance ceased, and no objections were raised to the friendship which the Vice Consul struck up with the Spanish air pilot who flew the Governor's private aircraft. The Vice Consul was a keen photographer, and indulged freely in his hobby during flights over the harbour.

Humorous though it may now sound it is undoubtedly true that, thanks to this incident, by the end of 1941 relations between the British Consulate and Government House had, superficially at least, improved substantially. As a result, the British Secret Service had a freedom of movement vital to Operation Postmaster, which they had not enjoyed before.

Equally importantly, perhaps, excellent aerial photographs were obtained of the Santa Isabel harbour. If it was Michie who photographed and blackmailed the Governor, then it must also have been he who took the harbour shots, which proved invaluable to Operation Postmaster. Under the guise of pleasure flights, Señor Alacon, the Governor's pilot, flew Michie over Santa Isabel harbour, enabling him to take a series of detailed photos of the harbour, showing the *Duchessa d'Aosta* and the *Likomba* at anchor. Combined with other intelligence received from the agents on the island, Agent W4 in Lagos was able to use these photographs to give a detailed briefing to the Maid Honor Force before the operation. All the significant buildings around the harbour were marked, so the members of the Force would know where to watch for danger. The British chaplain's house, from which it was intended that an 'approach now' signal would be given to the ships entering the harbour, was also clearly marked. Photographs had also been taken from ground level of the two target ships and of the surrounding harbour and buildings. If Michie accomplished not only the blackmail of Governor Soraluce, but also the taking of these vital intelligence images of the harbour and the target ships, then it is no surprise that M was so keen to recruit him after Operation Postmaster was over.

Richard Lippett, W25, also struck up a close friendship with the Governor's pilot. He paid over to Señor Alacon the sum of £50 (a substantial sum at that time, equivalent to 5,000 Spanish pesetas) from SOE funds, which can only have been a payment for the flight during which the photographs were taken.

Richard Lippett was given the responsibility of arranging a distraction to ensure that the officers of the *Duchessa d'Aosta* and the *Likomba* were not on their ships at the time of the raid. M and W4 eventually approved a plan for a dinner party to be held in Santa Isabel on the night of the raid, to which all the officers of both vessels would be invited. Even if the dinner was disturbed by the goings-on in the harbour, the guests would hopefully already be sufficiently befuddled by drink to be incapable of effective action. In any event, they would be some distance away from their ships.

The plan sounded simple to put into effect. It was in fact the opposite, since the British could hardly invite their enemies, the Italians and Germans, to sit down to dinner with them. Furthermore, if an intermediary were used it needed to be done in such a way as to give no cause for suspicion in advance, and to leave no concrete evidence afterwards that the British had been involved. Santa Isabel contained only a small ex-patriot community made up of Spanish, Italians and Germans, plus a very few British. All social activity took place in something of a goldfish bowl.

Lippett set about arranging the distractionary dinner party with consummate skill.

CHAPTER 15

The Plan of Attack

Back in Lagos, everything was being put into place for the military operation. In the absence of W in London, his deputy Major Victor Laversuch, W4, with the assistance of March-Phillipps and Appleyard, was required to perfect and submit the detailed plan for final approval to the local army and naval commanders (Giffard and Willis), to the Governor of Nigeria and, once Vice Consul Michie had departed on leave, to his deputy then in Fernando Po, Godden.

W4's orders came by cable on 28 November 1941. He had already called Richard Lippett, W25, to Lagos, and now called the other significant players there for planning meetings, and to prepare for the raid. This, of course included the entirety of Maid Honor Force. The date of the operation was provisionally set for 22 December. Lippett, having reported and been briefed, returned as quickly as he could to Santa Isabel. As it happened, he had difficulties in securing a ship and did not finally arrive back until 12 December, which reduced the time left for preparations. Lippett used his time in Lagos to do some significant shopping, and to draw a quantity of cash in Spanish pesetas from Secret Service funds. W4 had made clear to him the importance of his role, saying that 65 per cent of the chance of success of the venture depended on Lippett getting the officers away from their ships on the night of the raid. If he failed, total disaster might follow.

Having at last received their orders to proceed to Lagos, March-Phillipps and his Maid Honor Force eagerly packed up their camp at Lumley Beach and prepared their ship. From everybody's point of view, the sooner that they got to Lagos the better. March-Phillipps and Appleyard had to attend the planning sessions and the operation was scheduled for the next moonless period (22 December). However, they would have to leave Lagos some days earlier than that, in order to disguise any obvious connection between the departure of the Maid Honor Force and the mysterious disappearance of two enemy ships from Santa Isabel harbour. The *Duchessa d'Aosta* and the

Likomba would be a timely Christmas present to M and SOE from the Maid Honor Force, but must be a secret one.

There was a farewell party thrown for the Maid Honor Force by their hosts, the Anti-Aircraft Battery at Lumley Beach (the Log records: 'Seen off, gunners presented us with a silver mug, a jolly good send off'), and the *Maid Honor* sailed from Freetown on 30 November, with March-Phillipps and his ten fit men on board. It was a journey of 1,300 miles, but at a speed of seven or eight knots an hour (and the *Maid Honor* was capable of appreciably more), they should have reached Lagos in little more than a week. Unluckily, the ship's engine packed up yet again early in the voyage, and then a few miles short of Lagos she found herself becalmed. They eventually arrived on 14 December, far later than expected. The only excitement on the voyage had been that they managed to catch a nine-foot shark. As it swam near the ship, André Desgranges harpooned it with a home-made weapon and hauled it alongside, where Hayes shot it through the head with an automatic pistol. With considerable effort they managed to get the shark on board, where they discovered that it weighed about two hundred pounds. Appleyard described it as 'a filthy brute, as ugly as sin, it stank like a sewer'. They cut off the long fin of the tail and, upon Hayes or Lassen's advice that it would bring good luck and wind, mounted it on the end of the bowsprit. In fact it proved useless, and the *Maid Honor* was becalmed. Still, as Appleyard put it, 'it looks jolly fine'.

During their voyage, and unknown to them, the course of the war changed totally. On 7 December 1941 the Japanese bombed Pearl Harbor and the United States entered the war. It was a great mistake on the part of Japan – as indeed Tiger Tanaka was to say to James Bond in *You Only Live Twice* (1964).

In Fleming's books, James Bond often works closely with the Americans and with the CIA. Although the stories are set in the 1950s and 60s and perhaps at that time cooperation between American and British secret services was inevitable in any story about a modern agent, Bond's friendship with Felix Leiter and the CIA is another indicator that Fleming's Secret Service was based on the SOE. The Central Intelligence Agency (CIA) evolved from the wartime Office for Strategic Services (OSS), which was the American equivalent of the British SOE, and the two often worked together after the US entered the war. Their common goal was to foment resistance behind the lines in enemy-occupied countries and generally to do as much damage there as possible.

Although March-Phillipps and the Maid Honor Force did not work with the OSS in West Africa (Operation Postmaster was planned before the United States entered the war, and was executed far too early for active participation by the OSS), M was on good terms with Colonel W. J. Donovan, whom President Roosevelt had put in charge of Special Operations and the OSS, from an early stage. In July 1940 Gubbins (not yet appointed as M) had met Donovan when the latter was visiting London, and once in post as M he entertained Donovan on a visit to SOE's paramilitary training school at Arisaig, Scotland, in December 1940. This apparently so impressed Donovan that he later encouraged members of his organization to undertake training at the paramilitary school that SOE set up in Canada. Once the USA had entered the war, the OSS established its London Headquarters in Brook Street, Mayfair, in early 1942, and with M's active encouragement close cooperation ensued. Colonel Louis Franck, who had left his post as W in Lagos and returned to London in the autumn of 1941, travelled on from there to the United States to spend time with his family. He was in due course appointed as a liaison officer with the Americans and their newly created OSS, and SOE's United States presence became known as U Section. Thus, cooperation between SOE and the OSS, forerunners of the CIA, post-dated Operation Postmaster, but was a regular feature of later SOE operations.

When Fleming created Bond in the 1950s, the international scene was such as to demand a healthy cooperation between the British and US secret services, as continues to be the case today. Thus it was inevitable that Fleming should give Bond some American friends. At the time that the real M's Secret Service, SOE, was in business, the OSS (now CIA) were their friends, partners and protégés. A photograph of General Donovan hangs on the stairs of the Special Forces Club in London, which M founded after the war for the purpose of maintaining contact and friendship between the agents of many different nationalities with whom he had worked.

The late arrival of the *Maid Honor* in Lagos immediately threw the plans for Operation Postmaster into disarray and led to the cancellation of the intended date of 22 December. The operation would now have to wait for the next moonless period, in January 1942.

Consul Michie arrived in Lagos on 7 December, on his way home on leave. His replacement in Santa Isabel, Agent 51 Godden, was already in situ, and his assistant, Agent 53 Lake, was expected shortly. Guise, W10, got to Lagos on 10 December. In the frustrating and continuing absence of March-Phillipps and Appleyard, Laversuch, Michie and Guise got on as best they could. They held a series of detailed planning sessions. They considered various options and decided that the most sensible tactic would be to divide their force once it was inside Santa Isabel harbour, so as to seize both the *Duchessa d'Aosta* and the *Likomba* simultaneously. This would preserve secrecy until the last possible moment and offer the maximum chance of success, though the risks remained extraordinarily high. The three men went into the plan in detail, so it would be ready for discussion when the Maid Honor Force finally arrived.

Once the *Maid Honor* had finally reached Lagos on 14 December, March-Phillipps and Appleyard went into conference with Laversuch, Michie and Guise. The simultaneous seizure of the two ships was agreed, and the conference set down a list of points that they felt were fundamental to the operation and its success, and which they then demanded that London accept. They were:

- The operations must take place at night.
- They must consist of a simultaneous combined action on both ships
- One tug must be employed for each ship to be taken.
- The European Captain of the tug and native stokers and trimmers must take part in the operation.
- Additional personnel must be obtained, as the crew of *Maid Honor* were not, on their own, sufficient to ensure the success of the venture (they had only eleven fit men).
- If necessary, force would have to be used.
- 'Bangs' were unavoidable in connection with stern moorings and anchor chains.
- There would not be any doubt in the minds of the Spanish authorities as to the nationality of the cutting out party (although no evidence would be found to confirm their suspicions).

London accepted all eight points, and notified Lagos to that effect on 20 December. A new date of 14 January 1942 was proposed and agreed for the operation. March-Phillipps and Laversuch also decided that Agent W10, Guise, should return to Fernando Po immediately for a final reconnaissance, and be back at Lagos before the departure of Operation Postmaster with the latest intelligence he could obtain. Owing to his knowledge of the harbour and general local conditions, Guise was held to be indispensable to the Operation, and would accompany it when it sailed. He could help to guide the tugs into the harbour and alongside the target ships, which hopefully Lippett would have denuded of as many of their officers and crew as possible.

Even if Lippett was successful in this, more men than those presently available to Laversuch and March-Phillipps would be needed. Therefore, General Giffard was to be approached and asked for the loan of an additional seventeen men. Governor Bourdillon and the Nigerian Colonial Government would also be approached to request the loan of the two tugs needed for the Operation, together with their crews. One tug would need to be particularly powerful to tow the *Duchessa d'Aosta*.

For a while, progress was good. London was happy, Guise went off on his final reconnaissance, and Lippett was busy in Santa Isabel preparing the diversionary dinner (due to the postponement of the operation he had had to change the original date). The splendid Governor Bourdillon and his staff were very helpful. The large government tug *Vulcan* was made available, together with her Commander, Tugmaster Coker. A smaller tug (or barge), the *Nuneaton*, was also offered, under the captaincy of Lieutenant J. Goodman. The latter vessel had recently undergone a refit. Two experienced engineers of His Majesty's Nigerian Marine, Lieutenant Commanders Oldland and Duffy, were to help run the tugs, together with their necessary quota of stokers and trimmers.

All seemed set fair for Operation Postmaster. Finally, Maid Honor Force was going to do what they had come to West Africa to do – steal two enemy ships from under the noses of the 'neutral' Spanish. The ban on bangs was gone, and March-Phillipps and his men were elated at the prospect of a real commando raid, however heavily the odds might seem to be stacked against them. Nobody realized that yet another spanner was about to be thrown into the works, bringing the entire operation to a halt.

Even with London's support, Operation Postmaster required the final blessing of the two local commanders, General Giffard and Admiral Willis. This should not have presented any problems, since each would have had his orders from London. However a commander on the ground may, on occasion, disregard an order from above if there are local developments or circumstances that he knows about but his superiors do not. Therefore, it was necessary for Laversuch, standing in for W, to go and see the Army's Commander in Chief, General Giffard, who was in Lagos at that time. Apart from formal approval for the final plan, Laversuch needed a loan from Giffard of seventeen of his men. Maid Honor Force numbered eleven fit men, to whom a further six SOE officers based in Lagos were to be added (including Agent Guise). That still made only seventeen, and it had been decided that Operation Postmaster would need double that number to carry out the operation successfully, particularly since there might be a crew of thirty or more on board the *Duchessa d'Aosta.*

General Sir George Giffard KCB, DSO, was, inevitably, a First World War veteran, and a career soldier with considerable African experience. Born in 1886, now fifty-five years of age, he had been commissioned into the Queen's Royal West Surrey Regiment in 1906, at the age of nineteen. He had served in East Africa in the First World War, and in the Royal West African Frontier Force between 1920 and 1925. He was to be moved from his post as Commander in Chief West Africa in August 1943 to become ADC to King George VI.

Giffard appears to have been a man of strong views and something of a martinet. He had even fallen out from time to time with the Governor, Sir Bernard Bourdillon. In the early days after the British defeat at Dunkirk and the fall of France, when the first Free French delegation had arrived in Lagos in 1940 (described by Bourdillon as 'keen as mustard and very intelligent'), Giffard did not want anything to do with them. According to Bourdillon, '[he] looks upon the French as a defeated nation, rotten to the core, from whom no good can come, and thinks that we ought to let them stew in their own juice, and have nothing to do with de Gaulle or anybody. This. . . colours all his ideas, and he would rather let the Germans get into the Cameroons, and then turn them out when we are strong enough.'

Giffard was also implacably hostile to the SOE mission in West Africa. On a visit to London in May 1941, he had made clear that he had been strongly opposed to the idea of W Section from the first, saying: 'To be candid, the trouble with the SOE representatives was that (a) they did not know enough French and (b) they had not the knowledge of what will get under the skin of the African. In general, these SOE representatives are very able, but they are not round pegs in round holes.' Giffard's own objective was to keep the West African territories quiet, and not to provoke a local war by subversive activity. He complained that he was inevitably very intimately concerned in any action that W and SOE might take in West Africa, and that it was very unsatisfactory that he was not involved in the authorization of such activity. Another irritant for Giffard was SOE's cavalier attitude to military rank. When, in September 1941, Giffard heard that W and an SOE colleague of his at that time in Lagos called R. E. L.Wingate had both been given the military rank of Lieutenant Colonel, he was furious, and cabled the War Office, specifically in relation to Wingate, stating that he considered it, 'eminently undesirable that gentlemen not employed in any way on military duties should be granted military rank'. In short, General Giffard was one of those old-fashioned commanders who strongly disliked the sort of independent, irregular force that M's Secret Service was. This was the man Laversuch now had to approach for the loan of extra men for Operation Postmaster.

Major Laversuch's meeting with General Giffard was an unhappy one. He later described it: 'The G.O.C. in C's attitude was exceedingly difficult and he stated frankly that he could not countenance the operation without getting in touch with C. in C. South Atlantic [Admiral Willis], and further he did not like it for reasons which he could not disclose. He promised to let me have a reply by 25 December.'

One of the reasons that Giffard 'could not disclose' was that he had earlier been asked by London to look at the possibility of a British invasion of Fernando Po. This had no doubt been prompted by the obvious fear that Germany might themselves take possession of the island, which was of considerable strategic value. Therefore, the British should grab it first. Had that sort of action been in the offing, certainly a raid such as Postmaster would have put the Spanish on their guard and made a British invasion far more difficult. However, the diplomatic repercussions of an invasion of Fernando Po would have been substantial, and Giffard must have known that the suggestion was little more than an intelligence exercise. The truth undoubtedly was that he hated the idea of SOE carrying out a major operation on his territory.

Despondent, and no doubt sick of the see-saw of high-level decision-making, Laversuch and March-Phillipps waited to hear from Giffard on or before Christmas Day. March-Phillipps would no doubt have loved to simply disregard General Giffard and set off for Santa Isabel then and there – answering questions afterwards, if he were still alive. Major Roy Farran, the very successful 2SAS commando leader, did exactly that later in the war when he 'fell out of a plane by accident, with his parachute on', directly contrary to orders, to take command of Operation Tombola behind German lines in Northern Italy.

However, in this case such impetuous action was not possible. Maid Honor Force not only needed the extra men, they also needed the cooperation of the Royal Navy to formally seize the *Duchessa d'Aosta* and the *Likomba* on the high seas after the raid. March-Phillipps and Laversuch had no option but to wait and hope. Laversuch cabled London to inform M and Caesar of the problem. M took the matter to the highest level, and the War Office drafted a Top Secret telegram to Giffard at 1935 hrs on 23 December. It read:

> The Foreign Office have authorised SOE to take action against enemy shipping and Vichy ships working for Vichy interests, except those engaged in the trades approved by the Ministry of Economic Warfare. . .
>
> Local representative SOE has been instructed to obtain concurrence of C in C Atlantic (Admiral Willis) where maritime action is proposed.

> *Admiralty have requested C in C South Atlantic to afford all assistance possible in projects involving seizure of certain Axis ships in Fernando Po and Lobbito* [author's italics].
>
> Cover must ensure that collusion with British authorities or forces will not (repeat not) be apparent.
>
> *Request you will give any assistance possible in Fernando Po project.*

Such orders were, for Giffard, unequivocal. However, nothing was ever going to be easy for Maid Honor Force. Through clerical incompetence, probably because it was Christmas time, this vital telegram was not sent until some days after Christmas. Unaware of that, London cabled Laversuch on Christmas Eve, indicating that an appropriate telegram had been sent to Giffard and wishing them all a Happy Christmas. Wrongly, everyone in SOE and the Maid Honor Force now believed that the problem had been solved. In fact, Giffard, not having received the telegram, remained obdurately against Operation Postmaster and on Christmas Eve he went to see Admiral Willis and informed him of his objections.

Acting Vice Admiral Algernon Usborne Willis DSO was another First World War veteran. Born in Hampstead in 1889, therefore now fifty-two, he had gone to sea at the age of fifteen. He had fought in the Battle of Jutland, and had served throughout his career in a variety of ships and training schools. He was appointed Commander in Chief, South Atlantic in August 1941, with the principal duty of providing protection for convoys. He was to remain in post in West Africa only until February 1942, when he was transferred to the Eastern Fleet to command the No. 3 Battle Squadron. He was more open-minded than Giffard, but nonetheless an old-fashioned sailor and not enthusiastic about SOE'S activities.

General Giffard persuaded Willis that he too should object to the scheme and Willis did so. He cabled London at 2305 hrs on Christmas Eve, informing them that Giffard had been to see him and had said he was much against the seizure of the Axis ships in Fernando Po on three grounds: (a) Giffard had been instructed by the War Office to examine a plan for the capture of Fernando Po (which apparently had come as a surprise to Willis), (b) the origin of the raid would become known whether it was successful or not, and would have a bad effect on the Spanish attitude towards Great Britain, (c) such an action would be unnecessarily provocative unless the value of the ships was so great as to offset the damage of repercussions. Admiral Willis said that he concurred with

Giffard and had suspended the operation pending further instructions. Thus, both of the 'big guns' in West Africa had now placed an embargo on Postmaster.

Meanwhile, Laversuch, March-Phillipps and the Maid Honor Force had no idea of the trouble that was brewing. They were simply awaiting General Giffard's consent to the loan of seventeen of his soldiers, which they believed must follow the telegram from London ordering Giffard to give '*any possible assistance*' to them. Laversuch and March-Phillipps were also putting in place the last details of the plan of action.

On Christmas morning, Laversuch sent Appleyard and most of Maid Honor Force up country for a few days. Longe and Eyre had been called in as experts to advise on the amount of plastic explosive needed to sever the cables that Guise had so carefully measured. They had now been fully briefed on the operation, and Maid Honor Force needed somewhere away from prying eyes to carry out certain vital experiments with the plastic explosive they were going to use. Also, Laversuch thought the men might become a little too conspicuous if they remained hanging around in Lagos during the holiday season, and tongues might become loosened during the celebrations. So they went with Agent W30, Desmond Longe, to Olokomeji, a small settlement which Appleyard described as a 'tiny place in the bush', where Longe and Dismore ran their training school for black African guerrillas and agents.

Desmond Longe was determined to go on the Postmaster raid, although he was not officially fit. He had suffered injuries to both hands when a soda bottle exploded as he was endeavouring to treat a colleague injured in a road accident, and a tendon in his left thumb had been severed. He was awaiting repatriation to have it operated on. However, Longe was right-handed and thus felt able to 'get by'.

Appleyard and his party stayed in the only European house in Olokomeji (once a holiday home for the Governor of Nigeria) for three nights. They arrived in time for lunch on Christmas day, but the main meal was provided in the evening by their hostess, the only woman present in their group of nine. Appleyard described it in one of his many letters home: 'We had a grand Christmas dinner at night, with turkey and etceteras, plum-pudding (on fire!), mince pies, etc, and all the additions of crackers, a Christmas tree (with presents!), chocolates, nuts etc. Great fun and all very unexpected.'

Maid Honor Force thoroughly enjoyed their time at Olokomeji, where the climate was far more comfortable than in Lagos or Freetown. Very hot in the middle of the day, it became cool at night, with the temperature dropping to about 70 degrees Farenheit. Longe and Dismore clearly looked after them well and Maid Honor Force went on expeditions into the bush, hunting wild pig and monkeys. They even tried crocodile shooting one day, but as Appleyard put it, 'the crocs were apparently away for Christmas and didn't appear'. Longe also took them fishing – a hazardous affair which involved paddling on the nearby river in two-man canoes and tossing four-ounce sticks of plastic explosive on a very short fuse into the water. The resulting explosion would stun the fish, and bring them floating to the suface, where the men could catch them before they recovered. The only problem was, particularly in the canoe that contained the six-foot-four Captain Desmond Longe and Geoffrey Appleyard, that the explosions caused violent turbulence in the water, more than once threatening to throw them out of their canoe. It was lucky, as Appleyard noted, that the crocodiles were away for Christmas. It was a pleasant break for all concerned, although heavy sessions of physical training ensured they all reamained at peak fitness.

Whilst at Olokomeji, Maid Honor Force also carried out some vital training and 'experiments'for their mission. These involved testing the plastic explosive on various specimen widths of chain, to see how much would be required to sever the anchor chains and mooring cables of the *Duchessa d'Aosta* and the *Likomba*. The plan was for the chains to be severed by explosives on board the ships (thus ensuring that no commando agent had to set foot on Spanish soil), and it was therefore important that there be as little as possible collateral damage to the ships themselves, at the same time ensuring that the cables were parted. Using Guise's invaluable information on measurements, Maid Honor Force was able to discover in the privacy of the Nigerian bush exactly how much plastic explosive to use for each charge. It had been decided in consultation with Eyre and Longe, to use a hinged bracelet, or 'handcuff' charge. This could easily be slipped around the anchor chains and cables, fixed into position, and fired by a detonator and fuse. The bracelets would be attached in sets of three per cable, which would be wired to explode simultaneously. Each of the necessary charges was prepared in advance, subject to the final heating and moulding of the plastic explosive itself, which would need to be done on board ship. The detonators were stored separately in waterproof tins.

Meanwhile back in Lagos, while Laversuch waited to hear from General Giffard he prepared and sent a cable to London explaining further details of the final plan. Put simply, the objective of Operation Postmaster was to board, capture and tow out both the *Duchessa d'Aosta* and the *Likomba* from the small harbour at Santa Isabel, as quickly and unobtrusively as possible. The real difficulty of the task seems always to have been deliberately understated. The *Duchessa d'Aosta* was a great rudderless whale, and there was an enormous potential for things to go wrong. She had been built in Trieste in 1921. Her exact weight was 7,872 tons, she was 464 ft long, and 57 ft wide. She had two steel decks and a steel shelter deck, and was fitted with refrigeration machinery. Armed resistance was very possible on board the *Duchessa* herself once she came under attack, particularly if officers were on board, and running battles might ensue. It would be important for the boarding party to take immediate and total control of the bridge and upper decks, to blow the mooring cables and to attach the towing hawsers, but it might well be that a firefight would continue below decks for some time before the entire ship could be secured.

There would be no opportunity for the *Duchessa d'Aosta* to get up steam in Santa Isabel harbour and there was, in any event, no guarantee that her engines were still in working order after sixteen months at anchor in the tropics. She might even be stuck on the bottom. She would have to be towed as a dead weight, without use of her own rudder or steering gear. If the tug that towed her made any mistake in choosing a passage out of Santa Isabel harbour, the big ship was likely to run aground. During the operation, Maid Honor Force was likely to come under fire from the shore, just a short distance from the *Duchessa d'Aosta*'s mooring. And as soon as the explosives severing the anchor cables went off, all hope of secrecy would be lost. There was a danger that the garrison's four-inch guns might be brought to bear and they, of course, were capable of doing very substantial damage to the tug towing the *Duchessa d'Aosta* out of the harbour, or to the *Duchessa* herself.

The *Likomba* was a 199 ton steel tug, diesel-powered, built in Hamburg in 1939. She had been only a few months old when she took refuge at Santa Isabel. But she too had been at anchor in Santa Isabel harbour for well over a year, and there was no intelligence as to the state of her engines. Guise's careful survey of the harbour and ships had stopped short of boarding the tug and visiting her engine room. Therefore, it was envisaged that she too would have to be towed out of the harbour. She was as close to shore as the *Duchessa d'Aosta*, and within easy range of small-arms fire or anything larger that the Spanish might use. The layout of the *Likomba* meant that a small but determined unit could defend her against boarding without great difficulty. Surprise would be of the essence.

The *Bibundi*, which was moored beside the *Likomba*, was considerably smaller at 70 tons. She was unimportant, but the Maid Honor Force would take her too if the opportunity presented itself.

The plan was that if challenged on the approach the British ships would reply in Spanish or Italian, gaining sufficient time to get close enough to the target ships for the heavily armed boarding parties to make their move. The two British tugs would steer directly alongside their objectives and no small craft would need to be used (this was later changed during the operation because of mechanical difficulties on the *Nuneaton*). Since the mooring chains on both the *Duchessa d'Aosta* and the *Likomba* were to be blown from on board the ships themselves, there was a danger of collateral damage to both the British and enemy ships. Hopefully, Guise's measurements were good, and the trials at Olokomeji would result in appropriate amounts of plastic explosives being used. If any of the charges failed to sever the mooring cables, or, worse, failed to fire, time would quickly run out for Operation Postmaster. Spanish vessels could easily block the channel, thereby trapping the British ships inside the harbour.

The boarding parties for each ship would be divided into three: (i) to quell resistance; (ii) to blow the fore and aft mooring chains; and (iii) to attach the tow ropes from the tugs. All three sections would set about their tasks simultaneously, in order to ensure maximum speed. Thus the extra seventeen men that Maid Honor Force was expecting to be provided by Giffard were essential. But there were still so many things that could go wrong.

Caesar received Laversuch's Christmas Day cable in London, and duly passed on the details to M on Boxing Day. He requested a meeting with M to discuss the problem of General Giffard, but commented in his memorandum to M that on the whole the plan appeared to be sound. Caesar raised only two points, saying: '(i) The wireless set on the Duchessa d'Aosta is in use and therefore probably works off an independent generator. I consider that either the wireless or the generator or both should be put out of action in the very early stages of the operation. (ii) From the information at our disposal, the harbour of Fernando Po is very tricky, as the sole means of approach to the shore is through an extremely narrow channel. In consequence it might be as well to advise our people to secure a first-class pilot with a thorough knowledge of local waters to accompany the tug.'

Caesar concluded his memorandum by raising again the question of who was to be in command of Postmaster, reminding M of their meeting with W on 21 November, when W had 'expressed certain misgivings about March-Phillipps on temperamental grounds and felt that it might be hazardous to put him in charge'. It seems that even at this stage it was still not certain that March-Phillipps would be allowed to lead Operation Postmaster.

Back in Lagos, by 27 December Agent W4, Laversuch, had still not received the expected approval from General Giffard (promised by Christmas Day), or his confirmation that he would supply the seventeen men requested by Maid Honor Force. W4 was becoming worried about the lack of time available if they were to launch the operation in mid-January. He complained in a telegram to London, on 27 December, that if they did not have a decision at once their plan would be upset and the success of the operation jeopardized.

Laversuch finally heard from General Giffard on 28 December 1941, three days later than promised and the day that Appleyard and his party returned from Olokomeji. Giffard had still not received London's cable dated 23 December. His message was terse: 'Have consulted C.-in-C. South Atlantic who does NOT repeat NOT agree operations should take place at present.'

Rather than the seventeen men, Giffard had sent seventeen words that yet again appeared to stop Operation Postmaster in its tracks. Having experienced such an uncomfortable meeting with the General before Christmas, it seemed pretty obvious to Laversuch that Giffard had persuaded Admiral Willis to oppose the scheme, thereby avoiding being solely responsible for blocking it. Despite London's assurances on 24 December, Operation Postmaster could still not go ahead. The hopes of the SOE team and Maid Honor Force, recently so high, were once more dashed. What more did they have to do? London were saying 'yes', but Lagos were still saying 'no!'

London, of course, had to sort it out and they did. On 29 December, Admiral Willis received a telegram from London in response to the one he had sent late on Christmas Eve objecting to Postmaster. The orders to Willis, as they had been to Giffard, were unequivocal. The raid was to go ahead and he was to support it. Admiral Willis now had the clearest of orders (again) that he was to support and help Operation Postmaster. Agent W5, SOE's Head of Mission in Accra, Gold Coast, spoke with Admiral Willis whilst he was in Accra on New Year's Eve, after Willis had received that telegram. W5 then cabled Laversuch in Lagos to the effect that although Willis still disliked the idea of Operation Postmaster, he was prepared to discuss it and he now wanted to know every detail of the plan from the leader of the expedition. W5 strongly recommended that W.01, March-Phillipps, or possibly W.02, Appleyard, should come to Accra as soon as possible to meet with Willis, and if possible Laversuch should come too.

Laversuch realized it was essential that he accompany the inspirational but short-tempered March-Phillipps to meet Willis. The two men decided to fly from Lagos to Freetown (where Admiral Willis now was) in order to speak to him face to face as soon as possible. Time was of the essence if they were to have everything in place for the next moonless period, and the cover of Agent W25, Lippett, their vital man in Santa Isabel, would soon begin to wear a little thin. They took a flight out of Lagos on 3 January and arrived in Freetown the following day.

Admiral Willis held talks with Laversuch and March-Phillipps on the evenings of 4 and 5 January. He knew he would have to obey his orders but wanted to know about Operation Postmaster before he finally consented to it. He could see both the enormous difficulty of the plan and the dangers if it went wrong. The Royal Navy had an important role to play. Their cooperation in the international deception that was to follow a successful 'cutting out' of the enemy ships from Santa Isabel harbour was essential to the operation. The plan was that after the enemy ships had been seized they would be towed out to sea, well away from the island of Fernando Po. At a distance of at least forty miles from that island, they would be 'happened upon' by a Royal Navy warship, which would officially seize them on the high seas (well clear of Spanish territory), and escort them as prizes of war into Lagos harbour. It would be suggested that German radio traffic had tipped off the Royal Navy as to the presence of the ships in their area and that the Navy knew absolutely nothing about how the ships had come to leave Santa Isabel, other than what the crews of the captured ships told them.

Laversuch and March-Phillipps managed to satisfy Willis that the plan could work. The meetings were lengthy, but when they were over Admiral Willis at last gave his consent to Operation Postmaster. Further, he agreed to supply a Royal Navy Corvette, HMS *Violet*, under the command of Lieutenant Herbert Nicholas RN, to carry out the task of officially capturing the *Duchessa d'Aosta* and the *Likomba* on the high seas. Laversuch later reported: 'We found C-in-C and his Chief of Staff most helpful and courteous in every way.'

Admiral Willis also contacted and spoke with General Giffard and reported back to Laversuch and March-Phillipps that the General had now also given his consent to Operation Postmaster. Obviously, Giffard had finally received the 23 December telegram ordering him to give Postmaster every assistance possible. Laversuch requested another meeting with General Giffard, who as it turned out was now also in Freetown – he had every expectation that at last the General would give him the seventeen men Postmaster needed. Giffard agreed to see Laversuch and March-Phillipps that same evening, 5 January. But it became immediately clear that General

Giffard strongly resented being overruled. Laversuch later reported: 'The proceedings were exceedingly brief and the following conversation took place:

> Laversuch: "I was informed by the C-in-C South Atlantic that you had agreed in principle to the operations taking place, for which we are grateful."
>
> Giffard: "I have agreed, but I tell you frankly I do not like the scheme, and I shall never like it."
>
> Laversuch: "I am very sorry to hear this, but thank you for having given your consent. There is a question of personnel. Could you assist us on this subject?"
>
> Giffard: "No – most definitely – no. The only thing I can offer you is my best wishes for the success of the operation."
>
> Laversuch: "Thank you very much, sir. Goodnight."

Put bluntly, General Giffard had accepted the order that he should not block Operation Postmaster, but was not prepared to do anything at all to help towards its success. No doubt he believed he could justify his refusal to loan any of his men on the basis that all were needed to carry out their normal duties (his orders said, 'every assistance possible' and he could argue that it had not been possible). Perhaps also he thought that by refusing to supply the men Laversuch needed he could still bring about the abandonment of the plan. In fairness, General Giffard had the heavy responsibility of guarding the borders of Nigeria, the Gold Coast, Sierra Leone and the rest of the British West African colonies. He was no doubt concerned as to the effect Operation Postmaster might have on his 'neighbours' and the balance of power in the region. He may well have believed, understandably, that the operation had no real chance of success and could only result in a bloody disaster.

The confusion and muddle of the Christmas and New Year period had wasted a lot of time. It was now late evening on 5 January 1942. The next moonless period, for which Operation Postmaster had been scheduled, was days away. The planned night for the raid was 14/15 January and Operation Postmaster would have to leave Lagos harbour some days before that. There was still a lot to do and little time to do it in.

CHAPTER 16

The Final Pieces of the Puzzle

Final arrangements for Operation Postmaster had to be hurriedly put into place. The question of who was to lead the raid was rapidly resolved. There was no doubt that Gus March-Phillipps, Agent W.01, was an inspirational leader of a type rarely seen, and that the men of Maid Honor Force would follow him anywhere. To those in Lagos it seemed beyond argument that he was the only man to lead Postmaster, even though there were officers senior to him in rank from SOE Lagos who would be going on the raid. Major Laversuch cabled London: 'We feel strongly that W01[March-Phillipps] must be in command for the following reasons: (i) his sea faring and general experience, which are most valuable in an operation of this nature; (ii) personnel of the Maid Honor are backbone of whole party and they have the utmost confidence and trust in him; (iii) W29 [Major John Eyre, the senior Lagos SOE officer] volunteered to act under the command of W01 in any capacity; (iv) in view of the above, we submit that it is fundamentally wrong to change, especially at this late stage.' Following Laversuch's telegram Gus March-Phillipps was confirmed as the commander of Operation Postmaster. It would have been a nonsense for anyone else to lead it. It was, of course, what M had always intended.

Laversuch and March-Phillipps arrived back in Lagos on the morning of 7 January 1942. Time was now extremely short. The target date for the departure of Operation Postmaster from Lagos was fixed for 11 January, and somehow they had to find an extra seventeen reliable men. There could be no question of adjourning the operation again. It was essential that it took place in a moonless period (otherwise the entry of the two tugs into Santa Isabel harbour would easily be visible), and if this 'slot' were missed the operation would suffer substantial further delay. Further, the Maid Honor Force had now been hanging around in Lagos for some weeks and there was a risk it might become known that they were a commando force. There were always enemy spies about.

In Santa Isabel, Lippett, now the key player, had already had to extend his stay once as a result of the cancellation of the original 22 December date. He had done so on the basis that the premises of John Holt's in Santa Isabel needed some maintenance and redecoration, but that work would not last for ever and he could not postpone his departure again. He was booked on a steamer to leave the island on 23 January. Guise, having performed his final reconnaissance, had returned to Lagos and was ready to sail with Maid Honor Force.

A last minute scare sent Guise hurrying back to Santa Isabel. Lake, newly arrived in the port, wired Lagos on 7 January that he had observed machine guns being posted all round the harbour, surely a clear indicator that news had reached the Spanish of the intended operation. Guise flew straight to Douala, filled his diplomatic pouch with newspaper to provide some excuse for a trip to Santa Isabel, and set out in the *Bamenda*. Happily, he discovered on arrival that it was a false alarm – the guns were old ones, which could not be readied and manned in less than forty-five minutes and which would be very difficult to bring to bear on any target in the harbour. Guise hurried back to Lagos to report accordingly.

Meanwhile, Laversuch and March-Phillipps decided that (presuming all was well in Santa Isabel) it was essential for Operation Postmaster to leave Lagos as planned, in the early hours of 11 January. They confirmed that zero hour for the raid on Santa Isabel would be 2330 hrs on 14 January, just one week away. Somewhere, somehow, the seventeen extra men would simply have to be found.

As soon as they landed back in Lagos on the morning of 7 January Laversuch and March-Phillipps requested, and were immediately granted, an interview with His Majesty's Governor of Nigeria. Sir Bernard Henry Bourdillon, born in Tasmania in 1883, was the oldest of the three 'heavyweights' in the area, at the age of fifty-eight. He had been brought up in England and South Africa, and had graduated from St John's College, Oxford, in 1906. He joined the Indian Civil Service in 1908 and gained a reputation as an excellent linguist. During the First World War he transferred to the Army, reaching the rank of Major. He left the Army in 1919. In 1929 he transferred to the Colonial Civil Service, and in due course was appointed Governor of Uganda in 1935, then Governor and Commander in Chief of Nigeria in the same year. He was a man of considerable intellect and vision and he had been in favour of SOE's endeavours in West Africa from the start. It probably helped that he held a low opinion of General Giffard.

At their interview with the Governor, Laversuch and March-Phillipps explained the problem of personnel and asked whether they might borrow suitable men from within the Colonial Service in Nigeria. They were of course all civilians, but many had had military experience of one sort or another. The Governor at once agreed and instructed Laversuch to prepare a list of personnel who were thought to be suitable, and to submit it for his approval. He would then take a decision as to whether each man could be spared for the period of operation. With Guise's help, Laversuch drew up a list of seventeen names. Eleven were in Lagos, six were up country or on the frontier. They were selected from all the branches of the Colonial Government: four were police officers, three came from the Administrative branch, three from the Education branch, four from the Public Works Department, and one each from Land & Survey and Accountancy. March-Phillipps also needed a doctor in case of casualties, and one was duly selected. He was Dr J. G. MacGregor, the Senior Surgeon Specialist in Lagos, who was in fact currently treating one of the SOE officers already going on Operation Postmaster – the enthusiastic Agent W30, Captain Desmond Longe.

The men on the list were later described as being the 'toughest individuals in the public service in Nigeria'. Miles Clifford, the Governor's Acting Deputy Chief Secretary endorsed every name on the list, it was passed on to the Acting Chief Secretary, Hoskyns-Abrahall, who also gave his support, and it then went to the Governor. Sir Bernard Bourdillon approved all of the names submitted.

Bourdillon was acting with not just enthusiasm, but courage. If Operation Postmaster had gone badly wrong and the men from his Colonial Service had been captured, then not only would he have been subjected to considerable international embarrassment, but almost certainly his own career would have been over. Laversuch and March-Phillipps, in their subsequent reports to London, were to emphasize how vital Bourdillon's support had been.

The list of seventeen suitable 'amateurs' having been drawn up (the eldest was fifty-two years of age), a telegram was sent to each of them by Miles Clifford, requiring them to attend a gathering at 32 Cameron Road, Lagos, at midday on 10 January for further instructions. The cover story was that there was to be some sort of 'party' and they were to take two weeks 'leave'. The telegrams were courteous but firm, while telling the recipients nothing of what they were about to be asked to volunteer for. It is this section of Operation Postmaster that had yet to be formally recruited when M sent his final telegram of good wishes to W.01 on the morning of 10 January.

The group was duly assembled at Cameron Road. Although the seventeen men had, in effect, been ordered to attend, once they were there it was made clear that their status was purely that of potential volunteers. They were addressed in very general terms by Laversuch and March-Phillipps, who explained that volunteers were wanted for a job of military character which might last two weeks, would be arduous, might be dangerous, had the approval of His Excellency the Governor, and was aimed to assist the war effort. Only volunteers would be taken. For those who wished to opt out, invitations to a party at the nearby Ikoyi Club had been arranged, to provide a cover for the gathering. Every man volunteered. A champagne toast was then drunk to success, good luck and a safe return. Next, the volunteers had to be kitted out in suitable clothing. Everyone on Operation Postmaster was to wear dark clothing and plimsolls.

Agent W10, Guise, commented afterwards: 'The situation on 7 and 8 January was not too good. . . The question of man power looked serious. Owing to intense enthusiasm from His Excellency, and the Deputy Chief Secretary, Miles Clifford, the entire matter was solved in some twenty-four hours, and at midday on 10 January, as choice a collection of thugs as Nigeria can ever have seen was assembled at 32, Cameron Road. None of these volunteers had any accurate idea of what they were to do, and guesses varied from blowing up objects in Dahomey to the kidnapping of the Vichy Governor. Some of them, in fact, convinced that they were to trek for hundreds of miles, had been practising walking in thick boots for the previous twenty-four hours.'

Finally, March-Phillipps had his full force in place and was ready to go. The volunteers would not be further briefed until they were on board the tugs and well clear of Lagos. The meeting at 32 Cameron Road, went on until the evening and then the volunteers were taken in small inconspicuous groups on board the two tugs, the *Vulcan* and the *Nuneaton*, which were moored side by side at Apapa Dock, in Lagos harbour.

At 0530 hrs on 11 January the two tugs sailed, with the larger *Vulcan* towing the *Nuneaton*. They would have four days at sea before the raid. This was far more time than was necessary for the journey, but it reflected the importance of the departure of the tugs not being connected in any way with the attack on the night of 14/15 January. It also allowed March-Phillipps time to give his new men a full briefing on the operation, and some thorough training.

Agent W4, Laversuch, had wanted to go with them but was ordered not to. It was felt necessary that he stay in Lagos to coordinate the operation, and to fully brief both his local commanders and London on developments. The total European party that sailed for Santa Isabel numbered forty-one. Eleven were the Maid Honor Force (two of their total of thirteen were sick), six were SOE Lagos (including Eyre, Dismore, Longe and Guise), seventeen were civilians from the Colonial Service, and four were from the Nigerian Marine. There were also three Spaniards whom Agent W10, Guise, had recruited in Victoria, Cameroon. All three had served with the French (later the Free French) Foreign Legion, but when Guise came across them they had resigned from that unit and were looking for action. Guise had reported back to W on 17 October 1941: 'It occurs to me that you might have a use for them later on – at least on a dark night they could answer a challenge in the right accent. They are prepared to do anything, and one was previously an engineer cum street fighter.' No names appear for them in the SOE records. They are referred to as (and obviously were) 'very friendly' Spaniards. They were much needed fighting men and, as Guise had suggested, their presence on the ships could help support the bluff that the darkened *Vulcan* and *Nuneaton* were Spanish vessels, should identification be required in Santa Isabel harbour. Bearing in mind their background in the Foreign Legion, it seems highly likely that they eventually played some part in the action of the raid.

In addition to the Europeans there was a full complement of black African stokers and trimmers for the each of two tugs. These men would face many of the same physical dangers as their European companions on the voyage.

All was now ready. The ships would carry with them the expectations of all on board, of W4 in Lagos, and of M and Churchill's War Cabinet far away in London. For W.01 and his men, there was also the heavy burden of knowing that if it all went wrong the consequences could be disastrous, not only for themselves, but for their country. Armed with the words of M's final telegram: 'Good hunting. Am confident you will exercise utmost care to ensure success and obviate repercussions. Best of luck to you and all Maid Honor and others', March-Phillipps and Operation Postmaster sailed out from the relative safety of Lagos harbour into the unknown.

CHAPTER 17

The Cover Story

Once it had been decided that Operation Postmaster would go ahead, high level consideration had to be given to the international storm that would undoubtedly follow the taking of the *Duchessa d'Aosta* and the *Likomba* from neutral waters. There were bound to be repercussions, in particular from the Spanish, and of course from the Germans and Italians. The British Ambassador in Madrid was particularly sensitive to the potential consequences of any action affecting Spain's neutral waters – understandably so, since he would be the first target of any outrage. Until Hitler turned on Russia in June 1941 it was believed that an attack on Portugal was imminent, and that Spain might be recruited, by armed persuasion if necessary, into the Axis alliance. The objective would be to take Gibraltar and close off the Mediteranean to all Allied shipping. Even after the Russian campaign had started, that threat, although lessened, remained.

Britain's Ambassador to Spain at that time was a very experienced politician and man of international affairs, Sir Samuel Hoare, then sixty-one years of age. Hoare was for many years the Member of Parliament for Chelsea, and had filled the posts of Home Secretary and Foreign Secretary in the Conservative Governments of the 1930s. He was a close ally of Neville Chamberlain's, and when Churchill replaced Chamberlain in May 1940, Hoare lost his seat in the cabinet. In August 1940 he was appointed British Ambassador in Madrid and his specific brief was to keep Spain out of the war. Obviously, he was keen to prevent any unnecessary acts of provocation. On 8 January 1942, Hoare cabled that he was most anxious to assist with any venture, but felt obliged to point out the need for great care to avoid any incident which might prejudice His Majesty's Government in Spain. In the event, it appears that Hoare was told nothing of the planned action until after it had taken place.

W4 cabled London on 9 January 1942 with details of the plan that had been agreed with Admiral Willis for HMS *Violet*'s intervention and formal seizure of the enemy ships, plus a suggestion for a possible disinformation campaign and cover-up. Secrecy remained essential and a strict 'need to know' policy was in place.

HMS *Violet* was to leave Lagos with a prize crew on board, the justification for this being that she had orders to collect a tug from Douala. Lieutenant Nicholas and his crew would know nothing of Operation Postmaster at that stage. Once at sea, Nicholas would open a sealed envelope containing his real orders and the necessary instructions regarding the operation. W4 would then arrange for a dummy radio message to be received from Calabar, Nigeria, speaking of unidentified vessels in that general area, and HMS *Violet* would be given instructions to proceed to a set position to investigate. There she would find the *Duchessa d'Aosta* and the *Likomba*. With only her Captain knowing it was all a sham, HMS *Violet* would go through the complete drill for identifying and boarding her prizes, and would report to base in the usual way. The prizes would then be brought into Lagos under escort, with the prize crew on board.

Obviously, once the *Duchessa d'Aosta* and the *Likomba* had been seized, it would become pretty clear to HMS *Violet*'s crew that the two ships had already been in British hands, but at least secrecy would be preserved until the very last moment and the number who knew what was really going on would be kept to a minimum. The cover story was designed to operate not only in enemy and neutral countries, but also upon the minds of the substantial majority of the British and Allied forces. Very few would ever know the truth.

Of course, the cover story had to be in two parts – the first to preserve secrecy until the ships were safely in official British hands; the second to quieten the inevitable international outcry afterwards. So far as part two, the cover story after seizure, was concerned, W4 suggested that it be represented that the crews of the enemy ships had mutinied because of local conditions and lack of pay in Santa Isabel, and had left the harbour under their own steam, heading for the Vichy French port of Cotonou. They had subsequently been intercepted by a British warship and surrendered without a struggle. The announcement would be made on the evening of the day that the liaison with HMS *Violet* took place. The scheduled time for that liaison was 1400 hrs on 15 January 1942. A simple message would be sent by W4, 'Postmaster successful', and that would trigger within a few hours the launch of the cover story.

W4 suggested that the BBC should broadcast the cover story by way of a press release based on an Admiralty communiqué, in Spanish, Portuguese and English. He accepted that the Spanish authorities were unlikely to believe the story, but suggested they might wish to adopt it to avoid embarrassment.

Gus March-Phillipps and Geoffrey Appleyard on the *Maid Honor* (*courtesy of the Estate of the late Major General Gubbins, KCMG, DSO, MC*)

Major Gus March-Phillipps, DSO, MBE (*courtesy of the Special Forces Club*)

Major Geoffrey Appleyard, MC and Bar (*courtesy of the Special Forces Club*)

Captain Graham Hayes, MC (*courtesy of the National Archives, Kew*)

Major Anders Lassen, VC, MC and two Bars (*courtesy of the Special Forces Club*)

Maître André Desgranges, CGM (*courtesy of the National Archives, Kew*)

Major Victor Laversuch, OBE (*courtesy of the National Archives, Kew*)

Captain Peter Lake, MC, Legion d'Honneur, Croix de Guerre (*courtesy of the Special Forces Club*)

Lieutenant Colonel Leonard Henry 'Dizzy' Dismore, OBE, TD (*courtesy of the Special Forces Club*)

Photograph of the *Maid Honor*, with portraits of Appleyard, Desgranges and March-Phillipps superimposed (*courtesy of the National Archives, Kew*)

The *Duchessa d'Aosta* and the *Likomba* at their moorings in Santa Isabel Harbour (*courtesy of the National Archives, Kew*)

Santa Isabel Harbour, November 1941, photographed by Vice Consul Michie from Pilot Alacon's plane (*courtesy of the National Archives, Kew*)

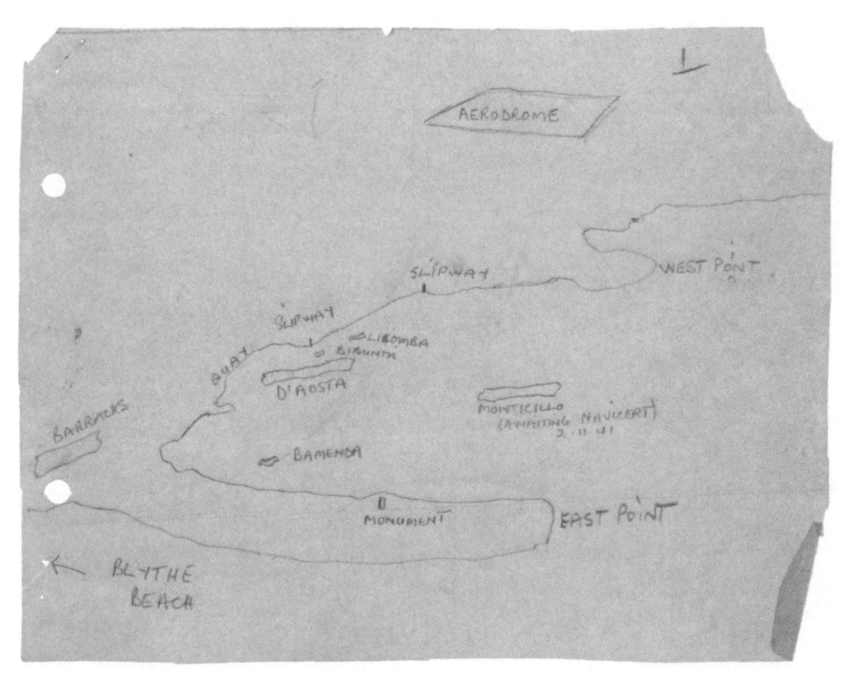

Tracing showing relevant buildings and features on the above photograph, prepared by SOE for Operation Postmaster briefings (*courtesy of the National Archives, Kew*)

The *Duchessa d'Aosta* at her mooring in front of the Cathedral Square, Santa Isabel, photographed by Vice Consul Michie from Pilot Alacon's plane (*courtesy of the National Archives, Kew*)

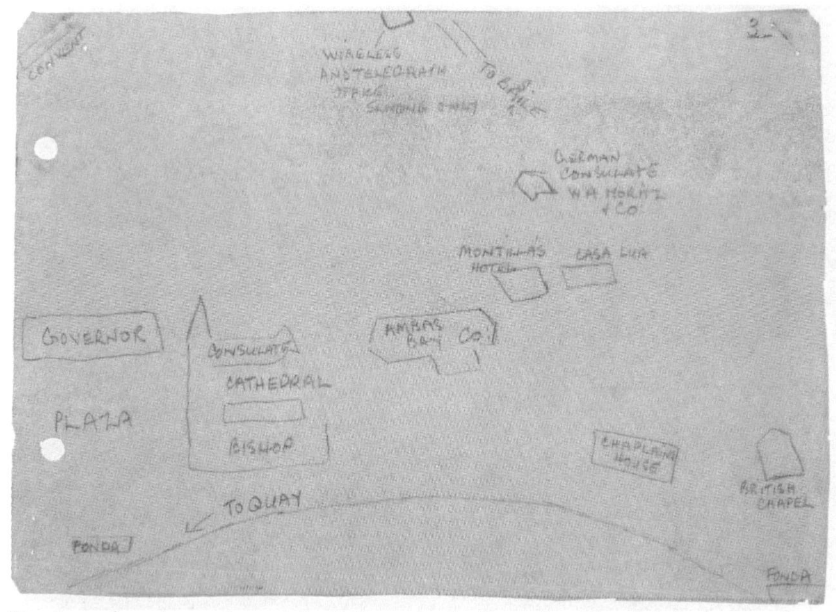

Tracing showing relevant buildings including the Chaplain's house from which the all-important 'Go ahead' signal was to be given, taken from a similar but poor quality photograph prepared by SOE for Operation Postmaster briefings (*courtesy of the National Archives, Kew*)

Photograph of the *Duchessa d'Aosta* at anchor, photographed covertly from the land (*courtesy of the Estate of Lieutenant Colonel L H Dismore*)

Nautical map of Santa Isabel Harbour, with the depths marked, and the *Duchessa d'Aosta* and *Likomba* ['tugs'] (*courtesy of the National Archives, Kew*)

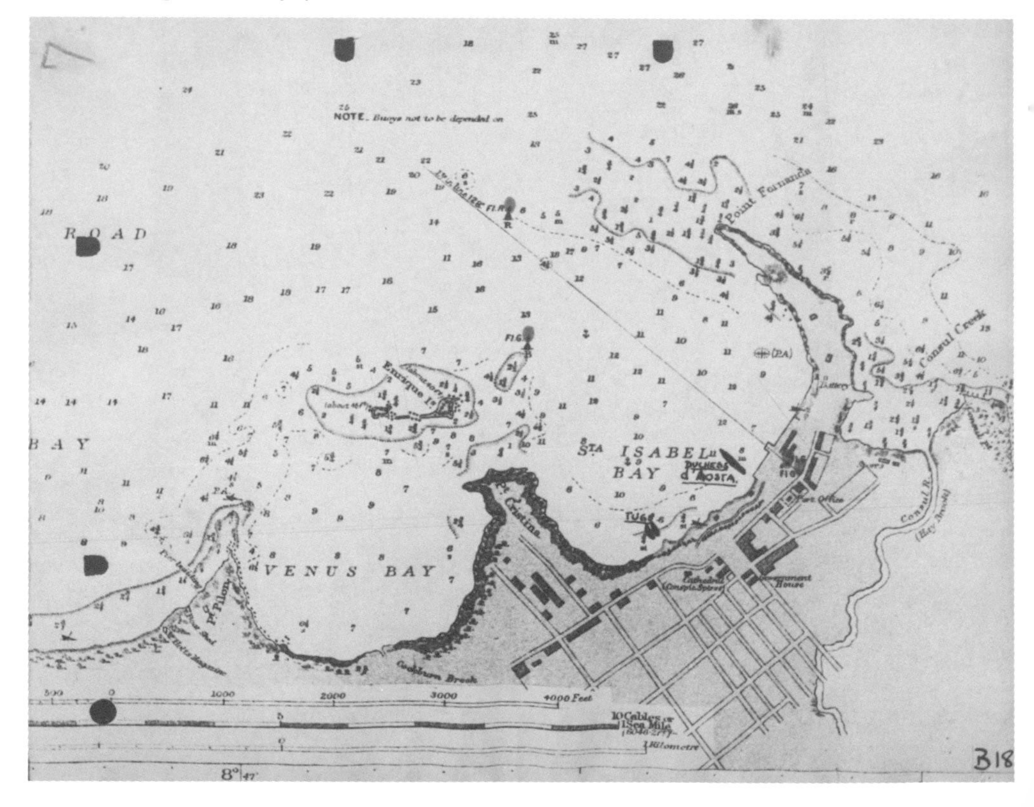

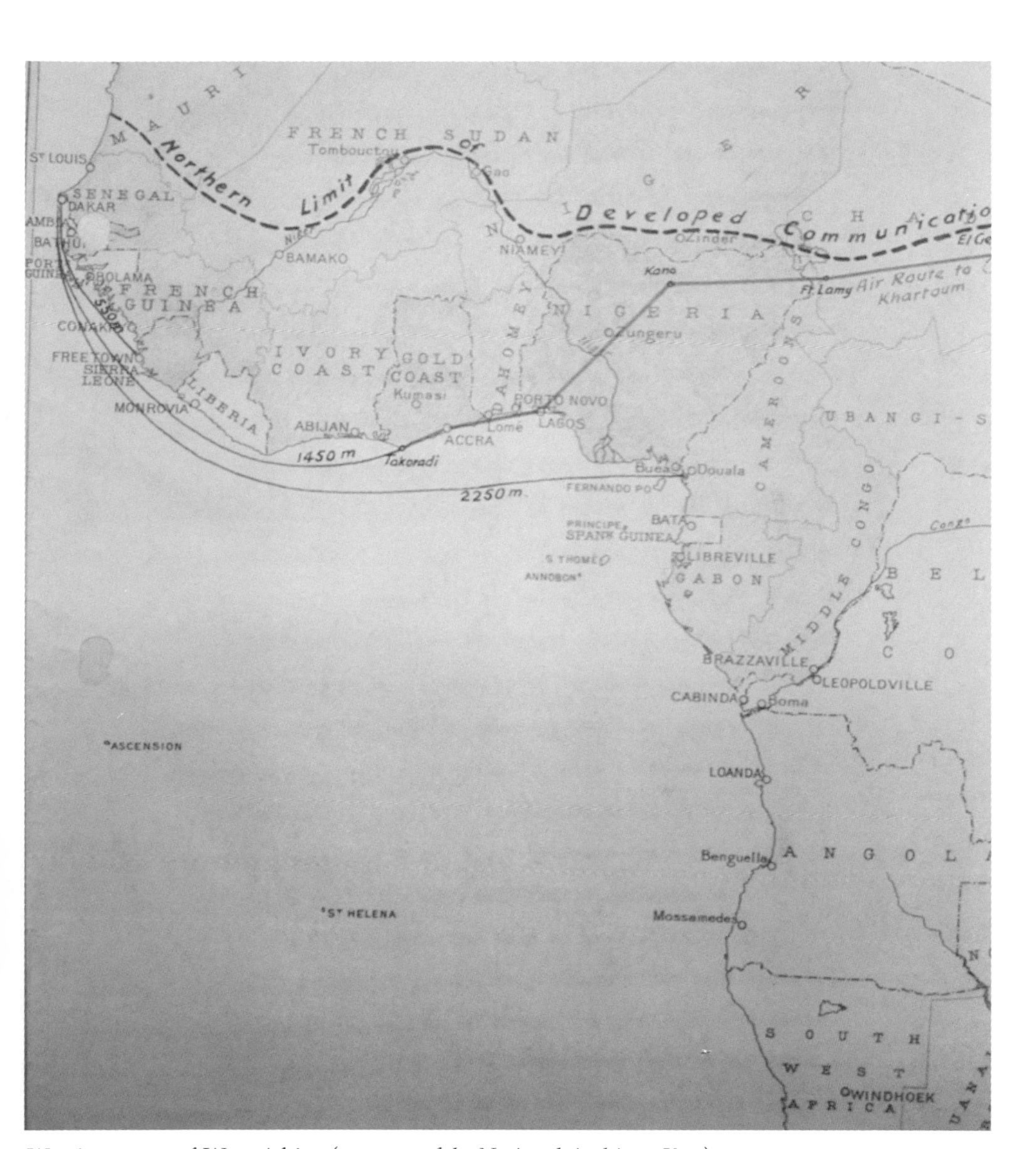

Wartime map of West Africa (*courtesy of the National Archives, Kew*)

The headquarters building of SOE, 64 Baker Street, as it is in modern times (*author's private collection*)

Inset: Plaque to SOE at 64 Baker Street (*author's private collection*)

Military identity card of Major General Sir Colin McVean Gubbins, 'M' (*courtesy of the National Archives, Kew*)

Lieutenant Colonel Julius Hanau, OBE, 'Caesar' (*courtesy of the National Archives, Kew*)

General Sir George Giffard, KCB, DSO, SOE's problem in West Africa (*courtesy of Surrey Heritage*)

General William J. Donovan, DSC, DSM, head of the OSS, which later became the CIA (*courtesy of the Special Forces Club*)

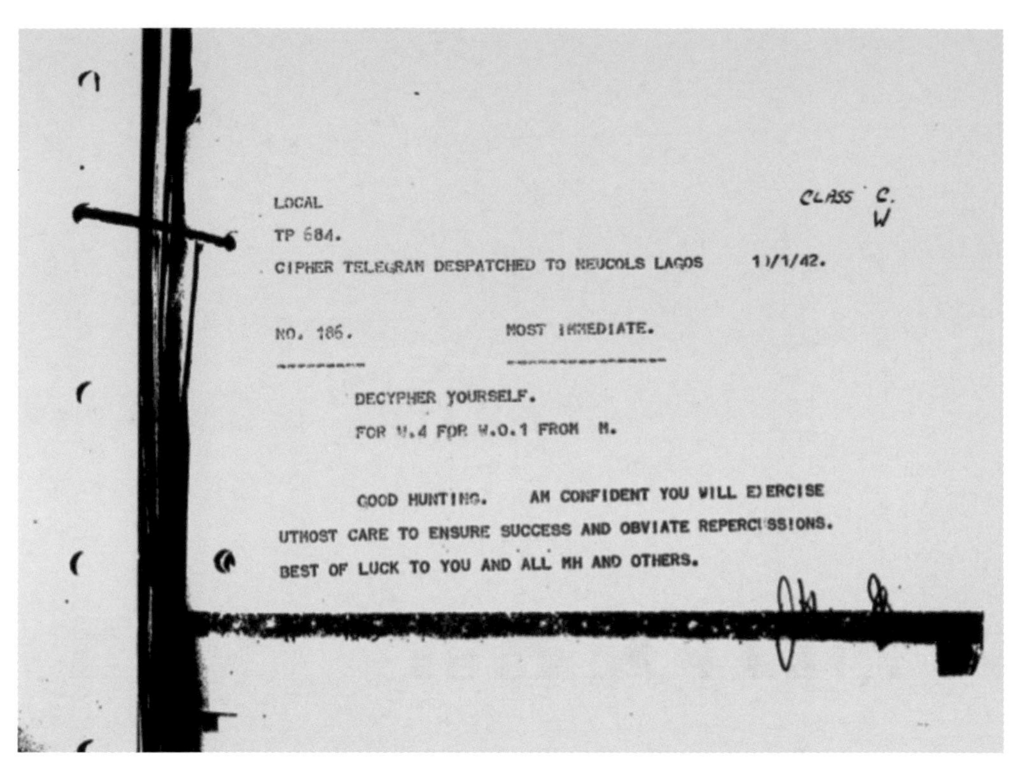

LOCAL

TP 684.

CIPHER TELEGRAM DESPATCHED TO NEUCOLS LAGOS 1)/1/42.

NO. 186. MOST IMMEDIATE.

DECYPHER YOURSELF.

FOR W.4 FOR W.O.1 FROM M.

GOOD HUNTING. AM CONFIDENT YOU WILL EXERCISE UTMOST CARE TO ENSURE SUCCESS AND OBVIATE REPERCUSSIONS. BEST OF LUCK TO YOU AND ALL MH AND OTHERS.

CLASS C. W

M's telegram to Agent W.01 (March-Phillipps) via Agent W4 (Laversuch), 10 January 1942 (*courtesy of the National Archives, Kew*)

W.01's telegram to 'M' in reply, sent by W4 on 12 January 1942 after Operation Postmaster had departed, 12 January 1942 (*courtesy of the National Archives, Kew*)

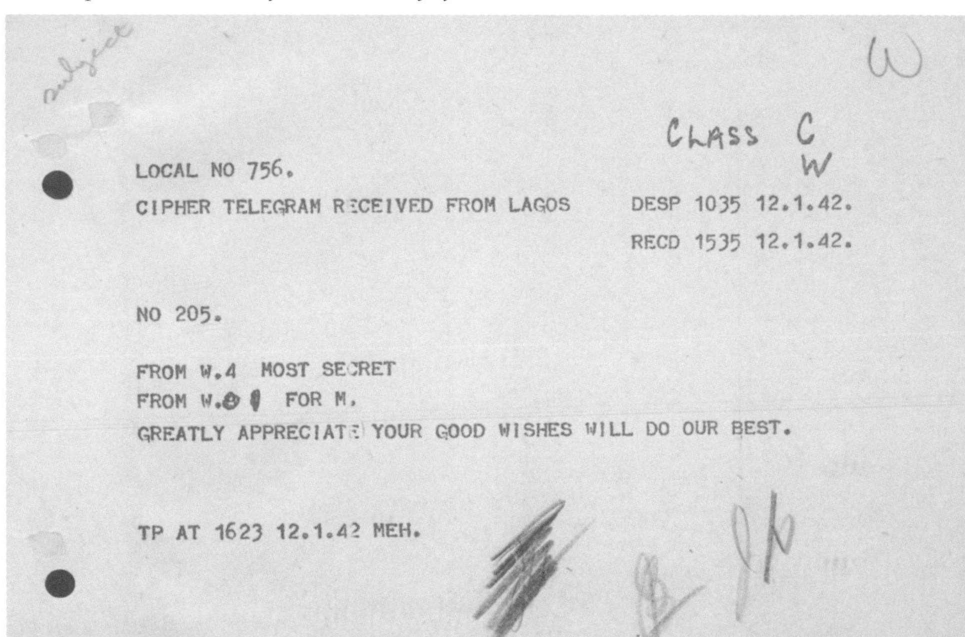

CLASS C W

LOCAL NO 756.

CIPHER TELEGRAM RECEIVED FROM LAGOS DESP 1035 12.1.42.

RECD 1535 12.1.42.

NO 205.

FROM W.4 MOST SECRET

FROM W.01 FOR M.

GREATLY APPRECIATE YOUR GOOD WISHES WILL DO OUR BEST.

TP AT 1623 12.1.42 MEH.

The *Maid Honor* under sail before the war (*author's private collection, original source unknown*)

A Vauxhall Velox 30/98 Tourer, one of the fastest cars of its day. Appleyard described the one that March-Phillipps owned as 'terrific' (*author's private collection, original source unknown*)

SLEEVE GUN

Catalogue No. N 254.

DESCRIPTION. Like the Sleeve Gun Mk. I the Mk. II is a short length, silent, murder weapon, firing 0·32 inch ammunition. It is a single shot weapon designed for carriage in the sleeve with the trigger near the muzzle to aid unobtrusive firing when the gun is slid from the sleeve into the hand. The gun is intended for use in contact with the target, but may be used at ranges up to about three yards; the silencing element cannot be removed for replacement since the gun is not intended for prolonged use.

The gun is fitted at the rear end with a ring to which the carrying lanyard can be attached.

In appearance the main difference between the Sleeve Gun Mks. I and II, is in the cocking tube of the Mk. I, which runs parallel to the main cylinder of the gun for its whole length; the depth of the weapon is thus near to its maximum value of 1¾ inches throughout the length of the gun. The Mk. II has no cocking tube and the only considerable protuberance from the main cylinder is the trigger; except for the foremost inch of the gun, the depth is therefore little more than the cylinder diameter of 1¼ inches. As a result, the Mk. II is a slimmer weapon than the Mk. I and much neater in appearance.

METHOD OF USE. The gun is carried up the sleeve until required, it is then slid into the hand and the muzzle pressed against the victim, at the same time operating the trigger with the thumb. After use, the gun returns to its position up the sleeve and all evidence such as the empty case is retained in the gun.

DIMENSIONS. Overall length 8¾″. Diam. 1¼″. **WEIGHT.** 26 ozs.

A sleeve gun, a 'murder weapon' available to M's agents, as advertised in their secret catalogue (*courtesy of the National Archives, Kew*)

Catalogue No. NS 304.

INCENDIARY BRIEFCASE (SINGLE LOCK)

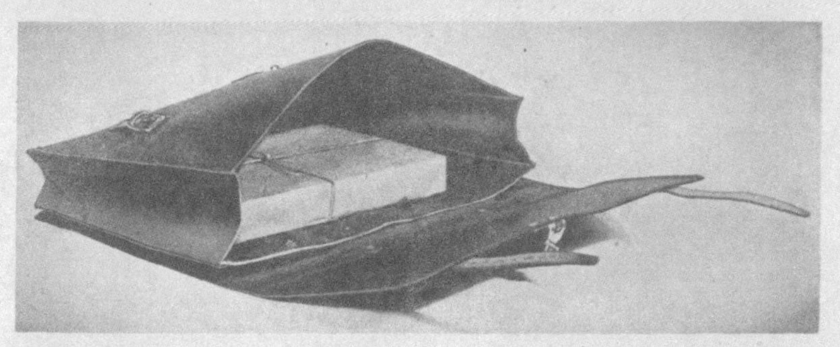

DESCRIPTION. The external appearance is that of an ordinary Briefcase. A camouflaged parcel inside the case contains a thermit charge, battery and arming switch. The electric wiring is concealed in the lining of the case. One quilt of potassium nitrate is provided to assist in combustion of documents. The lock is converted to act as a switch. Another switch, under a patch of rexine inside the case, takes the place of the right hand lock on double lock types.

METHOD OF USE. The arming switch is set to "ON" position. To close and open the case safely, the switch under the patch of rexine must be depressed to its full extent and held thus while the outer lock is manipulated. If this is not done the charge will fire when the external lock is moved.

SHIPPING CLASSIFICATION. Explosive Group - XI.
Storage and Stowage IV. O.A.S

PACKING AND SPECIAL NOTES. Instructions for use are provided with each case.

Catalogue No. NS 302.

INCENDIARY CIGARETTES

DESCRIPTION. This device consists of a small incendiary pellet placed inside any type of cigarette. The incendiary pellet is nearer one end of the cigarette than the other and can easily be located by touch.

When ignited the pellet gives a hot flame for about five seconds.

If the cigarette is lit at the end near the pellet the delay will be about two minutes. If lit at the other end the delay will be about three or four minutes. At each end of the pellet there is match composition and the flame produced lasts for about three to five secs.

METHOD OF USE. To obtain the best results it should not be buried more than one inch in the kindling, preferably placed near the surface, thereby assuring a good supply of oxygen.

SHIPPING CLASSIFICATION. Explosive Group - XI.
Storage and Stowage IV. O.A.S.

PACKING AND SPECIAL NOTES.
As required. It is not intended to make this a standard store, but numbers can easily be made to meet special demands.

Exploding briefcases and cigarettes depicted here were two of a wide variety of devices on offer to M's agents in the catalogue. Others included incendiary tyre busters, itching powder, underwater swimming suits, silenced Sten machine guns and thumb knives (*courtesy of the National Archives*)

'M' with the author's father, Major Gordon Lett, DSO, representing SOE at Dachau Concentration Camp in 1964 (*from the author's private collection*)

It was believed by M and his Secret Service that Spain did not really want to enter the war, since it was still recovering from its own damaging and recent civil war.

London was obviously extremely sensitive to the danger of adverse international reaction. M was involved at ministerial level and, since the Royal Navy was to 'capture' the two ships in international waters and any communiqué must therefore come from them, Admiral Godfrey was required to finalize and approve the cover story. Godfrey handed the brief to his assistant, the trusted Commander Ian Fleming, and Fleming was instructed on 10 January 1941, both orally and in writing. The written instruction still exists. It is from someone who styles himself D/Q.9., and reads:

> Dear Fleming,
> This is to confirm our verbal agreement made today, and to give you the full facts about the operation projected. . . [a summary of the operational plan is then set out]. I understand that you will arrange in advance that as soon as the signal is received announcing that the operation has been successfully carried through, the Admiralty will release to the BBC and the Press a communiqué on the lines of the attached story, and that this release will be so framed that the BBC and the Press will understand that it is a definite request by the Admiralty that the story will be given prominence, particularly through such media as will reach the Spanish Government. . . I have given the most solemn undertaking that there shall be no danger of a slip in this matter, so I should be very grateful if you would confirm to me on the 14th that all is prepared.

Agent W4, Laversuch's suggested cover story was attached to the instruction.

Ian Fleming, a safe pair of hands, sought to improve and perfect Laversuch's suggested communique. He duly submitted an initial draft which read:

> Axis Ships Intercepted off West African Coast
>
> The Admiralty announced tonight that early this afternoon a Naval Patrol ship intercepted off the West African coast two Axis vessels whose crews had mutinied and were attempting to reach the Vichy French port of Cotonou. Neither of these vessels, a cargo boat of some 8,000 tons and a tug of 200 tons, made any attempt to resist capture. One of the crew stated that the ships had been lying in Spanish territorial waters since 1939 and explained that, owing to

> dissatisfaction with their living conditions and lack of pay, they had decided to take advantage of the absence of their senior officer to raise steam and slip out to sea under cover of darkness.
>
> This story throws interesting light on the low state of Axis morale abroad and also emphasises once more the unceasing vigilance of the Royal Navy.

Fleming's suggested communiqué would therefore achieve two objectives: disinformation to cover up the British raid on Fernando Po, and good propaganda as to the vigilance of the Royal Navy in the South Atlantic. The fact that it would be total nonsense did not seem to trouble anyone on the British side. The only question that troubled anybody about Fleming's piece of creative writing was whether it would be believed.

The content of the proposed press release was approved by the Admiralty, but then had to be considered by the Ministry of Economic Warfare (MEW), Hugh Dalton's department. On 12 January in a high level meeting at the MEW some reservations were expressed. Despite the Admiralty having agreed to Fleming's communiqué (which was really only a question of Godfrey approving his assistant's work), the MEW was nervous. Gladwyn Jebb, Dalton's Under Secretary of State, subsequently drafted a memorandum expressing the view that it would be a wiser course,

> for the Admiralty merely to announce, on receipt of a telegram saying: 'Postmaster successful', that two Axis vessels had been intercepted off Fernando Po in unusual circumstances, and that a further statement would be issued later. This would force the Spaniards to show their hand, and we would then be better placed for issuing a subsequent statement in the light of what they said, (if they said anything). It might conceivably be, for instance, that although our people were confident that the Spaniards possessed no evidence, they might after all possess some, and that it would therefore be unwise for us to tell about the 'mutinous Italian crews', when the Spaniards could prove that they weren't mutinous at all. We have also, I need hardly say, given much anxious thought to the problem of what we are to do in the event of Postmaster being unsuccessful, or partially unsuccessful, and have come to the conclusion that it is really impossible to provide a story covering every situation in advance, and that, if approached by the Spaniards, the Foreign Office should merely say that an investigation is being made. If the worst should happen (e.g. if our men were left behind or our tug got stuck in the mud) it would, we suggest, always

> be possible for His Majesty's Government to say eventually that, on investigation, they find that 'irresponsible elements' did in fact make an attempt to get the two ships out, and that disciplinary action will be taken against these irresponsible elements.
>
> Finally, in the event of the two ships being successfully got out, but the Spaniards nevertheless being in possession of irrefutable proof that the operation was the work of British agents, we could always, as a last resort, hand them back again.

Thus, at the highest level, the concern was not about the fact of breaching international law, breaching neutrality, and telling lies, but about the danger of being caught doing it. The last comment by Jebb, that His Majesty's Government might return the ships if caught out, is reminiscent of the schoolboy who tries to put the sweets that he has stolen back in the jar.

Jebb went on to set down his confidence that such a situation would not in fact arise, and that the operation would be a success, and finally commented: 'In any case, seeing that the Spaniards are behaving in a thoroughly un-neutral manner in regard to the re-fuelling of German submarines, I do not think that His Majesty's Government need necessarily put themselves in a white sheet, even if they have to talk about "irresponsible elements".'

Gladwyn Jebb's reservations about the cover story are understandable. Of course, the last thing that His Majesty's Government wanted to do was to make an official announcement that was provably false. If everything went wrong and the Maid Honor Force was caught, responsibility for the raid would be denied by the British Government so long as they thought that they could get away with such a denial. The British Government would prefer to leave March-Phillipps and the rest of his Maid Honor Force, the men of the Nigerian Marine and the civilians of the Colonial Service, to their fate, despite the real possibility that they would simply be given the status of pirates or spies and might be shot out of hand. Only if a British connection was proved would the Government be forced to accept the truth, and even then the action would be described as unauthorized and overenthusiastic, the action of irresponsible elements. It would certainly never be admitted that Operation Postmaster had been carefully planned, considered and approved at the highest level.

A memorandum from Caesar dated 11 January, under the heading, 'Note on problem of repercussions' said pertinently: 'Perhaps it would not be out of place to observe that one of the chief reasons for the creation of SOE was the desirability of an organization whose actions could be disowned by His Majesty's Government.'

One piece of luck did come the way of SOE and Operation Postmaster.

Whilst Laversuch and March-Phillipps had been away in Freetown, Agent W10, Guise, had been in Santa Isabel. Guise had been approached there by a Señor Avendaño, the President of the Spanish Chamber of Commerce, who was believed to be well connected in Spain and who was certainly known to have plenty of influence locally on Fernando Po. He handed Guise a letter which he requested that Guise, the British diplomatic courier, pass on to his lords and masters. The contents of the letter, duly translated, reached London by cable from Lagos on 5 January 1942: 'In the event of the peninsula (mainland Spain) being invaded by German forces, I consider within twenty-four or forty-eight hours of the fact becoming known, or at the latest forty-eight hours, we should have English assistance in Fernando Po to prevent this colony passing into German hands. If this assistance is given, it must be expressly understood that Spanish sovereignty will be respected.'

In his accompanying report, Guise added that there was a strong feeling in Fernando Po that Spain would be involved in the war, through German aggression, within a month or two. London was delighted. An internal memorandum dated 7 January comments: 'This is a timely communication, coming as it does just before our operation. In the event of there being any trouble we can now if necessary say that we were taking steps to ensure that the island would not easily come under German control. If we had left the two ships in the harbour they would have assisted in a coup d'état.'

In effect, Señor Avendaño had gifted the British Government with a possible 'Plan B'. Should things go utterly wrong, and should the complicity of the British Government became known, it could be said that they were after all only acting for the benefit of the local Spanish citizens on Fernando Po, and the letter could be used to back that up.

London thought this news might help the Governor of Nigeria, Sir Bernard Bourdillon. The memorandum continues: 'I do not know whether it is worthwhile putting this thought into His Excellency's mind, especially as he may be having a slightly rough time with his GOC [Giffard] and C in C [Willis], who appear to be conscience-stricken to a regrettable degree.' SOE were well aware of the pressure that Governor Bourdillon might be under through giving them his unqualified support and, most importantly, seventeen of his sturdiest men.

The cover stories were prepared. Government ministers had been briefed. The Maid Honor Force and Operation Postmaster were on the high seas. Only the final preparations for their arrival in Santa Isabel remained to be completed.

CHAPTER 18

Final Preparation in Santa Isabel

Gus March-Phillipps and his Maid Honor Force were undoubtedly very fortunate that M's Secret Service had such a good team working for them on Fernando Po. In the same way that Ian Fleming shows his hero 007 relying on efficient local agents to prepare the way for his missions, so the Maid Honor Force relied on their outstanding local agents, Guise, Lippett and the unofficial agent Vice Consul Michie, on Fernando Po. As the experienced Company Sergeant Major Tom Winter later put it, 'the spadework that had been done was really something'. Winter praised in particular Guise's efforts in obtaining the measurements of the all-important anchor chains, the arrangements that Lippett made for the party, and the 'old fashioned' signal that was arranged to indicate to Maid Honor Force that the time was ripe to enter the harbour (see below).

The work in Santa Isabel continued after the Maid Honor Force and Operation Postmaster had set sail on 11 January, right up until their arrival in Santa Isabel harbour. Richard Lippett, having left Lagos after his briefing in early December, had much to arrange. He arrived back in Santa Isabel later than intended, on 18 December, so it was fortunate the 22 December date for the operation had by that time been cancelled. However, the postponement meant Lippett had to spend a further period on the island. He ordered renovation works on John Holt's premises in Santa Isabel, to give him a reason to stay on. Lippett had to arrange further funds for the work and in due course 10,000 pesetas arrived, officially sent from John Holt, in fact from SOE. The plan was that once the raid was over, Lippett would remain on the island only for as long as was necessary to allay suspicion, and would then leave Fernando Po for the safety of British Nigeria.

Whilst in Lagos, Lippett had drawn a substantial quantity of cash funds in pesetas and had also bought a number of gifts. The latter he could give to members of his network under the pretence that they were Christmas presents, in his role as a man who was well off and generous – they would in truth serve to grease palms. The cash was intended to fund the diversionary party for the night of the raid. The rescheduled date of 14/15 January gave Lippett more time to perfect his arrangements, but had the distinct disadvantage of being outside the Christmas party season, when another one would not have excited comment. A party in mid-January would be more conspicuous.

The main difficulty remaining was how Lippett could arrange the party without showing his hand, and how the Italians on the *Duchessa d'Aosta*, and the Germans on board the *Likomba* could be persuaded to accept the invitations. Lippett's plan was to persuade some of his new Spanish friends to hold the party for him. He also decided that there should be two parties – one over the Christmas period, and another on the night of the raid. The first one would be an unexceptional seasonal gesture, and of course nothing would happen to the *Duchessa d'Aosta* or the *Likomba* while it was going on. It would also be a trial run to see who could be persuaded to come, and how it all went. Provided the first party was a success, it would be a good excuse for a second party in January, on a 'that was fun, why not do it again' basis.

One of Lippett's newfound friends, Abelino Zorilla, the assistant manager of the hardware store, was chosen by Lippett to arrange the parties for him. Lippett got on well with Zorilla and believed him to be an anti-Falangist, therefore not in sympathy with the Germans on the island. He told Zorilla that he had been approached by a shipping company in Lagos regarding the entertainment of the officers and men of the *Duchessa d'Aosta* over the Christmas period, and as there was considerable sympathy between international shipping companies over the difficulties their ships faced on the oceans in time of war, the owners did not want the crew of the *Duchessa* to feel neglected on this, their second Christmas in Santa Isabel.

Lippett further explained that he himself could not be seen to be openly entertaining enemy seamen – his consulate would report him and he would be in a lot of trouble. Therefore, he was asking Zorilla to look after the matter for him with money that he, Lippett, would provide. Zorilla agreed to help with the project, and said that he would get the Governor's pilot, Alacon, and Dr Sola to assist him. It was important that the invitations came from the right sort of people. Lippett had in fact already paid Alacon 5,000 pesetas (for the photographs of the harbour) and Alacon was recruited to host the first party. Lippett had presented Dr Sola with a gold bracelet he had bought in Lagos, nominally as a Christmas present for his wife, and he too agreed to attend the party.

The intention was to invite the officers of both ships, together with a number of members of the local German and Italian community. A shipping agent had been appointed as nominally responsible for the *Duchessa d'Aosta* whilst she remained in Santa Isabel. He was a German called Heinrich Luhr, who lived with his wife in the town. He was apparently quite wealthy, and described as being a vain man with a very high opinion of himself. He is also said to have been the local Nazi party agent.

Herr Luhr had already invited the officers of the *Duchessa d'Aosta* to dinner at his house on Christmas Eve, so Lippett's first 'decoy' party was arranged for the night of 27 December. Zorilla performed his tasks extremely well and managed to secure the attendance of a number of leading members of the local European community. The pilot Alacon and Dr Sola were, of course, there, as were Herr and Frau Luhr. Thirty people attended, including all the officers of the *Duchessa*, and for those who could not leave the ship, a large quantity of wine, whisky and brandy was sent on board. The crew apparently got very drunk and some were still drunk the next day. Herr Specht, the Captain of the *Likomba*, did not attend.

The party was held on the upper terrace of the Casino Restaurant, which had a fine view over the harbour. It went on until 0400 hrs on 28 December, and was a great success.

The pilot Alacon was nominally the host at this first party and Lippett had given him the money to pay for it, but careful manipulation of the proceedings by Zorilla left many with the impression that in fact Luhr was giving the party. When the time approached for the bill to be paid, Zorilla made an excuse to leave early and, taking Luhr aside, asked him if he would be good enough to deal with the bill. Somehow, he managed to arrange for 2,000 pesetas to pass from Alacon to Luhr. Herr Luhr, vain as he was, was only too happy to help and to make sure that people noticed it was he who gave the money to the restaurant for the bill – with the result that many thought that Luhr had funded the party. Richard Lippett, of course, was not there and had retired to bed at the hotel at his normal hour. Nobody suspected that it was Lippett who had paid for their entertainment, with SOE funds. It was a masterpiece of manipulation.

As one of the few British citizens on the island, there was nothing suspicious in Lippett visiting the British Consulate, which was only a short distance from Montilla's Hotel where he was living. He did so regularly. He also made a habit of reading a lesson at the Sunday service each week in the British church in Santa Isabel. He therefore had plenty of opportunity to communicate with other SOE agents on the island when he needed to, and also with the many Nigerian plantation workers who attended the church, some of whom were in his pay.

In late December Guise, W10, was back on the island and Godden, W51, was installed in the Consulate as Michie's temporary replacement. Lake, W53, arrived on 6 January 1942. Lippett could liaise with any of them without giving rise to suspicion. After the success of the first party in December, he was waiting for final instructions confirming the raid for the night of 14/15 January. Meanwhile the Italian officers of the *Duchessa d'Aosta* were so happy with the hospitality they had received at the Casino restaurant that they gave a return party on the ship on 6 January. It was noted by some of the guests that much of the refreshment seemed to consist of the wine and spirits that had been sent on board as a gift on 27 December.

When word eventually reached Lippett that the raid was definitely on for the night of 14/15 January, he was able to put phase two of his plan into action. Again, he used Zorilla to make the arrangements, and to use his ingenuity to obscure the identity of the real host of the party. Obviously the Casino Restaurant could not be used again, since its terrace gave a fine view of the harbour where the action was to take place. Zorilla (presumably at Lippett's request) asked for Frau Luhr's help in finding a suitable restaurant that was less 'conspicuous'. 'Conspicuous' to Frau Luhr probably meant somewhere rather less public than the terrace of the Casino – somewhere the guests could get roaring drunk until four o'clock in the morning without attracting attention. For Lippett of course, it meant somewhere away from the harbour front, in the hope that any action in the bay during their dinner might go unnoticed.

Frau Luhr duly came up with what she believed to be a suitable restaurant, the Valencia. A booking was made for the night of 14 January, and invitations were sent out. With Frau Luhr involved, the impression that her husband Heinrich had been the real host at the first dinner party was reinforced. To help things along, Frau Luhr paid a personal visit to her fellow countryman, Captain Specht, on the *Likomba*, and persuaded him on this occasion to accept the invitation. In the event, all eight officers of the *Duchessa d'Aosta* accepted, as did both officers of the *Likomba*. From Lippett's point of view, it was going to be a 'full house'.

Zorilla, obviously, had quickly realized that there was something of significance going on. As an anti-Falangist, he had no sympathy for either Hitler's Germany or Mussolini's Italy, both of whom had given military support to Franco during the Spanish Civil War, and clearly Lippett had won his personal friendship. Zorilla was happy to help an Englishmen who liked the Spanish with a ruse against the Falangists, Germans and Italians. Nonetheless, as time went by, Zorilla began to be a little concerned for his own safety. A few days prior to the second dinner, he asked Lippett if he was running himself into danger by helping to arrange the parties – adding that if he was, then at an appropriate time he was prepared to leave Santa Isabel by canoe and take his chances in Nigeria. Such a passage was somewhat hazardous, but could be achieved by hiring a native canoe and crew. Lippett was surprised that the question had not come earlier. He could not tell Zorilla that there was no danger; also it occurred to him that if Zorilla did secretly flee the island after the second party, it might carry certain advantages for him and the other SOE agents on Fernando Po.

Lippett discussed this with Agent W51, Godden, at the Consulate. Lippett believed that Zorilla was a reliable ally. He had checked and re-checked his bona fides and, as he put it to Godden and in a later report, Zorilla had come through every test with flying colours. Lippett felt that if he confirmed Zorilla's suspicions, Zorilla would keep the matter to himself, and would keep his word and disappear from the island after the party. Lippett did not think it would be very healthy for either Zorilla or himself if Zorilla remained in Santa Isabel after the raid had taken place, when inevitably a careful post mortem would be undertaken by the Spanish authorities. The dinner party that took the officers from the ships was bound to be suspect. In order to avoid confirming any suspicion that the British had been responsible for the raid, Lippett himself would have to remain on Fernando Po as normal, at least for a short time. But if Zorilla fled, he might well prove a useful scapegoat for those such as Lippett who remained. The finger of suspicion would be pointed at the anti-Falangist Spaniard. Lippett and Godden decided it would be to everyone's advantage for them to encourage Zorilla to leave.

A plan was therefore agreed that Zorilla should flee the island secretly by canoe once the party was in full swing. Lippett put this to Zorilla, but gave him no explanation as to why it was necessary. Zorilla, for his part, did not ask, but told Lippett that he would make his own private arrangements to disappear when the time came. He added: 'The reason why I am assisting you is that I am certain that the British will win the war, and the Spanish Government will have to change. When that time arrives, I will go back to Spain in a better position than I have previously held. I will help my country more than I do by being an assistant manager of a hardware store here in Santa Isabel.' Sadly for Señor Zorilla, his faith in the early fall of General Franco and his Falangist party proved to be misplaced. Franco ruled Spain for many years after the Second World War, and remained in power until his death in 1975.

The English chaplain, the Reverend Markham, was persuaded to leave Fernando Po for a short time, to attend a Church Synod that was conveniently taking place in Calabar, Nigeria. It was thought by M's Secret Service that the raid might lead to reprisals in Santa Isabel against the small British community, and that Markham, as a protestant, might prove to be a popular target. Also, it would no doubt be remembered that he had visited the *Duchessa d'Aosta* under slightly false pretences when the crew had given a party the previous year. But there was a more pressing reason why M's Secret Service wanted the Reverend out of the way. His house was in a prime position overlooking the harbour, and it had been decided that it should be used as a signalling point to inform the British ships that they should enter the harbour. Operation Postmaster had been supplied with photographs and a plan that clearly showed Markham's house, where they should look for the 'all clear' signal. But if enemy eyes were to spot the signal it would be preferable that the Reverend Markham was well away from the island.

When Operation Postmaster took to sea in the early hours of 11 January, the diversion was in place and all appeared as well set as it could be for the success of the venture. However, fate was determined to set as many obstacles in the way of Postmaster as she possibly could. On 12 January, the owner of the Valencia Restaurant cancelled the booking for the dinner party because his wife had fallen ill. All of a sudden, the carefully crafted distraction plan was in pieces.

Lippett was no doubt already under considerable stress as the night of the intended raid approached. There was much that might go wrong and he himself faced many dangers. But the news that the Valencia had cancelled with only two days to go was a hammer blow. The town of Santa Isabel was small, and there were not many establishments capable of laying on a fine dinner for a large party, particularly not at two days' notice. Lippett knew that the only real alternative to the Valencia at this late stage was to return to the Casino Restaurant, on the terrace overlooking the harbour.

Lippett's most vital task was to get the officers off their ships on the night of 14 January. Those were his orders and, as Laversuch had put it to him during his last visit to Lagos, 65 per cent of the chance of success of the raid depended on him achieving it. Lippett did not know the details, but had been left in no doubt as to the importance of his diversionary ruse. To move the party to the Casino restaurant (where the previous one had proved such a success) seemed his only option. At least the officers would be away from their ships. But what if they spotted what was going on in the harbour below? Or heard something of the raid across the relatively short distance between the terrace and the ships? Hopefully, if they did, it would at least take them some time to do anything about it. Perhaps a surfeit of alcohol might blind them to whatever action was taking place, or render them incapable of effective response. Also, once the island's lights were out, with no moon the harbour would be dark, and the movement of the raiders would be difficult to see.

Lippett took the decision to move the party to the Casino and hope for the best. He also decided to design a seating plan for the dinner that would place all the officers from the *Duchessa d'Aosta* and the *Likomba* with their backs to the harbour. If there were pretty ladies on the other side of the table, hopefully they would be content to look in that direction and not turn towards the sea. The officers would have spent long enough on their ships looking out at the harbour, and would surely be only too happy to look at something more attractive. On the other hand what would happen if someone opposite them, with a view of the harbour, saw something strange happening and brought it to the attention of the officers? Most of the guests would be sympathetic to German and Italian interests, not to British ones. Perhaps if he could ensure that the terrace continued to be very brightly lit once the town's electricity was switched off sometime after 2300 hrs as usual, then the guests would lose their night vision, and would not see anything that went on in the darkness of the harbour below them.

One SOE report has it that some of the money provided for the distraction found its way into the pocket of the proprietor of the local brothel. It is difficult to imagine Mrs Luhr being prepared to have such ladies of easy virtue as her dinner companions, so if prostitutes were employed by Lippett and Zorilla it must have been for the purpose of getting some of the Italian and German officers to leave the terrace for a while during or after the party. Perhaps unsurprisingly the location of the town brothel is not marked on the maps and photographs prepared for Operation Postmaster, but Santa Isabel was a very small town, and it could not have been far from the Casino. No doubt the male party guests would have had the chance to pop away to visit the local ladies, particularly if someone else was paying.

With all these and other possibilities running through his mind, Lippett passed on the necessary instructions to Zorilla that the venue should be changed to the Casino Restaurant. He then carefully drew up a seating plan, and gave this without explanation to Zorilla to infiltrate into the restaurant in readiness for the dinner. Lippett also took steps to ensure that the lights of Santa Isabel would go out as early as possible on the night of 14/15 January. Amongst the 'Christmas presents' that he had brought with him from Lagos were a diamond ring and a watch. These were intended for the wife of the chief electrician at the Santa Isabel power station. Zorilla again acted as go-between, and delivered the gifts. This fine lady had an admirer, one of the power station employees who would be on duty that night. She guaranteed that the admirer would cut off the current at the appropriate time. History does not tell us what reason Lippett (through Zorilla) gave for wanting to ensure the lights went off. Since there was a lady involved, perhaps the excuse was a romantic assignation, more easily carried out in the dark.

A party of twenty-five sat down to dinner at the Casino Terrace Restaurant on the evening of 14 January. Eight officers came from the *Duchessa d'Aosta*, including Acting Captain Umberto Valle and First Mate Antonio Bussani. Two came from the *Likomba*, including Captain Specht. Again, the guests did not of course include Richard Lippett. Zorilla was present at the start to ensure that the party got well under way and the alcohol was flowing freely. The carefully prepared seating plan was accepted without objection by all the guests, so that when they sat down all the officers had their backs to their ships and to the harbour. Zorilla eventually made an excuse at about 2200 hrs, and slipped away. He was not seen on the island again. He had done all that Lippett asked of him and did not attempt his escape until everything was in place and running smoothly. As anticipated, his absence was to prove very useful to Lippett after the raid. Apparently, the dinner party was once more a great success, and much alcohol was consumed. So caught up in the congenial company were the guests that no one on either side of the table paid any attention to the harbour that lay below them. Lippett's enforced gamble seemed to be paying off.

At the Consulate, every scrap of potentially incriminating evidence that could be destroyed had been. Godden and Lake were both there – Godden with the excuse that he was settling in the recently arrived new Assistant Consul, Peter Lake. Telegrams and re-cipher pages had been burnt immediately they were received or despatched. Should the Consulate be searched (in breach of international law), nothing incriminating would be there to be found. There had been an incident in 1940 when six angry Germans had invaded the Consulate building, and Godden and Lake appreciated that after the raid had taken place diplomatic immunity might not prevent the same thing from happening again.

Lippett spent the evening as usual, in company with one of his Spanish friends, Señor Ruiz, the bank manager. At 1900 hrs they went to the club at the Casino and played cards. At 2100 hrs, when Lippett and Ruiz went to the Casino bar to settle their accounts as usual, the manageress commented that there was a dinner party for about thirty Italians and Germans going on. Ruiz quite innocently asked who was giving the party, and the manageress (to Lippett's satisfaction) said that she did not know, but thought it was just a party of friends like the previous one, and it had all been paid for in advance. Zorilla had done his work well.

It may be pure coincidence that Ian Fleming set much of the plot of his first Bond book in a casino and named the book after it, *Casino Royale*. But he certainly knew that in Operation Postmaster the Casino of Santa Isabel had played a vital part in the plan, and that Lippett had spent some of the last nervous few hours before the operation playing cards there.

Ruiz and Lippett went to Montilla's Hotel for some dinner and afterwards, at about 2200 hrs, they left together on foot for the Bank House, where they parted company. Lippett, on the pretext of aiding his digestion, now took his customary walk along the front. He observed no preparations of any kind and no untoward activity. He noted that a number of the Colonial Guard sentries were asleep. The night was very dark, with occasional flashes of lightning. Lippett then walked back to his hotel, entered through a side door and went to his room. He felt exhausted and went to bed, actually managing to fall asleep for a while. Like the consummate professional that he undoubtedly was, Richard Lippett had done a superb job and there was nothing more he could do. It was now up to Maid Honor Force and the men of Operation Postmaster.

CHAPTER 19

Maid Honor Attack

The Maid Honor Force and SOE Lagos knew very well the dangers that they faced, and how the odds were stacked against them if anything went wrong in Santa Isabel harbour. They all experienced the fear that precedes a particularly dangerous operation, but were able to overcome it. Another poem that Gus March-Phillipps wrote during his time in West Africa perhaps sums up how he was feeling as he led his men into mortal danger:

If I must die in this great war
When so much seems in vain,
And man in huge unthinking hordes
Is slain as sheep are slain
But with less thought; then do I seek
One last good grace to gain.

Let me die, O Lord, as I learned to live
When the world seemed young and gay,
And 'Honour Bright' was a phrase they used
That they do not use today
And faith was something alive and warm
When we gathered round to pray.

Let me be simple and sure once more,
O Lord, if I must die,
Let the mad unreason of reasoned doubt,
Unreasoning pass me by,
And the mass mind, and the mercenary,
And the everylasting 'why'.

Let me be brave and gay again
O Lord, when my time is near,

Let the good in me rise up and break
The stranglehold of fear.
Say that I die for Thee and the King
And what I hold most dear.

The *Vulcan* and the *Nuneaton* cast off from No. 2 Wharf in the Apapa dockyard at 0440 hrs on Sunday, 11 January, and crept out of Lagos harbour. They had four days to do such final training as was necessary and to make the journey to Fernando Po, where they would attack shortly before midnight on 14 January.

The Steam Tug *Vulcan* was a tough coal-driven vessel of the Nigerian Marine. She was under the command of Mr T. C. T. Coker, Tugmaster. Coker had the two engineers on board, Lieutenant Commanders J. A. K. Oldand and J. O. C. Duffy, and a Lieutenant Duff as his Chief Officer. Dennis Tottenham RNVR, of the Maid Honor Force, acted as quartermaster. March-Phillipps and Appleyard retained military command of the *Vulcan* and of the expedition itself. Desgranges, Lassen, Prout, Evison and 'Haggis' Taylor were with them on the tug, as were the volunteer medic Dr J. G. MacGregor, and the 'three friendly Spaniards'. Thirteen black Africans made up the engine room crew. The latter were accustomed to short haul work – none of them was used to being at sea for more than three days. Little did they know this would be a far longer voyage. The *Vulcan*'s task was to capture and tow out the 8,000 ton 'rudderless whale' that was the *Duchessa d'Aosta*.

The Motor Tug *Nuneaton* was the smaller ship, belonging to Elder Dempster Lines Ltd. She was commanded by Lieutenant J. Goodman, Nigerian Marine, and crewed by two black African 'drivers' from Elder Dempster, O. Hanson and Olu David. Her military commander was W.03, Graham Hayes. Leonard Guise was on board the *Nuneaton*, as were Tom Winter and Buzz Perkins of the Maid Honor Force, and W. F. H. Newington and A. F. Abell, two District Commissioners, were amongst the civilian volunteers. The *Nuneaton*'s target was the 200 ton *Likomba*.

The *Nuneaton* had recently undergone a major refit and was no doubt thought to be in tip-top condition. The reverse however proved to be true. The engines had not been properly run in and were to cause major difficulties, while conditions on board, difficult anyway, were considerably worsened by the fact that the fresh water tank had recently been relined with cement which had not set properly. The result was that the 'fresh' water throughout the voyage was unpleasant to drink, and caused discomforting conditions of the digestive system. In a climate where it was necessary to drink large quantities of water (Appleyard estimated between one and one and a half gallons per man, per day), this was a problem those on the *Nuneaton* could happily have done without.

As the two ships left Lagos harbour the *Vulcan* had the *Nuneaton* on tow alongside. Once they reached the Bar the *Nuneaton* was dropped astern onto a long tow, but still made heavy weather of the lumpy sea caused by the ebb tide running against the swell. The weather was foul and in the words of Guise, as the *Vulcan* wallowed along slowly, the *Nuneaton*, at the end of her tow rope was 'dancing along behind her like a naughty puppy on a lead'.

It was a very difficult start. The ebullience and excitement of the previous evening had gone and many of the volunteers became extremely seasick. Guise describes *Nuneaton*'s contingent as being 'hors de combat' by midday, trying desperately to stay in the fresh air above decks. The poor performance of the *Nuneaton* on the tow slowed the *Vulcan* down, until at last Coker managed to get her sheered onto his port quarter, where she towed more comfortably. On the evening of 11 January March-Phillipps took pity on the volunteers on the *Nuneaton*, and invited them aboard the rather steadier *Vulcan* for the night. Thankfully, Monday, 12 January saw the return of better weather, calm sea and the warmth of the sun. The *Maid Honor* cook, Ernest Evison, produced 'magnificent' food for them all and morale rose accordingly. The 'amateurs' returned to the *Nuneaton*.

Coker described his crew as 'shaking down', and breakfast as 'in great demand'. He himself had had no sleep since leaving Lagos, and longed to take a nap. However he dare not yet leave the bridge since his deputy, Lieutenant Duff, was not used to steering a large tug like the *Vulcan*. Under Coker's watchful eye, Appleyard had a go at the wheel and eventually, at 0930 hrs, Denis Tottenham took over. Tottenham learned quickly and by 1100 hrs Coker was sufficiently confident to leave the bridge in the charge of Duff and Tottenham, and to suggest to March-Phillipps that they muster the hands aft for tow wire drill. This was the first part of the necessary training that the new men had to undergo. It was obviously critical to the operation that the towing cables on both the *Duchessa d'Aosta* and the *Likomba* should be made fast and secure, so that they might be successfully hauled out of Santa Isabel harbour.

On the *Nuneaton*, meanwhile, Hayes took advantage of the better weather to gather his men together on the sundeck in order to initiate the amateurs in the intricacies of Tommy Gun drill, which they much enjoyed. The 'Tommy' was the Thompson machine gun, which had found great popularity with American gangsters such as Al Capone before the war, and was now a favoured weapon for British commandos. It could spray a lot of bullets all over the place, though not often with great accuracy.

One of the many remarkable features of Operation Postmaster was the way it was constantly challenged by bad luck. March-Phillipps and his men had to battle against unexpected adversity on a regular basis. Already, there had been innumerable difficulties in obtaining the necessary authority and manpower. The carefully arranged diversion in Santa Isabel almost came to grief when the restaurateur's wife fell ill. The concrete in the *Nuneaton*'s fresh water tank had not set so the water was foul. The weather as they left Lagos had been dreadful. Now at last, everything appeared to be going well. The weather was set fair and the crews were undergoing necessary training exercises in preparation for the operation. The *Nuneaton* was bobbing happily along at the end of its tow line from the *Vulcan*, with her Captain, Lieutenant Goodman, relaxing in the wheelhouse.

Suddenly, the *Nuneaton* keeled over on to her starboard side. The sea poured into the wheelhouse and the engine room, and Goodman quickly found himself up to his neck in water as he clung on to the wheel. In the engine room, the African drivers, David and Hanson, thought their final moment had come as the water level quickly rose. A variety of the ship's supplies went straight over the side into the ocean. What had happened was that the *Nuneaton* had drifted too far out to the port side on her tow rope, and with the swell of the sea the powerful *Vulcan* had pulled her over on to her side. Now, the *Vulcan* was pulling the *Nuneaton* further into trouble, dragging her along on her side as she filled with water. As the men on the *Nuneaton* scrambled to the port side to try to right her, Guise privately put the odds on the ship's survival at 100 to 1 against. It was Anders Lassen's swift action that saved them. He was standing on top of the wheelhouse of the *Vulcan*, and saw the *Nuneaton* go over. A professional seaman, Lassen immediately appreciated the enormous danger that the ship and her crew were in. He leapt down from the wheelhouse, grabbed an axe, ran to the stern of the *Vulcan* and hacked through the tow line, setting the *Nuneaton* free and preventing her from being dragged further under the water. At the same time, Coker ordered the engine room of the *Vulcan* to stop engines. As her human cargo gained her port side the *Nuneaton* thankfully righted herself on the swell, without taking in further water. Relief swept over the crews of both ships as they realized that total disaster had narrowly been avoided.

Coker brought the *Vulcan* alongside and all hands turned to bailing out the substantial quantities of seawater that *Nuneaton* had taken on board. Much equipment had been lost, including mattresses, forty fathoms of hawser, clothing, beer and other consumable supplies, but at least she was still afloat. Had she sunk, not only would there have almost certainly been loss of life, but Operation Postmaster would have failed before it had properly begun. As it was, the seawater did the *Nuneaton*'s engines no good at all, and no doubt added to the troubles that she was to experience later.

The bailing out took time, but allowed some of the materials that had been swept overboard to be salvaged from the sea. Eventually, order was restored and the *Nuneaton* was able to proceed. It had been a very close run thing, but at least the smaller tug had not ended up on the bottom of the ocean. The *Nuneaton* started her engines and Operation Postmaster was able to continue on its way, this time in convoy with each ship travelling under her own power.

For the next twelve hours, all went well. The training was continued on both vessels. Two Folbot canoes, which March-Phillipps and Appleyard now decided should be used to board the *Likomba*, were assembled and painted grey for night camouflage. On the *Nuneaton*, Lieutenant Goodman finally was able to leave the bridge and take a well deserved rest.

Lieutenant Duff impressed the men of Maid Honor Force by taking the helm of the *Vulcan* in unusual attire. From the waist up he was in full uniform, and appeared as such to those seeing him from elsewhere on the tug, or from the *Nuneaton*. From the waist down he wore only his underpants, to allow for the excessive heat during the day. Another eccentric dresser was the Frenchman André Desgranges. He customarily wore nothing but a loin cloth and a multi-coloured handkerchief over his shock of black curly hair, playing the part of a bloodthirsty pirate of old.

On the *Vulcan*, Coker continued his instruction of the tow wire/hawser party for the towing of the *Duchessa d'Aosta*, and Lieutenant Commander Oldland, the Chief Engineer, instructed the engine room party on what they would have to do when the time came. Even for a large and sturdy tug like the *Vulcan*, hauling the huge *Duchessa d'Aosta* was going to be a major task. Every bit of power that could be coaxed from the engines would be needed. Oldland was concerned about how the engine room stokers might behave, below decks, when they heard the explosions intended to sever the cables securing the *Duchessa*. The stokers were not aware of the plan and were bound to think their own ship was under attack – they might panic or decide to abandon ship. After discussion, it was decided that Leslie Prout of the Maid Honor Force should stay and take command of the *Vulcan*'s boiler room during the attack, in order to ensure that the stokers kept loading on sufficient coal, whatever distractions might occur. Prout had been looking forward to being in the boarding party and was disappointed to be condemned to the engine room, but he fully appreciated the importance of the role now assigned to him.

Coker and Duff, working with the aerial photographs taken by Michie from Pilot Alacon's aeroplane, and from the other information M's Secret Service had gathered, drew a plan of the layout of the *Duchess d'Aosta*, which was then made available for all to study. Deck watches were organized from amongst the Maid Honor Force, supplemented by Major Eyre and Captain Longe. Ernie Evison did the cooking on the *Vulcan*, and the volunteers dealt without complaint with all the more tedious duties – galley fatigues, cleaning mess decks and cleaning the ship. After the foul weather and sickness of the first day there was much to do. However, by the end of the day, as Guise put it when he visited her: 'The Vulcan looked like a new ship. Decks were clean, bedding and baggage stowed away and everything looked ship shape. Immaculate officers from the Maid Honor strolled the bridge, our three tame Spaniards were peeling onions, an outsize police officer was taking a bath, an opulent District Officer was washing dishes, and a prominent Treasury official with the air of a retired Field Marshall was shovelling coal.'

After twelve hours the *Nuneaton* came to a stop. Hanson in the engine room reported that the engines were running dangerously hot. March-Phillipps later reported to M that the problem had been the small end bearing. It seemed that in her efforts to keep up with the speedier *Vulcan* the Nuneaton had put too much strain on her engines, which apart from their recent dowsing in seawater, had not been run in sufficiently. All of a sudden, once again, Operation Postmaster was in trouble.

After two hours' work and an opportunity for the engines to cool down they were on their way again. The *Vulcan* tried taking the *Nuneaton* back on a short tow but this was not a success, so the two ships continued under their own power, going much more slowly. Happily there was no pressure. They still had more than enough time to reach Santa Isabel by the night of Wednesday, 14 January. The night of 12/13 January was blessedly calm and the ships made steady progress. A complete blackout was enforced on both ships, and the only hazard was the danger of getting lost in the dark on board.

Tuesday, 13 January was spent on more serious military training. Fighting knives were sharpened in the sunshine on deck. All guns were checked, fired and cleaned. Fusillades of Bren and Tommy gun fire swept the open sea, as the amateurs in particular learned to master the weapons. Evison found that attendance at galley fatigues dropped off considerably in the face of the rival attraction of practising with weaponry. Practice targets were not difficult to find. The two ships were always accompanied by a number of inquisitive sharks, and now their usually unwelcome presence became useful. A lump of meat was tied on the end of a length of rope and hurled over the side, into the ocean. It was then hauled back in as rapidly as possible, so that it jerked and bounced across the surface of the waves. The waiting sharks would raise their heads out of the water and snap their jaws to catch it, thereby presenting themselves as fleeting targets for the Tommy guns, Bren guns and side arms to shoot at. It was good sport and good practice, although no record exists to show how many, if any, sharks were actually hit.

Now at last March-Phillipps gave a thorough and detailed briefing, running through the entire plan. This was the first time that the volunteers learned the full truth of what they were to be asked to do. March-Phillipps selected the final parties and assigned them their special duties for the night of the attack. On the *Vulcan*, two L-shaped brackets had been mounted outside the guardrail on the port side of the wheelhouse, with a plank of wood fixed firmly across them, protruding beyond the brackets at each end. This had been done to facilitate the boarding of the *Duchessa d'Aosta*, since the *Vulcan* was a much smaller ship, and lower in the water. Four men could stand shoulder to shoulder on the plank, and the plan was that boarding would take place in waves of four at a time. The boarding parties practised throughout the day in full kit and in their designated order of battle. They tried to prepare for every possible eventuality at the moment when they landed on the deck of the *Duchessa d'Aosta*. Nobody knew what resistance they would actually meet.

Once dark had fallen the ships came to a halt. The crews were fed at 2100 hrs, then March-Phillipps ordered boarding drill to commence, and the *Nuneaton* lowered its two Folbots for a rehearsal of the attack on the *Likomba*. Hayes and Winter were to man the first Folbot and would be first aboard the *Likomba*. Two of the 'amateurs', District Commissioner W. F. H. Newington and District Commissioner A. F. Abell, would be in the second Folbot and would back them up as necessary. In this training session, the *Vulcan* played the part of the *Likomba*. Paddling the Folbots was an acquired skill, and though Hayes and Winter were old hands at it, Newington and Abell at first found manoeuvring the small craft very difficult. Bill Newington was a large and cheerful man, accustomed to taking life's mishaps in his stride. He was also a bit of a showman. He customarily wore a pork pie hat against the strength of the African sun and enjoyed smoking a pipe. Invited to try out one of the Folbots, paddling away from the *Vulcan* on to the open sea, Bill Newington set to his task with the pork pie hat still on his head and pipe firmly clamped between his teeth. An audience on board the *Vulcan* watched him with interest.

Newington did not get very far before his Folbot capsized and he was thrown into the sea, much to the amusement of his audience. Undeterred, and with his hat and pipe still miraculously in place, Newington began to swim back to the *Vulcan*, pushing his Folbot in front of him. Encouraging banter came from the audience, which Newingon did his best to ignore. However, as he swam rather slowly towards safety, those on board saw a shark appear in the water not far from him and begin to show interest in his progress. Urgent shouts of warning about the shark reached Bill Newington's ears, but he simply dismissed them as part of the heckling and continued at a steady pace towards the *Vulcan*. Happily, he reached the ship and hauled himself out of the water before the shark made the decision to attack, much to the relief of his colleagues on board. When Newington realized that his friends had not been joking, and saw how close the shark was, in the words of Desmond Longe, he looked like a ghost. It took a lot of courage for him to get back into the Folbot and try again, but that was exactly what he did. He and Abell kept practising until they had mastered the Folbots, and were able to carry out a mock attack on the *Vulcan*.

To Maid Honor Force's satisfaction, the Folbots proved almost invisible at night against the black of the sea. Although it was difficult to board the *Vulcan* from them, because of her size (relative to the Folbots) and the projecting ledge beside the wheelhouse, no such problem would be experienced with the *Likomba*, and both March-Phillipps and Tugmaster Coker regarded the practice session as very successful.

The ships then both went to Action Stations, with the men wearing full equipment, and they practised on the open sea as best they could the manoeuvres they would make in Santa Isabel harbour the following night. Finally, after a lot of work by all concerned, March-Phillipps was satisfied and the two ships started up again and continued slowly on their way to Fernando Po. Coker was happy that all the training had allowed his boiler room men to have a fairly easy time that day. He knew how hard they would have to work when the moment came to tow the *Duchessa d'Aosta* out of Santa Isabel.

The weather worsened during the night, and an easterly wind sprang up, which pushed the ships closer to Fernando Po than their crews had intended. However, the day of 14 January dawned fine and clear. At 1000 hrs Santa Isabel Peak, the 10,000 ft volcanic high point of Fernando Po, was sighted, and Coker judged that it was only forty miles away. At 1110 hrs, Tom Thumb Peak in the Cameroons was also sighted.

Zero hour was 2330 hrs, and as the day slowly passed tension mounted inexorably on both ships. Fortunately, due to a change of weather visibility became poorer as the hours passed, which at least meant that there was no danger of being spotted from Fernando Po. After midday the ships stopped again and final preparations began. A cold lunch was served on the *Vulcan*, because the galley was being used to prepare the plastic explosives that would be used to blow the mooring lines. After lunch the engineers on the *Vulcan*, Oldland and Duffy, ordered that the engines be checked over and all tubes cleaned. All the towing and boarding gear was also checked.

On the *Nuneaton*, Lieutenant Goodman gave his engines a thorough trial. He could only pray that they would behave themselves in Santa Isabel harbour, and provide consistent power to manoeuvre and to pull out his target. If the engines broke down in the harbour, there would be no chance of a tow from the *Vulcan*. She would be fully occupied with the *Duchessa d'Aosta*. They would be on their own, at the mercy of the Santa Isabel garrison. By 1630 hrs the *Nuneaton* had been reprovisioned and had taken on fresh water, albeit that much of it had to be stored in the same cement spoiled tank. She was as ready as she was ever going to be.

March-Phillipps again briefed his men on the detail of the plan. He made a few minor adjustments based on what he had learned of their abilities and as a result of his discussions with Appleyard. All kit and weapons were checked. Torches, pistols and Tommy guns were issued to the boarding parties, but strict instructions were given that firearms were to be used only if absolutely necessary. The men were issued with silent weapons – twelve-inch metal bolts encased in rubber to act as coshes – and told to use these in preference to their guns. The Maid Honor Force commandos also carried knives and other weapons of personal choice. Anders Lassen liked to carry a Beretta pistol as his personal reserve, concealed in the small of his back. Years later, Ian Fleming would give James Bond the same weapon.

Towards evening the weather cleared, and having restarted the engines at 1730 hrs, for a while the *Vulcan* and the *Nuneaton* had to adopt a course that suggested they were steering for River Cameroon, in case they were spotted from the shore or by an enemy ship. The *Nuneaton*, although under her own power, came up close to the *Vulcan* so that from a distance or from the air it might seem she was on tow, thus giving the *Vulcan* an apparent purpose for being at sea. Time now passed painfully slowly as the two ships dawdled along with engines running at dead slow. There was a sense of impatience and frustration. Operation Postmaster was still well ahead of time, but could not afford to reach Santa Isabel until at least 2330 hrs.

Once dusk had fallen, sailing without lights the two ships became hard to spot and felt it safe to change course, heading now directly for Santa Isabel. They were still ahead of schedule. The plan was to enter the harbour in the dark of the moonless night, with the smaller vessel, the *Nuneaton*, in the lead.

She had further to go in the harbour to reach her target and she had to launch her Folbots in time to ensure that her attack on the *Likomba* was simultaneous with that of the *Vulcan* on the *Duchessa d'Aosta*. If the ships were spotted before the Folbots reached the *Likomba*, they would be in obvious difficulty. Guise, with his detailed knowledge of the harbour, was the appointed lookout and pilot, standing in the bows of the *Nuneaton* to help steer a safe course. Even in the near pitch dark he was confident that he would be able to recognize the bouys and markers for the channel. About four miles out from Santa Isabel harbour the *Nuneaton* took her place in the lead.

As they quietly crept towards the island of Fernando Po, trouble began to brew up on the *Vulcan*. March-Phillipps and Appleyard were informed that they had made a very elementary mistake. They had misjudged the time. Their plans for the arrival had been based upon the reasonable assumption that Fernando Po and Spanish Guinea kept the same time as Nigeria and the Cameroons, only a few miles away. They didn't. Fernando Po kept Madrid time, which was one hour behind Nigerian time, so midnight in Lagos was only 2300 hrs on Fernando Po. The lights in the harbour were not expected to go out before 2330 hrs, Madrid time. Guise and the Nigerian contingent had always known this and had wrongly assumed that the Maid Honor Force knew it too. Only late in their approach to Santa Isabel did March-Phillipps and Appleyard realize the problem and initially they were very reluctant to accept that they were wrong. The matter, however, was put beyond doubt when the town of Santa Isabel and its harbour finally came within sight of the two ships. Although the force commander, March-Phillipps, still believed the time must be approaching midnight, the lights of the town and harbour were blazing – in Santa Isabel it was not yet 2300 hours and Maid Honor Force had arrived an hour too early.

A major row immediately broke out on the *Vulcan*'s bridge, shouts of anger reaching Guise and Hayes on the bridge of the *Nuneaton*. The intelligence supplied to Maid Honor Force and Operation Postmaster by M's Secret Service had been nigh on perfect until now. There had been hour upon hour of careful planning. How could it have possibly happened that nobody told March-Phillipps and Appleyard about the time difference? As always where there is an elementary breakdown in communications, what seemed obvious to one side seemed far from obvious to the other. For Gus March-Phillipps, after the numerous trials and tribulations that had beset him and the Maid Honor Force since their departure from Poole harbour the previous August, this silly, unnecessary breakdown of communication was the final straw.

As the row raged, the *Nuneaton*, in the lead, slowed right down to ensure that she did not arrive before the lights of Santa Isabel were switched off. Happily, the ships of Operation Postmaster still could not be seen out on the black moonless ocean by the inhabitants of Santa Isabel. As the two ships began very slowly and carefully to approach closer to a harbour that was still ablaze with lights, the moment that W, Head of West Africa Station, had feared all along arrived. Gus March-Phillipps' temper finally snapped. Angrily, he bellowed across from the *Vulcan* to the *Nuneaton*: 'Will you get a b-b-bloody move on or get out! I'm coming in.'

To steam into the lighted harbour would have brought instant disaster. All surprise would have been lost, and the Spanish authorities would have been able to see clearly what was going on – namely that no warships were attacking, but merely two civilian vessels without significant armament. They would have had very easy targets to shoot at. For a moment, March-Phillipps' always short-lived temper caused him to lose control.

Hearing March-Phillipps' shout, Lieutenant Goodman, at the helm of the *Nuneaton*, immediately took decisive action and swung his ship across the bows of the *Vulcan*, stopping his engines and blocking her path. There followed a short and furious argument between those on the bridges of the two ships, but as was his way March-Phillipps' temper soon calmed under the influence of Geoffrey Appleyard, and the row abated. A moment of apparent danger had passed. Agent W4, Laversuch, who himself had insisted that March-Phillipps should be in command of Operation Postmaster, commented later: 'Without distracting from the good work done by March-Phillipps (W.01) and the crew of the Maid Honor, without the restraining influence of Guise and others I have a feeling that the original plan and schedules would not have been strictly adhered to, particularly in regards time, and this, in my mind, would have been fatal.' It is unfair to March-Phillipps, however, to presume that he would actually have sailed into Santa Isabel harbour while the lights were still on. He had put so much into the creation of the Maid Honor Force and the planning of Operation Postmaster that he was unlikely to have thrown it all away through momentary loss of control. It was M's judgement that eventually proved right. With Appleyard by his side, March-Phillipps was soon able to control his temper and a very short time later carried out the attack on Santa Isabel with nerve, verve, and considerable courage.

The Maid Honor Force accepted they had no choice but to wait for darkness. Both vessels crept to within about 200 yards of the harbour lights where, shrouded by the dark of the ocean, they lay low. It was a tense and difficult time, as always in the lull before a violent action. Layered upon that tension was some concern on the part of the non Maid Honor Force men, who did not know March-Phillipps well, at what had just occurred. However March-Phillipps' now had his temper in hand and was back in effective command. Each man had his appointed task. Each knew what he had to do. If it all went like clockwork, they would pull off an extraordinary coup. If it went wrong – well, nobody thought too much about that.

Happily, thanks to Lippett's good work (and no doubt also to the gift of the ring and watch), the engineer's wife's admirer ensured that the lights went off a little early, not long after 2315 hrs Madrid time, so the wait was not as long as the Maid Honor Force had feared. A few lights went out, then more and more, and within moments the entire town and harbour of Santa Isabel were plunged into darkness. A wave of relief flooded over the men of Operation Postmaster. On the larger tug *Vulcan*, a mug of rum was passed around the boarding party intended for the *Duchessa d'Aosta* as they lay face down on the deck, with their faces blackened. The *Nuneaton* began to creep forward under the lea of the cliffs that surrounded the harbour, which would hopefully obscure any view of their approach from hostile eyes until the last moment, moving as quietly as she could between the buoys that marked the channel leading into the small harbour.

For Operation Postmaster, one advantage of entering the harbour as soon as possible after the lights had gone out was that the men's eyes were already adjusted to the dark of the ocean, whereas those who had been enjoying the bright lights of Santa Isabel would not, for a while, be able to see very well in the dark. As the *Nuneaton* nosed into the channel Guise was leaning forward in the bow, scanning the water for any marker or hazard. The *Vulcan* followed a short distance behind. The targets ships were at the far end of the harbour. The *Duchessa d'Aosta* was moored at right angles to the shore, a little less than 50m from the quayside, and the *Likomba* was a similar distance from the quay, about 200m to the east of the *Duchessa*.

Bren gunners were in position on both the *Vulcan* and the *Nuneaton*. They were instructed to deal with any boats that sought to interfere by firing across their bows. The order was, 'No useless slaughter'. This reflected the fact that the action was to take place in a neutral port, and the last thing that the British Government wanted was any loss of life among Spanish citizens.

Meanwhile, the Colonial Guard relaxed at their posts around the harbour. Some dozed or slept in the relative cool of the night. The monotony of wartime colonial life had taken its toll on their efficiency and discipline. The Colonial Guard were island troops, passing the war quietly on neutral territory. For them, the *Duchessa d'Aosta* and the *Likomba* had long since become a permanent part of the harbour landscape. The *Likomba* had now been moored in the harbour for over two years, the *Duchessa* for eighteen months. For the guards the evening had passed as hundreds of other evenings had passed in this peaceful colonial backwater. They had no reason to expect any trouble, other than perhaps a few drunks.

On the upper terrace of the Casino Restaurant, the dinner party was in full swing. Zorilla had slipped away, but all the other guests remained (except for those who may have been temporarily in the brothel). Captain Umberto Valle of the *Duchessa d'Aosta* and Captain Specht of the *Likomba* relaxed in their chairs, backs to the harbour, well oiled by the contents of their frequently refilled glasses. The electricity had, as planned, been replaced by bright and cheerful Tilley Paraffin Pressure lamps and by candles, and had they looked behind them, to the officers of the enemy ships the harbour would have appeared merely a pool of blackness.

In that blackness, the *Nuneaton* and the *Vulcan* were creeping towards their prey. Once in the harbour, both cut their engines and drifted gently towards their targets. Goodman and Coker were showing their true skills as tugmasters.

Graham Hayes and Tom Winter, leading the way into the harbour on the *Nuneaton*, watched for the expected signal from the window of the Reverend Markham's house. Sure enough it came. A blind was raised and lowered on a light in the window. There remains a genuine mystery as to who it was that signalled to Operation Postmaster that it was safe to enter the harbour. The Reverend Markham was in Calabar, Agents W51 (Godden) and W53 (Lake) were in the Consulate watching from the dining room window. Agent W25, Lippett, was in bed in Montilla's Hotel. Agent W10, Guise, was on board the approaching *Nuneaton*. Abelino Zorilla had already slipped away and in any event, according to Lippett, did not know about the plan. Whoever signalled from Markham's house knew enough about the planned attack to judge the time to perfection, and he (or she) was fulfilling a vital role in Operation Postmaster. Either it was one of Lippett's Spanish friends, or an African, or else M had another agent in Santa Isabel that night whose identity remains a secret to this day.

Agents Godden and Lake had positioned themselves at the dining room windows of the Consulate, watching the bay, after the lights had gone out. They could at first see nothing, but within a very few minutes they heard the sound of a tug's engine. Then the engine was cut and there was only silence as the two British ships drifted in. From their window, Godden and Lake could not see the *Likomba*, but the *Duchessa d'Aosta* was in their full view as she lay at anchor a few metres from the quay.

CHAPTER 20

The *Nuneaton* Takes the *Likomba*

Well inside the harbour, the *Nuneaton* stopped. The two camouflaged Folbots were quietly and gently lowered to the sea, one from each side of the *Nuneaton*. Hayes and Winter settled with practised ease into theirs. Their weapons were concealed. They would be the first to board the *Likomba*, and might encounter a watchman. Guise pointed out the direction of the *Likomba*, since visibility was virtually nil, and silently they paddled towards it. They expected the smaller *Bibundi* to be moored on its starboard side.

The second Folbot, crewed by District Commissioners Newington and Abell, heavily armed with revolvers and a Tommy gun, set out rather less confidently. They were to act as immediate back-up in support of Hayes and Winter, should those two experience any resistance once they had boarded. However, Newington and Abell at first appeared to be heading off in the wrong direction, towards the *Duchessa d'Aosta*, until Guise on the *Nuneaton* called out to them urgently, and they corrected their course and followed Hayes and Winter. So dark was it that before they found the *Likomba* they happened upon a totally innocent Spanish launch moored nearby, and imagined she was their target. Their raid on that happily empty vessel was unopposed, they quickly realized their mistake and left, heading at last for the real *Likomba*.

All four of the men in the Folbots prayed that the distraction had worked and that the ship's officers were not on board. For Hayes and Winter in particular, it would be difficult to board the *Likomba* from a Folbot if their identity was discovered and someone started shooting at them. They had a bluff ready, and were counting on any watchman not suspecting that they were enemy commandos with hostile intent until it was too late for him to take effective action or raise the alarm. For a watchman, as for the Colonial Guard, the evening so far had been identical to hundreds spent in this sleepy little harbour.

As their Folbot came alongside the *Bibundi* (which was tied up to the *Likomba)*, a black African on board the *Likomba* challenged them and flashed a light. Graham Hayes grunted non-committally in response, and the watchman, obviously thinking that it was his Captain returning from his night out, came forward to help with the painter and to assist them to board. However, when he saw the two men close up, he realized that neither was Captain Specht. Hayes forestalled any protest by proffering a letter which he claimed, in pidgeon English, was a missive for the Captain, using the pre-planned ruse to get himself and Winter on board the *Likomba*. The watchman told Hayes and Winter that the Captain and Second Officer were both on shore. Then, to Hayes and Winter's concern, another crew member then appeared behind the watchman.

Happily, at that moment Abell and Newington arrived in the second Folbot, armed to the teeth – and seeing the Tommy gun and revolvers both the *Likomba*'s crewmen fled forward, made no attempt to raise the alarm but jumped into the sea, preferring to face the possibility of sharks on the short swim to dry land than to remain in the close vicinity of the armed boarders. Guise, watching from the nearby *Nuneaton*, described the night watchmen as 'popping over the side like performing gymnasts over a horse'. Thus the *Likomba* and the *Bibundi* were seized without the need for violence, but, presuming that the night watchmen successfully made it to the shore, it would be only a matter of time before the alarm was raised.

Hayes rapidly dispersed his small force to their appointed tasks. The anchoring cables had to be blown fore and aft, the ship had to be searched, a watch placed, and the all important towing hawser from the *Nuneaton* had to be attached. Hayes and Winter had the specialized task of blowing the anchoring cables. Each of them carried a rucksack containing enough explosives to do not only their own but the other man's job, should he be put out of action. The same was true of the explosive teams assigned to the *Duchessa d'Aosta*.

The *Nuneaton* now approached, with Guise still in the bows acting as pilot. It was known from the charts that there was a shoal immediately to the stern of the *Likomba*, which was moored less than fifty metres from the shore. Therefore Guise had advised that Goodman bring the *Nuneaton* round in a wide sweep to come alongside her. Guise called the directions from the bow, but miscalculated, telling Goodman to swing the wheel a second or so too early and nearly causing the *Nuneaton* to over-run her target. Happily, Goodman's seamanship saved the day and the *Nuneaton* safely arrived alongside the *Likomba*.

The *Bibundi* was not an official target of the raid. It was the 200 ton tug *Likomba* that mattered. The *Bibundi* was a small pleasure cruiser of some seventy tons, and Hayes was initially minded to cut her free and to leave her behind, feeling she would add to the complexity of the tow (it was only later discovered that she had no fitted engine, her own engine was in fact in the hold of the *Likomba*). One of the difficulties, of course, was that the Maid Honor Force could not afford to take a neutral Spanish vessel by mistake. Both the *Duchessa d'Aosta* and the *Likomba* had been clearly identified as enemy vessels. Little was known about the *Bibundi*.

Both the *Likomba* and the *Bibundi* were now thoroughly searched. The only occupants were found to be two cats. It fell to Tom Winter to search the *Bibundi*. Winter found on display in her cabin a photograph of the ship flying a swastika from her jackstaff, with a lady who was later assumed to be the owner's wife posing beside it. Armed with clear evidence of the *Bibundi*'s nationality, Winter was able to persuade Hayes that it was worth taking her too. Happily, it later turned out that Winter was right and both ships were German, although the *Bibundi* proved of little value as a prize and undoubtedly did add to the difficulty of the tow.

All had so far been accomplished as silently as possible. The pitch dark provided anonymity, but sound carries easily over water, particularly in a small harbour such as Santa Isabel. The original plan had called for a simultaneous blowing of the anchor chains and cables on both target ships, thereby giving each the best possible chance of escaping the harbour before the Spanish realized what was going on. However, the unreliability of the *Nuneaton* on the outward journey had forced a change of plan. Hayes had orders to blow the stays of the *Likomba* as soon as he was ready, and the *Vulcan* was to take her chances with the *Duchessa d'Aosta*. The Admiralty had always taken the view that the *Likomba*'s capture was the more important of the two since she was a modern tug and potentially more dangerous (or useful) to British Naval interests. The cutting out of the *Likomba* was also, potentially, easier to achieve.

Hayes could now hear activity from the direction of the *Duchessa*, and correctly concluded that she too had been boarded. With the *Nuneaton* alongside the *Likomba*, Leonard Guise and Buzz Perkins now attempted to board the tug. Perkins carried the all important towing hawser needed to secure the *Likomba* and the *Bibundi* to the *Nuneaton*. Both men were heavily armed, carrying with them Mills bombs (hand grenades) and Tommy guns.

The greatest care had been taken to ensure that the right amount of plastic explosive would be used to sever the anchoring chains of both the target ships. Guise was now going to find out if his measurements had been accurate enough. However, no amount of careful reconnaissance and planning can guard against human error. The fuses for the explosive charges attached to the bow and stern cables were already burning as Guise and Perkins clambered aboard the *Likomba* with the towing hawser. The four men already on board were under cover, and their shouted warnings came too late. The bow charge went off with Guise and Perkins fully exposed to the blast. Both men were blown off the *Likomba*, propelled through the air by the blast, and landed back on the *Nuneaton*. One landed on the sun deck, the other on a bollard. Hayes and Winter thought they had killed them both, but miraculously neither Guise nor Perkins suffered more than a cracked rib. Thankfully, none of the Mills bombs they were both carrying (Guise had had one in his hand), which could have caused serious damage to men and ships, exploded.

Hayes and Winter, enormously relieved to discover that they had not killed their comrades, could not afford to pause in their work. Now that the first charges had gone off, it would not be long before the garrison of Santa Isabel reacted. The aft cable of the *Likomba* was still in place, the charge had misfired and not exploded. Moments later a second attempt at firing the charge succeeded and the cable was parted. Hayes and Winter breathed a sigh of relief. However, when Guise and Perkins had been unceremoniously ejected from the *Likomba* the towing hawser had gone with them, so the *Likomba* had yet to be secured to the *Nuneaton*. She and the *Bibundi* were now adrift, turning with the tidal swell. As quickly as he could, Goodman brought the *Nuneaton* back alongside the *Likomba*, and this time Perkins and Guise landed on board successfully, with the hawser. Perkins made it fast, then returned to the *Nuneaton* to ensure that the tow paid out evenly. Goodman allowed the *Nuneaton* to take the strain of the tow, and the three ships began to make their way as quickly as they could towards the harbour entrance and the open sea.Thankfully, the *Nuneaton*'s engines, for the time being at least, responded.

CHAPTER 21

The *Vulcan* Takes the *Duchessa d'Aosta*

Meanwhile, once the Folbots were away the *Vulcan* had come up alongside the *Nuneaton*, and then headed on towards her own target. On board, March-Phillipps handed over the command to Coker and Duff, and joined the boarding parties which had assembled on the mess deck and lower deck behind the iron bulwarks, waiting out of sight for the order to Action Stations. About twenty men were in the boarding parties. March-Phillipps' presence gave his men confidence. The storm of his temper had long since blown itself out and he was his usual calm and collected self. His own men were used to his 'bollums' and knew that they had no effect on his cool head in battle.

Although informality was an essential part of the ethos of the Maid Honor Force, that did not extend to March-Phillipps' orders – he expected total and immediate obedience, and his men were happy to give it. As they crouched in the dark, Appleyard, Lassen and the others of the Force who were with him knew that this moment was the culmination of all their effort and training so far. Forgotten now were the frustrations of their first four months in West Africa, and the numerous difficulties that fate had placed in their way. They focused solely on the large target looming in the darkness, the *Duchessa d'Aosta*. As Hayes and Winter had done moments earlier approaching the *Likomba*, March-Phillipps and Appleyard were praying to God that the distraction had worked and that the crew on board the *Duchessa d'Aosta* would be without their officers and off-guard. The window blind that had signalled the all-clear for them to enter the harbour hopefully also meant that the officers had been successfully lured away from the *Duchessa*.

Coker, exercising considerable skill in the confines of the harbour, brought the *Vulcan* round in a wide sweep, with the intention of placing her port side alongside the starboard side of the *Duchessa d'Aosta*. As he did so, numerous pairs of eyes on the *Vulcan* watched for any hostile activity on board the enemy ship. As they closed on her, a number of unidentifiable figures were observed moving about on the after deck and once a torch flashed briefly from there towards the outline of the *Vulcan*. March-Phillipps had his friendly Spaniards ready to reply to any challenge, in order to gain the time necessary to close the gap between the two ships. However, no challenge came. Lights were seen in some of the portholes of the *Duchessa d'Aosta*, indicating that some members of the crew were in their cabins. It seemed that nobody had any idea that their ship was about to be boarded. Clearly, no effective watch had been set.

As the *Vulcan* manoeuvred closer to the *Duchessa*'s starboard side, March-Phillipps ordered his men to Action Stations. The boarding parties filed silently up to the bridge deck, and moved on to the extended boarding platform on the side of the *Vulcan*, covered by two Bren guns that were positioned on the roof of her bridge.

In the boiler room, Lieutenant Leslie Prout, drawing on his great experience as an NCO, took command of the stokers, readying them for their big effort. He was armed with a Colt .45 and a Tommy gun, and as he put it: 'I was telling the sweating stokers the tale as I have never told it before, and promised them a big "dash" [money] if they worked well.' Engineers Oldland and Duffy were both in the engine room, ready to coax every ounce of steam and every revolution that they could out of the 2,000 hp engines of the *Vulcan* once the clang of the ship's telegraph sounded.

Still without any obvious reaction from the *Duchessa d'Aosta*, the *Vulcan* inched closer, until a gap of only two feet remained between the two ships. March-Phillipps gave the order to board, and leapt for the enemy ship. The diminutive figure of his batman, Haggis Taylor, followed immediately behind him, together with three others. Once on board the *Duchessa*, they headed directly for the bridge. Next aboard was Anders Lassen, carrying a line and as always armed to the teeth. He leapt for the rope ladder that hung down from the cabin decks. Grabbing it, he climbed on board, looped the line around a bollard, and hurled it back to Lieutenant Duff who was waiting on the bridge of the *Vulcan*. Duff, urged on by Lassen from the *Duchessa*, made the line fast. The two ships were now linked. Nonetheless, the impact of the *Vulcan* against the side of the *Duchessa d'Aosta*, and the swell of the sea in the harbour was forceful enough to cause the *Vulcan* to recoil, and a gap temporarily opened between the two ships. A second contact enabled another six of the Maid Honor Force to swarm aboard the *Duchessa*, but then the *Vulcan* drifted forward, opening the gap to about eight feet. Still there was only one line aboard.

Appleyard, who was in charge of the explosives party, was momentarily stranded on the *Vulcan*. Knowing there was no time to waste he boldly leapt the eight-foot gap, and successfully reached the *Duchessa d'Aosta*. A bamboo ladder was then placed across the gap and the remainder of the boarding party crossed precariously to the enemy ship. They included the civilian Dr MacGregor, with his medical kit. A fall from the bamboo ladder into the sea below would inevitably have meant being crushed between the sides of the two ships.

As the boarding party spread out over the ship, they met no resistance from the crew. There was a moment of concern as, in the dark, the tall figure of Agent W30, Captain Desmond Longe, was felled on the aft well deck by a body that hurtled out of the dark. As his 6ft 4in frame crashed to the deck, the boarding party realized that his attacker was in fact a pig – one of three that were running loose, enjoying a degree of freedom before eventually facing their undoubted fate in the *Duchessa d'Aosta*'s galley. Two black Africans were also found on the deck, one of whom was apparently meant to be the watchman. He speedily jumped over the side, hit the water in a classic belly-flop, and swam for the shore. The other man surrendered tamely to the boarders. The surprise of the attack was complete.

As Gus March-Phillipps and Haggis Taylor took command of the bridge, Geoffrey Appleyard and André Desgranges rushed forward to place explosives on the forward anchoring chains, whilst John Eyre and Desmond Longe (quickly back on his feet) ran equally fast to deal with the aft chains and cables. Longe, disregarding the handicap of an injured left thumb, worked feverishly, as did Eyre beside him. They had a total of six stern cables to sever, and March-Phillipps was later to commend them to M for the phenomenal speed at which they went about their work. All four of the explosives party heard the charges go off on the *Likomba*, and knew that time was now extremely limited. It was not known how long it would take for the lights of the town to be switched back on, but once that happened they would be like target ducks in a fairground shooting booth.

A very real sense of urgency pervaded the whole operation. With the bridge and upper deck secured, the *Duchessa d'Aosta* could be towed out to sea even if there was a battle royal raging below decks. It had always been recognized that it might take some time to secure the ship. Once March-Phillipps was satisfied that the *Duchessa* was secure above decks, he carried on with the next stage of the operation, which was to get her out of Santa Isabel harbour as quickly as possible.

Below decks, the assigned sections of the boarding party made simultaneously for the all important radio room, the officers' quarters, passenger quarters and the engine room. Each section knew its job and thanks to the careful planning and preparation knew the route that they had to take through the ship to achieve their objectives. To the crew of the *Duchessa d'Aosta*, they presented a fiercesome and totally unexpected sight as they stormed through the ship. With faces blacked commando style, and armed with their heavy coshes and other weaponry, it is perhaps not surprising that they encountered no resistance worthy of the name. The radio room was secured without difficulty, and there was nothing to suggest that in the few moments between the Maid Honor Force boarding the *Duchessa* and reaching the radio room any message had been sent out.

In total, they discovered twenty-eight European members of the crew still aboard, together with the one African who had not jumped over the side. As the boarding party moved through the ship's accommodation, they were in fact impeded by the number of prisoners who had to be secured. Coker, now preparing to take the tow, saw the first of the prisoners brought up on deck in their pyjamas and herded forward under guard. It was vital that each prisoner remained quiet and did not attempt to raise the alarm to others – on board or, more importantly, on land.

Although none of the crew offered any real resistance, the men of Operation Postmaster could take no chances, and had no time to be delicate with their prisoners. Any possible opposition had to be quelled immediately and no respect could be given to any language problems. Guise, who was now on the *Likomba*, later told of an incident when six of the Italians on the *Duchessa d'Aosta* were ordered to lie down on their bunks, but remained standing because the order was given in English and they did not understand it: 'A large Public Works Official had to take his "persuader" and play a quick arpeggio on their heads. The wounds were not grave, and the casualties served a very good breakfast next morning.'

To the surprise of Maid Honor Force, who had apparently not been briefed about it, one woman was found on board. She was Gilda Turch, a stewardess in her fifties. Hearing the disturbance outside her cabin, she had presumed it was just members of the crew coming back on board drunk, and locked her cabin door. When the raiders hammered on her door, she refused to answer it, so the door was at once kicked in. As the men of Operation Postmaster burst into her cabin, with their blackened faces and fiercesome coshes, Gilda Turch fainted dead away.

Meanwhile, Agents Godden and Lake had been watching from the window of the Consulate's dining room. They could only see the *Duchessa d'Aosta*. They heard what they thought was a challenge in Italian, followed by a gruff, 'Keep 'em up!' Then came the bangs from the explosive charges attached to the *Likomba*'s anchor chains. On the *Vulcan*, the Bren gun parties stiffened in anticipation and watched for any response from the shore.

For the diners at the Casino Terrace Restaurant, the initial explosions in the bay came as a complete surprise. The charges from the *Likomba* were not as large as those that were to follow from the *Duchessa d'Aosta*, but they were enough to bring the dinner party to an abrupt halt, and to wake the whole of Santa Isabel. The bangs and flashes were no more than 400 metres from the Casino terrace. Nobody had the slightest idea what was going on, and the large amount of alcohol that all had drunk added to the total confusion. It may well be that some of the male guests were passing a little time with the girls in the brothel. The officers of the two ships who were still on the terrace appreciated that the explosions had come from the harbour where their ships were anchored, but the harbour instantly returned to darkness afterwards, there were no flames to light the scene, and turning from the brightly lit dinner table, the officers could make out nothing in the bay below. Lippett's emergency plan was working to perfection.

The sound of a lone bugle rang through the night as the bugler at Government House frantically blew the alarm. For the moment, the lights of the town remained off, although small lights came on in various parts of Santa Isabel. It would take some time for the appropriate instructions to reach the power station and for the main lights to be switched back on, if the decision was taken that that was the appropriate thing to do. Until the authorities in Santa Isabel knew what was going on, they could not assess whether turning the lights on would help them, or make things worse.

Lippett was back in his hotel room and had been asleep. He heard the explosions at about 2335 hrs, and looked out of his windows to see the streets of Santa Isabel rapidly filling with people, as did the balconies of the hotel. Very wisely, he remained exactly where he was.

Deep in the bowels of the *Vulcan*, the first of the explosions caused a moment of near panic amongst the stokers. They, of course, knew almost nothing of the operation on the surface. Prout's steadying presence was now vital, as he calmed them and cajoled them into yet more frantic efforts. Prout knew, of course, that there were more explosions to come.

As the explosives party on the *Duchessa d'Aosta* were placing their charges, the *Nuneaton*, with her two prizes in tow, passed by heading for the harbour mouth. Hayes hailed them in English from the bridge, forgetting perhaps in the heat of the moment that the nationality of the attackers should not be known. There were calls in English heard by some of those on land. In the midst of the operation, it was inevitable that some English would be used.

With the charges all in place on the *Duchessa d'Aosta*, March-Phillipps gave the signal for them to be fired – a single blast on his whistle. Almost immediately, the ship and the harbour were shaken by a series of titanic explosions, far more violent than those on the *Likomba*. The telegraph clanged in the engine room of the *Vulcan*, and Chief Engineer Oldland opened the throttle of the tug's engines as wide as he could. The powerful engines shook the tug as they strained and pulled at their huge burden. The *Duchessa d'Aosta* did not shift.

Above decks, Agent W.02, Geoffrey Appleyard realized instantaneously what had happened. One of the major explosive charges attached to a forward cable had failed to go off. Without hesitating for a moment, despite the obvious danger of a delayed explosion, Appleyard shouted out, 'I am laying another charge', and rushed forward to do just that. Godden (who was a Scot) and Lake heard his call from where they were watching in the Consulate, and described it as being made in 'an ultra Mayfair or West End accent'.

Having fixed the fresh charge, Appleyard called a warning, 'I am going to blow', fired the fuse, and flung himself under the cover of a nearby winch. Moments later there was another enormous explosion, the last remaining cable parted, and the *Vulcan* lurched forward, propellers thrashing. Coker now demonstrated his expertise. With the *Vulcan* secured against the side of the *Duchessa*, he gave the liner a slew to starboard and then another to port, as though loosening her, and then drew her forward like a cork from a bottle. With a terrific grinding noise from her keel, the *Duchessa d'Aosta* came clear of her mooring. A shout rang out from March-Phillipps on the bridge, 'My god, she's free!'

For Coker, pulling the *Duchessa d'Aosta* free was only the start of his task. Now he had to get her out of the harbour. The liner had not moved from her mooring for well over a year, she had no power from her own engines, and no rudder. Using all of his expertise, and making the task look almost easy, Coker towed the *Duchessa d'Aosta* against a severe cross current at a speed of at least three knots, directly out between the harbour entrance buoys and into the open sea, passing the slower *Nuneaton* and her prizes as he did so.

Meanwhile, on shore the explosions on the *Duchessa d'Aosta* were having a dramatic effect. Many of those who had been making their way down towards the harbour turned and fled for cover. Cries of 'Alerta! Alerta!' rang out across Santa Isabel, and most people seemed to believe that they were being attacked from the air. That fear removed any question of the town's lights being turned on, and instead Santa Isabel's anti-aircraft guns started firing blindly up into the sky. The confusion was complete and the harbour remained in darkness. Eyre and Longe, their job with the explosive completed, took up position at the stern of the *Duchessa d'Aosta*, with their Thompson sub-machine guns covering the quay.

Prout's stokers were magnificent, heaping coal into the furnace, and the engineers, Oldland and Duffy broke all the safety rules of the Mercantile Marine as the engines threatened to shake themselves out of their beds. Oldland physically sat on the safety lever to prevent it from cutting in to reduce the revolutions of the hard-working tug. The *Nuneaton* followed the *Vulcan* away from the harbour and before long both had vanished into the night and out to sea. As they left the chaos in Santa Isabel behind them, it was noted that the whole operation had taken a mere thirty-five minutes. Throughout their time in the harbour the men of Postmaster had fired only one shot, the accidental discharge of a .38 pistol that happily did nobody any harm.

It was some while before the lights of the town came back on, and by that time the Maid Honor Force and the five ships were long gone from the harbour and shrouded by the comforting darkness of the ocean. Many of the dinner party guests, and indeed much of the population of Santa Isabel, began to make their way down towards the port, some on foot, some by motor car. Those of the Colonial Guard who had been dozing on duty were now wide awake, and there was a general rush to the armoury to grab weapons. It was immediately obvious to all that the *Duchessa d'Aosta* was gone from the harbour. The Captain of the Colonial Guard was left running around in confusion, asking what had happened. All of the Guard now turned out, but many were only half-dressed and some were without arms. Whatever guns there may have been covering the harbour had been not fired. Some believed that the attack had been from the air, others talked of having seen as many as five enemy battleships. The Governor had apparently been worried that if his own guns fired, the enemy battleships might fire back upon the town.

In short, the raid on the harbour and the seizure of the ships went totally unanswered. The preparations made by Lippett had been first class, and Maid Honor Force had executed its task to near perfection despite the difficulties thrown in its way. The Governor and authorities in Fernando Po simply didn't know what had happened, or who had visited their harbour. By the time the lights came on, it was all over.

As icing on the cake, Operation Postmaster had been supplied with a number of Free French naval hats, which they dropped into the sea as they left the harbour, in an exercise in disinformation. Since the Free French were already 'stateless rebels' fighting against Vichy France, there could be little or no international comeback against them. As things stood, the Spanish might suspect, but they would never be able to prove, that the British were responsible for the 'theft' of the ships.

However, all that could change if Phase Two of Operation Postmaster, the liaison with the Royal Navy's HMS *Violet*, did not go according to plan.

CHAPTER 22

Escape

If the raid on Santa Isabel had happened in one of Ian Fleming's James Bond stories, at least in the film version the next scene would have been of Bond, operation successfully completed, relaxing on a boat with a beautiful girl in his arms, waiting for the Royal Navy (or perhaps the Americans) to come and rescue him. So, in a sense, it should have been for Operation Postmaster after they left Santa Isabel harbour (except that Operation Postmaster was a wholly male affair with the exception of the unfortunate stewardess Gilda Turch). The plan was that they should head out to sea and liaise during the early afternoon with HMS *Violet*, who would take over the captured ships and sail them on to Lagos. The Maid Honor Force and the others of Operation Postmaster would have been able to relax and congratulate themselves. However, it was not to be.

As he rode the bridge of the *Duchessa d'Aosta* out of Santa Isabel harbour and into the relative safety of the darkened South Atlantic ocean, March-Phillipps was rightly triumphant. Operation Postmaster had captured all three ships, without a shot being fired in anger and without a single casualty being sustained. The sheer size of the *Duchessa d'Aosta* was brought home to him by the lofty position that he now occupied on her bridge. To seize her and take her out of the harbour had been a remarkable achievement. However, in the stark reality of the early hours of 15 January 1942, many hurdles still lay in the way before they could regard the operation as successfully completed. It was no time yet for celebration. March-Phillipps had to content himself by heading the page of the *Maid Honor*'s log book (which he had brought with them) for 15 January with the name 'S.S. Duchessa d'Aosta', and by stamping the log with the *Duchessa d'Aosta*'s Lloyd Triestino line rubber stamp. Obstinately, March-Phillipps recorded the time of the attack in the log as 0040 hrs (sticking to Lagos time), and recorded that the *Duchessa d'Aosta* had got under way at 0100 hrs.

March-Phillipps knew that he had to take all five ships as far away from Fernando Po as he could before daylight. There was a real possibility of pursuit from Santa Isabel and although it was not believed that the Spanish had any craft in the harbour that were capable of causing major damage to any of the Postmaster convoy, March-Phillipps himself had nothing bigger than a Bren gun to call upon to defend his ships. A greater danger might come from the air, should the Governor of Fernando Po call upon assistance from Spain's Axis friends. The sooner that Operation Postmaster was brought under the safety blanket of the Royal Navy, the better.

The tugs stayed under the command of their own officers, whilst March-Phillipps and Appleyard remained on board the *Duchessa d'Aosta* and Hayes remained on the *Likomba*, with the *Bibundi* adjacent. March-Phillipps took the sensible step of appointing Anders Lassen, the professional seaman, as Second Officer of the *Duchessa*.

The rendezvous with HMS *Violet* was set for 1400 hrs on 15 January, some forty miles away from the coast of Fernando Po. It was very important that March-Phillipps and Operation Postmaster make that rendezvous. Only the Captain of the *Violet* would be in on their secret and they would be boarded and seized in the normal way, as if the ships were genuinely still in enemy hands – but once 'seized' they would be under official Royal Navy protection. The *Likomba* bore the German colours on its funnel and one of the many dangers was that if she did not link up with the *Violet* quickly, she might prove a tempting target for a passing Allied plane. To a lesser extent, the same was true of the *Duchessa d'Aosta*. The need for absolute secrecy had again left Operation Postmaster very exposed. No British plane could yet be told that in fact the two ships were in British hands.

Unknown to Maid Honor Force however, in its hour of triumph disaster had struck elsewhere. HMS *Violet* had experienced her own problems and had somehow managed to run herself aground on the night of 14 January. For the time being she was 'out of the game', and would not be able to rendezvous with March-Phillipps at the appointed hour and place. This meant that the Maid Honor Force's five ships would remain unprotected on the high seas, not only throughout the daylight hours of 15 January, but potentially for some days thereafter. Because of enforced radio silence, moreover, March-Phillipps could not be told of the fact that there would be no Royal Navy ship at the rendezvous. It was a most unlikely accident and nobody could have foreseen it, but it was going to cause enormous difficulties not only for Operation Postmaster in the South Atlantic, but also for the British Government in London, and in particular for Commander Ian Fleming at the Admiralty, responsible as he was for the official cover story.

The *Nuneaton*, the *Likomba* and the *Bibundi*

The weather was wild and stormy, and there was a deep swell. The *Nuneaton* was labouring with her double tow, and the *Bibundi* and the *Likomba* were bumping forcefully against each other with dangerous regularity. Assessing that there was a real risk that they might break each other up, Lieutenant Goodman decided that the only thing to do was to put the *Bibundi* on an extended tow behind the *Likomba*. They stopped and *Bibundi* was manhandled to fall in behind the *Likomba* on the end of a tow rope. Goodman and Hayes also discovered a few tiny craft which had obviously been tied up to the *Likomba* in Santa Isabel harbour and had remained attached to the little convoy. Reluctantly, they cut these free and let them go, in the hope they would drift back to their rightful owners on Fernando Po.

However, when the *Nuneaton* set off again it was soon discovered that the problem was not solved. Within half an hour *Bibundi*'s tow rope began to fray, and it became clear that if it was not replaced or reinforced with a new rope, the tow would sever and the *Bibundi* would be lost. The difficulty now was that the *Bibundi* was fifty yards adrift behind the *Likomba* in increasingly violent seas. Somehow, a new line had to be fixed to her. Somebody had to try to get back on board the *Bibundi* with that line.

Graham Hayes, Agent W.03, had already proved a number of times during the life of the Maid Honor Force that he had no fear of the sea. He was the officer in charge of the three ships but, as was the ethos of the Maid Honor Force, that did not prevent him from now taking on the most dangerous of tasks himself. In an inky darkness broken only by torches shone from the *Likomba*, and with a fresh line wrapped around his waist, Hayes began to clamber along the fifty yards of existing tow rope, across the shark infested sea, from the *Likomba* to the *Bibundi*. Goodman, Guise, Winter and the others aboard the *Nuneaton* and the *Likomba* could only watch and hope. Probably Winter was regretting that he had persuaded Hayes to take the *Bibundi* in the first place. Such was the character of Hayes, however, that now that the *Bibundi* was their prize, there was no question in his mind of cutting her loose and letting her go.

Pulling himself forward inch by inch along a rope that behaved like a bucking bronco, Hayes was thrown alternately high into the air, then down into the sea. The physical strength required simply to cling on was enormous. He stuck doggedly to his task and eventually reached the *Bibundi*. Then he clambered aboard and started to haul in the new tow rope that was attached to the end of the line around his waist. This again was a hard physical task, since the rope was thick and heavy, and the sea remained wild. It threatened to swallow up the rope as Hayes hauled it across the fifty-yard gap. Eventually, he got the rope on board the *Bibundi*, and made fast the new tow. That done, he slumped exhausted on the deck and attempted to regain some strength.

Graham Hayes allowed himself a mere five minutes' rest before attempting the return. Tough as the outward journey had been, going back proved worse. The sea had not quietened, and much of his strength was gone. Raw courage and sheer determination got him back to the *Likomba*, where willing hands dragged him on board. Had those hands not been there, Guise was convinced that Hayes would have been lost to the sea. Guise reported to M later that those who saw it believed Hayes's effort to have been one of the bravest things they had ever seen. When Ian Fleming later read Guise's report (as he must have done), an enduring seed for his own heroic agent was sewn.

As Hayes lay exhausted, Goodman now began to make some progress with both his two prizes in tow, but the *Nuneaton* continued to struggle. As dawn broke, she was making a miserly one knot, and Fernando Po (and possible pursuit) was still only some five miles distant. The *Nuneaton* could see the *Vulcan* and the *Duchessa d'Aosta* about four miles ahead of her, apparently making good time. As the day progressed, *Nuneaton*'s engine threatened to overheat and Goodman had to stop, this time for about an hour. Once the engine had cooled they started up again, but not for very long. She broke down yet again a mere twelve miles off the coast of Fernando Po, now of course in broad daylight and within easy range of any pursuing vessels. Once more they got her started and she continued to crawl away from the island.

By 1000 hrs, the *Vulcan* and the *Duchessa d'Aosta* were out of sight, but the *Nuneaton* was still making little progress. At 1300 hrs she broke down once more. The problem this time was diagnosed as being that the piston rings were too tight, and had to be freed. The problem was solvable and the engine could be repaired, but it would take time – a commodity that the *Nuneaton* could not afford. With the sea now much calmer, Hayes and Goodman decided to see if it was possible to start the engines of the *Likomba*, so that she might proceed under her own power. Using the Folbot canoes, Hanson was ferried from the engine room of the *Nuneaton* to the *Likomba* to have a look. Sadly, after an hour of work, Hanson confessed to failure. He could not get the *Likomba*'s engine started, and they would have to continue to rely on the *Nuneaton*'s power, such as it was. Back down to the engine room he went, to rejoin Olu David, who had continued working on the *Nuneaton*'s engine while Hanson was on the *Likomba*.

The *Vulcan* and the *Duchessa d'Aosta*

On board the *Vulcan* and the *Duchessa d'Aosta* things were going far better. On the *Duchessa*, March-Phillipps had confirmed that any potential resistance was quelled, and pulled by the powerful *Vulcan* they were making good progress. Watches were organized, and the Bren guns that had been on the roof of the bridge deck were now set up on the boat deck in case of any pursuit by small boats. Anders Lassen efficiently fulfilled the role of Second Officer. March-Phillipps discovered that, like the *Likomba*, the *Duchessa d'Aosta* had been used as a convenient mooring point for small vessels in Santa Isabel harbour, and still had attached to her a selection of small yachts and boats. These were cut free and left to float away.

The twenty-nine prisoners had caused no trouble, and with a little encouragement many were now making themselves useful. March-Phillipps assembled and addressed them, telling them that they were now prisoners of war and to behave themselves. Dr MacGregor held a sick parade in the saloon once the liner was well clear of Santa Isabel, and ordered all casualties to report. No significant injuries were discovered, either to prisoners or to the raiding party. The stewardess, 54-year-old Gilda Turch, who had fainted at the sight of the men of the Maid Honor Force breaking into her cabin, and had later become hysterical when the charges were detonated, now appeared fully recovered. The worst 'injury' found was a wound to the foot of a large Italian, which upon examination and cross-examination by Dr MacGregor, the sailor admitted had been festering for at least six months. Gilda Turch was permitted to remain in her cabin, but the remaining prisoners, who turned out to include three junior engineer officers, were put under guard in the aft dining saloon. Mr Le Mare, from the Accountant General's department, took command of the guard on the prisoners.

Many of the Italians seemed happy to simply be at sea again. For the ordinary Italian, the war was not an ideological venture, merely a necessary inconvenience imposed on him by a Fascist government. The crew of the civilian liner *Duchessa d'Aosta* were world travellers who enjoyed life at sea. Their incarceration at Santa Isabel had no doubt been hard for them. Now they were, at last, back on the open sea again, even if they were destined for a prisoner of war camp.

Attempts were made to start the engines of the *Duchessa d'Aosta* so that she could proceed under her own power. It would look far more convincing at the moment of rendezvous with HMS *Violet* if the liner was making her own way across the ocean, and it would also have eased the burden on the *Vulcan*, leaving her free to help the *Nuneaton* if necessary. It was not to be.

After eighteen months of inactivity and neglect, the engines proved impossible to start. They would require a full overhaul when the *Duchessa* eventually reached Lagos.

Work parties were set to clean up the ship, which was also in a state of considerable neglect, to restore it to a state fitting for one of His Majesty's ships. A number of boxes of flowers that bedecked the ship, perhaps leftovers from the party that the crew had given after Christmas, were thrown overboard. The Italian cooks and stewards served breakfast to the men of Operation Postmaster with surprising enthusiasm and skill. The liner was big enough to ride the heavy seas in a way that was impossible for the *Nuneaton* and the *Likomba*, and life on board was relatively comfortable. One surprise problem that March-Phillipps and his men discovered was that the *Duchessa d'Aosta*'s fresh water tanks were virtually empty. According to Desmond Longe, there was nothing to drink on board except Chianti, Green Chartreuse and brandy, none of which were suitable to quench the sort of thirst created by the tropical climate. Fresh water was brought across from the *Vulcan*.

A feeling of elation at what they had achieved remained ever present amongst the Maid Honor Force as the *Vulcan* steamed towards their rendezvous. They did not yet know, of course, that HMS *Violet* would not be there.

Seeing that the *Nuneaton* was having trouble behind them, March-Phillipps took the decision to press on with the *Duchessa* to the rendezvous, and if HMS *Violet* was not already there, to leave her adrift and return to the *Nuneaton* to offer assistance. The *Vulcan* and the *Duchessa d'Aosta* made the rendezvous area south of the Calabar on time, but of course there was no sign of HMS *Violet* who, unbeknown to them, was still aground. Coker was far from keen on the idea of cutting loose his prize and leaving her, but March-Phillipps' view eventually prevailed. He believed that HMS *Violet* must soon appear and would look after the *Duchessa d'Aosta*. His priority was to go to the aid of the *Nuneaton*.

Having made his decision, March-Phillipps had to get himself across to the *Vulcan*, which was still side by side with the *Duchessa d'Aosta*, and attached by the hawser. There was a narrow gap between the two ships. March-Phillipps decided to take the quick route across – to jump the gap, aiming to land on the board that was still firmly fixed in place on the port side of the roof of the *Vulcan*'s wheelhouse. This was appreciably lower than the deck of the *Duchessa d'Aosta*, but seemed an easy target. March-Phillipps did not waste any time on safety precautions. No doubt, his confidence was high after the success of the previous night, but he must also have been tired.

His decision to jump the gap proved a reckless one. As March-Phillipps leapt for the plank on the *Vulcan*, the swell of the ocean dropped the *Vulcan* down even further below the height of the *Duchessa*'s deck. March-Phillipps found that he had mistimed the roll of the tug, and desperately stretched out in mid-air, reaching for the plank. Those watching from the two ships gasped in horror as, seemingly in slow motion, March-Phillipps landed out of control on the protruding forward end of the plank, beyond the metal bracket, and was flipped back, spinning into the air, as the end of the plank behaved like a diving springboard. He crashed down into the sea between the two ships and disappeared under the water, just as the swell brought the sides of the two ships bumping together. Those watching felt sure he was lost, crushed between the two ships by the force of the ocean.

Time seemed to stand still. Slowly the two ships rolled apart. Numerous pairs of eyes scanned the sea below. Suddenly, March-Phillipps popped to the surface 'like a cork', and Leslie Prout on the *Vulcan*, boat hook to hand, hauled him rapidly out of the sea, helped by some of the powerful African stokers, before the two ships could close again. March-Phillipps was shaken and bruised, but protested that he was otherwise unhurt. It had been a very close run thing, and a reminder to all those on both ships that irrespective of enemy action, the ocean itself always required very real respect. A moment of carelessness could bring death.

After his narrow escape March-Phillipps gathered himself together and gave Tugmaster Coker the appropriate order to set the *Duchessa d'Aosta* adrift. Appleyard was left in command of her, with the boarding party still on board. She could only drift, but it was already gone 1400 hrs, and March-Phillipps and Appleyard had every reason to expect HMS *Violet* to arrive at the meeting place shortly.

March-Phillipps and Coker now made haste to get back to the *Nuneaton*. In the event, it took the *Vulcan* two hours to reach her, as she and her prizes had remained stationary whilst work continued on her engine. She was still within easy sight of Fernando Po, with the current threatening to carry her closer to the shore. She was in the uncomfortable position of a burglar who, having successfully burgled a house, finds himself crippled in the roadway outside, with his stolen goods in plain view for all to see.

However, having abandoned the attempt to start the engine of the *Likomba*, Goodman was confident that the engine of the *Nuneaton* was repairable given another two hours, and that in due course they would be on their way again. When the *Vulcan* came alongside, Hayes passed this news to March-Phillipps, but asked for a tow for perhaps an hour, since he was worried that the current would carry them back closer to the Fernando Po coastline before the engine could be restarted.

March-Phillipps had the interests of all five ships to consider. He did not share Hayes' views about the danger of the prevailing current, believing that it would carry the *Nuneaton* safely beyond Fernando Po, not back into Spanish hands. Having ascertained that the *Nuneaton* would be able to get herself underway in due course, he decided after much debate that the *Vulcan* could not afford any more time with the *Nuneaton* and her prizes. It was by now 1700 hrs, and the *Vulcan* had already been away from the *Duchessa d'Aosta* for more than two hours. It would take her two hours to get back to her again, and she needed to find the liner before nightfall. Hopefully, HMS *Violet* would have taken charge of her by now, but there could be no guarantee of that. The *Duchessa*, like the *Nuneaton*, had no power, and was vulnerable to the elements as well as enemy attack. Coker had been loathe to leave her in the first place. There was a strong wind blowing, and she would be bound to have drifted some way from the point at which they had left her. Towing the *Nuneaton*, the *Likomba* and the *Bibundi* for the hour that Hayes requested would be a difficult exercise, and would slow the *Vulcan* down very considerably. Furthermore, presuming that HMS *Violet* had arrived by now (she had been due at 1400 hrs) and had put a prize crew on board the *Duchessa*, as soon as the *Vulcan* returned *Violet* could speed to the assistance of the *Nuneaton*.

It was not the most popular of decisions, since the *Nuneaton* had anticipated a rescue when she saw the *Vulcan* steaming back towards her, but it was made for sound reasons, and Hayes and Goodman accepted it with good grace. Because their journey was obviously now going to take much longer than planned, about fifty gallons of fresh water in clean containers, together with extra food, were taken on board the *Nuneaton* from the *Vulcan* before she left. Also, at Hayes' request, an extra crew member was assigned to them from the *Vulcan* to assist with the handling of the *Likomba*. The *Vulcan* then left, steaming with all possible speed to rejoin the *Duchessa d'Aosta*.

When eventually the *Duchessa* came back into sight March-Phillipps scanned the horizon anxiously for a sight of the Royal Navy ship that should have solved all his problems. Of course, there was no sign of HMS *Violet*. As they drew closer to the liner, March-Phillipps noticed that she now had a makeshift flag at her masthead, and was furious to see it was the skull and crossbones. The atmosphere on the *Duchessa d'Aosta* was still one of elation and triumph, and as she lay waiting for the Royal Navy to arrive and 'capture' her, her temporary captain, Appleyard, had seen no harm in flying a homemade 'Jolly Roger' made from two bedsheets and a pot of black paint.

March-Phillipps, after the expedition to the ailing *Nuneaton* and the non-appearance of HMS *Violet*, and burdened with the responsibility for the whole enterprise, was in a different mood.

Those on board the *Duchessa d'Aosta* felt the full force of his fury as he ordered that the flag be hauled down immediately and burnt. The Maid Honor Force and the men of Operation Postmaster were British Secret Agents, not pirates, and the *Duchessa d'Aosta* was now a British ship belonging to His Majesty the King. March-Phillipps also knew the importance of maintaining the pretence that the *Duchessa* was still in Italian hands at the moment that HMS *Violet* arrived. As always, March-Phillipps' temper was short lived. The unflappable Appleyard calmed him down, and together they began to plan their next move.

For the moment, the *Vulcan* and the *Duchessa d'Aosta* had no options. They were in the correct area for the rendezvous and could only hope that HMS *Violet* would shortly appear. March-Phillipps ordered that the two ships should proceed at half speed on a north westerly course, in the expectation of meeting the Navy vessel before too long.

The *Nuneaton*, the *Likomba* and the *Bibundi*

For the *Nuneaton*, the mechanical battle continued. As prophesied, they managed to get the engines started up again, and by 2000 hrs the *Nuneaton* was able to make some small progress against the current. However, the engines failed twice more during the hours of darkness. The Spanish lighthouse at Cape Formosa on Fernando Po winked at them throughout the night, seeming infernally near. The two stops during the night cost the *Nuneaton* two more hours of sailing and on the morning of 16 January, she broke down again. This time the cylinder head had to come off, and another two hours were wasted before the engines could be restarted. In the broad light of day, the view of the northwest coast of the volcanic island of Fernando Po was magnificent – but it was the last thing that any of the Maid Honor Force now wanted to see. Happily, no shipping appeared, and no planes passed overhead. Nonetheless, the feeling of living on borrowed time grew greater as the hours passed. Conditions on the *Nuneaton* and the *Likomba* remained cramped and unpleasant.

Lagos

Meanwhile, back in Lagos, Agent W4, Laversuch and his team waited and wondered what on earth had happened. Since the Maid Honor Force had left early in the morning of 11 January, SOE had heard nothing at all from them.

Up until the afternoon of 15 January this was to be expected, and although anxious to know whether all was going well, there had been no cause for any particular concern. But once the time of the intended rendezvous at 1400 hrs on 15 January had come and gone without news, Laversuch became seriously worried. If the raid on Santa Isabel had been successful, a signal should have been received from HMS *Violet* pretty soon after that time, saying she had seized the *Duchessa d'Aosta* and the *Likomba* on the high seas. If things had gone wrong in Fernando Po, he knew that a huge storm was about to break. Apart from anything else, quite a number of his friends and colleagues were with Operation Postmaster, and he had no idea whether they were now alive or dead. It is unlikely that Laversuch or any of his team remaining in Lagos got much sleep on the night of 15 January.

On the morning of 16 January, some good news arrived. Laversuch received a cable from Agent W53, Lake, at the Consulate on Fernando Po which said simply: '*Duchessa d'Aosta* and *Likomba* sailed midnight 14th'. The cable brought enormous relief to the waiting SOE team, although it did not supply any details of the operation, or indicate whether there had been any casualties. Later that same morning, another cable arrived that caused very mixed feelings. This was from the Royal Navy, informing Laversuch that HMS *Violet* had gone aground on the night of 14 January near Forcados. It followed that she had not made the rendezvous with Operation Postmaster. On the one hand, this explained the lack of any signal to say that the *Duchessa d'Aosta* and the *Likomba* had been boarded by the Royal Navy, but on the other it meant that Operation Postmaster remained 'adrift' and very vulnerable somewhere on the high seas. Laversuch remained a very worried man as the rest of the day passed without further news.

It was not just Laversuch in Lagos who was worried. M and Caesar in London needed to know what to tell their masters at the Ministry of Economic Warfare, the Foreign Office and the Admiralty. Spanish protests at the action in Santa Isabel had already started and were growing in number and volume. On the morning of Saturday, 17 January, with no further news, Laversuch despatched a plane to search for the Maid Honor Force and Operation Postmaster. The day passed slowly, and when the flight returned, its crew reported that they had failed to make any sighting of the Operation Postmaster flotilla. Where was Postmaster? Laversuch ordered that the plane should search again on the following Monday, 19 January.

The *Vulcan* and the *Duchessa d'Aosta*

Meanwhile, on board the *Duchessa d'Aosta*, life had settled down. March-

Phillipps had made clear there was to be no looting of the ship's possessions, since the *Duchessa* was now the property of His Majesty the King, but an exception was made in relation to provisions for their extended voyage. The three pigs that had been running free on the deck when the Maid Honor Force had boarded now fulfilled their ultimate destiny. They were slaughtered and roasted, providing the hard-worked men of Operation Postmaster with very fine fare, served up to them by the Italian prisoners.

The prisoners were all put to work without complaint. 'Second Officer' Anders Lassen and Captain J. W. W. Hallam of the Public Works Department led regular fatigue parties in order to ensure that the ship would arrive in British waters in good condition, clearing up the remains of the explosions, cleaning and polishing the ship's brass. The explosions had not surprisingly left a number of gaping holes in the deck, down one of which Lieutenant R. A. McKenny had almost fallen in the dark, after the *Duchessa d'Aosta* had left Santa Isabel harbour. Luckily for him he was spotted just in time, and a rugby tackle around his neck and upper body (which in the modern game would probably have attracted a yellow card) hurled him away from disaster.

The *Duchessa d'Aosta* was now a British ship and proper standards had to be observed. District Commissioner E. R. Ward took charge below decks and a very efficient mess and service was arranged. The Italians seemed very happy and willing, now that they realized that their fiercesome looking captors were not going to murder them in their beds. They were back in their element, doing the jobs that they were accustomed to doing, albeit for some rather unusual passengers.

There was, of course, a constant fear of discovery by an enemy plane or vessel. Also, as time went by Coker began to worry about coal stocks on the *Vulcan*, and the morale of the stokers, who were becoming tired and fed up. They had now been away from home for a week, far longer than the usual maximum of thirty-six hours. However, those concerns aside, life on the *Duchessa d'Aosta* was pretty good. As 17 January turned into 18 January, there was still no sign of HMS *Violet* so the *Vulcan* and the *Duchessa d'Aosta* continued slowly on their way.

The *Nuneaton*, the *Likomba* and the *Bibundi*

Life could not have been more different on the *Nuneaton*. During the daytime on Friday 16 January she finally reached the rendezvous area south of the Calabar and, like the *Vulcan* and the *Duchessa d'Aosta* before her, found no sign of HMS *Violet*. The *Nuneaton* was a day late, and could only presume that *Violet* had come and gone. Since the visit that March-Phillipps and the

Vulcan had paid them on the previous afternoon, Hayes and Goodman had had no contact with the other half of Operation Postmaster. They remained under strict orders to preserve radio silence. On the vastness of the ocean, the cluster of three small ships was totally alone. Hayes and Goodman were left with no option other than to continue to limp along on a course for Lagos, unable to average more than a knot and a half per hour.

During the midnight watch of 16/17 January, their solitude was disrupted. A large blacked-out ship loomed out of the night towards them. The men of the *Nuneaton* were unable to tell who or what she was as the gap between the two ships continued to narrow. They did not dare signal to her, in case she was an enemy. Hayes and his men held their breath as the unidentified ship passed dangerously near to them, but continued on its way without apparently noticing their presence. As she disappeared into the gloom, Hayes and Goodman could only hope that if she was an enemy her telegraph was not already chattering out their location to any listening enemy ears. Leaving the area of the Calabar, the weather worsened considerably and tornadoes sprung up. These might have little effect on the *Duchessa d'Aosta*, but dramatically affected life on the *Nuneaton*, the *Likomba* and the *Bibundi*.

On Saturday 17 January, during the afternoon, there was another scare for the *Nuneaton*. An aeroplane was heard approaching high above. Happily, it adopted no search pattern (it could not therefore have been Laversuch's search plane), and remained above the clouds of an overcast sky. The *Nuneaton* presumed that it must be the regular Sabena flight out of Douala.

On the Saturday night, there was yet another alarm, as a brightly lit liner passed on the port bow. Hayes and Goodman concluded that this must be the Spanish MV *Domine*, out of Las Palmas and headed for Fernando Po. The *Domine* was a regular visitor to Santa Isabel. Without incident, that ship too continued on its way, but again the worry was what her radio might be saying to others. If the *Nuneaton* and her two companions were identified for what they were, a radio message would quickly alert her enemies, be they German, Italian or Spanish, and an attack by air or sea was likely to follow. Hayes could not know what was going on in the world of his enemies, he could only assume that they were eagerly searching for them.

Each day brought its fresh batch of engine problems. On Sunday, 18 January, another cylinder head had to be removed and all the rings freed, which meant a long wait. The opportunity was taken to relieve the crew on the *Likomba*, where two men were now posted to supervise the tow. 'Changing the guard' was of itself a risky venture, since it had to be accomplished in the tiny Folbot canoes on the rolling ocean. Guise later described the changes as 'exciting'. Thankfully, there were no accidents.

The towing arrangements between the three ships also remained difficult, requiring regular attention. The fresh water taken on from the *Vulcan* was quickly exhausted and, through necessity, the crew went back to drinking the unpleasant water from the *Nuneaton*'s water tank. Progress was painfully slow and for days the island of Fernando Po remained in sight. All this put the crew's endurance severely to the test, but their cheerfulness and combined strength of character kept them going. Lieutenant Goodman, in naval command of all three ships, had the hardest job and won the admiration of the Maid Honor men for his skill, coolness, endurance and unfailing good humour in the face of every sort of difficulty, by day and by night.

The crew of the *Nuneaton* prayed their nightmare would be brought to an end by the appearance of HMS *Violet*, but the days went by and there was no sign of her. On Monday, 19 January, concern ran through the ships when yet another vessel was sighted on the horizon, closing on her from behind. This time it was broad daylight and there was no doubt that the *Nuneaton* and her two prizes would be seen. Depending on the nationality of the newcomer, would it be third time lucky – or unlucky? The *Nuneaton* with her snail's pace could take no avoiding action. The *Likomba* still bore German colours – which, depending on the nationality of the newcomer, could prove to be either a good or bad thing. As the vessel came closer, it quickly became clear that whatever she was, she was not the long awaited HMS *Violet*. She was a civilian ship.

When finally it was possible to make out her identification, enormous relief flooded through the crew of the three small ships. She was recognized as the Nigerian Government Collier, SS *Ilorin*. The *Ilorin* altered course to pass close to the *Nuneaton*, and the *Nuneaton* was able to speak with her by semaphore. Although the order for secrecy still applied, in the difficult situation they were in, and in the continuing absence of any sign of the Royal Navy, Hayes took the decision that he must ask the *Ilorin* to pass some sort of message to his bosses at SOE as to their whereabouts and well-being. When asked where she was bound, the *Ilorin* gave her destination as Port Harcourt, Nigeria, and upon Hayes' request, her Master promised to telegraph Lagos from that port to inform them that he had sighted the *Nuneaton*, and that all was well. The *Ilorin* then continued on her way and by the following day, 20 January, had arrived in Port Harcourt, where her Master kept his promise and cabled Lagos that he had passed the *Nuneaton* and her two smaller companions on the previous day, a mere five miles west of Formosa.

On the evening of 19 January an engine broke down again, another cylinder head had to be removed, and there was a further lengthy delay. The repair made, the *Nuneaton* continued, almost literally, to inch closer to Lagos. The next day, the sixth after leaving Santa Isabel, the *Nuneaton* finally enjoyed a little of the good fortune that she undoubtedly deserved. At about 1000 hrs yet another ship, this time the SS *Ajassa*, a British vessel whose Master was a longstanding personal friend of Lieutenant Goodman's, came up on them from the east. With their own engines still causing great difficulty, Hayes and Goodman decided to ask for some immediate help. Once Goodman had identified himself, the Master of the *Ajassa* agreed to give the three smaller ships a tow to Lagos. Initially, the tow proved problematic, and the three 'passengers' broke their tow ropes, but by nightfall the problems were sorted and the little convoy was under way. The emotions of the *Nuneaton*'s crew were mixed. They were of course relieved at the prospect of arriving home safely, and somewhat earlier than they had come to expect, but at the same time, having battled with adversity for so long, they rather wished they had been able to take the *Nuneaton* all the way back to Lagos themselves without assistance. Amongst the civilian volunteers, there was also a feeling that their remarkable adventure was soon coming to an end.

Now able to abandon their own troublesome engines, all aboard the *Nuneaton* and her prizes were happy at the prospect of making a little speed. They got rather more than they had bargained for. The SS *Ajassa* had been quite badly delayed by stopping for them and now wished to make up time. She steamed for Lagos at maximum speed, making some 10 or 11 knots and showing no mercy to the three far smaller ships that were bobbing along on the tow. Goodman tried to steal a little sleep, but was woken twice during the night because of fears that the *Nuneaton* might capsize. After what had happened to the *Nuneaton* at the start of their voyage to Fernando Po, the risk was a real one. Happily, however, all went well and by 1400 hrs on the following day, Wednesday, 21 January, the *Ajassa* was able to drop off her passengers at the Lagos fairway buoy. To their pleasure, the *Nuneaton*'s crew found that they were now ahead of the *Duchessa d'Aosta* and the *Vulcan*. They were the first back to Lagos, despite all the problems they had had.

A tug was sent out from Lagos to fetch them, but their difficulties were not quite over. The weather remained rough, and the *Bibundi* managed to break both a chain and two manila ropes, and to part company from the *Nuneaton*. When Goodman liaised with the tug at about 1600 hrs, after recovering the *Bibundi*, the tug decided that the priority tow was the *Likomba*, and took her alone into Lagos harbour. The *Nuneaton* tried to start up her own engines again, so that she could tow in the *Bibundi* herself, but they would not start. She had to suffer the indignity of waiting for the tug to come back for her. Eventually, the tug returned and towed the *Nuneaton* and the *Bibundi* into safe waters. It was an unsatisfactory ending to a very difficult voyage. The ships eventually tied up in Lagos harbour at 1930 hrs on 21 January.

The *Vulcan* and the *Duchessa d'Aosta*

Early on 18 January HMS *Violet* had finally managed to re-float herself and, no doubt discreetly urged on by his superiors, Lieutenant Herbert Nicholas RN headed at full speed for the rendezvous area. Having opened the sealed envelope addressed to him, he was the only one to know something of the truth about the ships they were now trying to find. For everyone else on board, the story was the one that had been cooked up and agreed by M, Laversuch, Ian Fleming, and the Admiralty – that a German signal had been intercepted indicating the presence of an unidentified civilian ship in the area and HMS *Violet* had been despatched with all speed to intercept her, and discover who she was. If she was an enemy ship, she was to be seized.

Not long after midday on 18 January, nearly three days late, HMS *Violet* sighted the *Duchessa d'Aosta* and the *Vulcan*, and came up on them. The *Vulcan* was towing the Duchessa, and it was to her that HMS *Violet* first paid attention. Just how pleased Operation Postmaster was to see HMS *Violet* at this late stage is debatable. Mr Coker was not particularly impressed when a shot was fired across his bows. At the same time, HMS *Violet* raised what Coker referred to contemptuously as a 'string of bunting' aloft, signalling: 'Stop. Heave to. Do not attempt to abandon or scuttle your ship.'

This order caused hilarity aboard the *Vulcan*. After all the effort that they had put in to steal the *Duchessa d'Aosta* from Santa Isabel harbour and haul her this far, they were hardly going to scuttle her now. Sensibly in the circumstances, Coker did not in fact stop. The *Vulcan* was travelling at a mere two knots, and Coker's view was that if she had stopped it was likely that the tow wire to the *Duchessa d'Aosta* would have fouled her propeller. HMS *Violet* then put a boat away containing a sub-lieutenant and four naval ratings, all armed, who boarded the *Vulcan*. The sub-lieutenant, who was not in on the secret, announced to Mr Coker that he was taking him prisoner in the name of His Britannic Majesty, and that the *Vulcan* and the *Duchessa d'Aosta* must now proceed to Nigeria. Having arrested him, the sub-lieutenant asked Coker where he was bound. Coker, keeping a straight face, replied according to a prepared script that they were from Bari bound for Cotonou. The sub-lieutenant remarked that Coker spoke English very well and asked if he had lived in London. There is no record of Coker's reply.

For the members of Operation Postmaster on the *Vulcan*, after all they had been through, the situation was farcical. However, they knew that it was necessary to conceal the true nature of their operation as far as possible, and to their considerable credit they did not at this stage seek to enlighten the unfortunate sub-lieutenant as to the truth. Coker and his crew remained, for the time being formally under the arrest of His Britannic Majesty, on board the *Vulcan*.

Leaving one of the armed ratings on the *Vulcan*, the sub-lieutenant and his remaining three men now took their boat on to the *Duchessa d'Aosta*. Little did they know that they were about to attempt the arrest of a body of heavily armed commandos. March-Phillipps and his men were coming to the end of a very difficult operation, and he was extremely worried about the fate of the *Nuneaton* and her two prizes, whom he had not seen for three days. All March-Phillipps wanted to do was to send HMS *Violet* as quickly as possible in search of the *Nuneaton*. No doubt he had great difficulty in controlling his notorious temper when confronted by the young sub-lieutenant and his boarding party. Their conversation went much the same way as that with Coker on the *Vulcan*. The sub-lieutenant, armed only with a sidearm and the rifles carried by his three ratings, but backed by the menacing guns of HMS *Violet*, placed the *Duchessa d'Aosta* under arrest, and forbade the crew to enter various parts of the ship including their own beer store (which cause some bitter comment later). March-Phillipps demanded to speak to the Captain of HMS *Violet* (whom he knew would have been properly briefed), and eventually the sub-lieutenant agreed to send a signal. It read: 'Captain of Italian ship wishes to speak to Captain of *Violet*. Italian Captain speaks good English.'

Lieutenant Nicholas of course agreed to speak with 'the Captain of the Italian ship', and March-Phillipps was ferried across to HMS *Violet*. He there made his report and asked that a message be sent to Lagos telling Laversuch what the position was. He also asked Nicholas to proceed with all possible speed to a position ten miles north of Fernando Po, and to search the Straits in case the *Nuneaton* had broken down again and was drifting there, short of water and food, and perilously close to enemy territory. Nicholas sent the message to Lagos and agreed willingly to search for the *Nuneaton*. However, he insisted that his prize crew stay on board the *Duchessa d'Aosta* to keep up appearances, and March-Phillipps could hardly refuse. Appleyard was put aboard HMS *Violet* to assist in the search for the *Nuneaton*, and March-

Phillipps was returned to the *Duchessa*. The *Vulcan* was then permitted to proceed with her tow to Lagos. March-Phillipps asked for a ship to escort them, now that they were officially under naval control, but it was two days before any arrived.

HMS *Violet* never found the *Nuneaton* and her companions. On Monday, 19 June, Laversuch sent up another plane but once more it failed to find any trace of the missing ships. Until it was known for certain that all the men and ships of Operation Postmaster were safely in the hands of the Royal Navy, the danger remained that they might be caught by one of their enemies, and that the truth of the whole operation would be exposed. London was becoming increasingly desperate to know what had happened to them. Again on 20 January the plane went up, yet again the search was fruitless. However, it was later that day that the Master of the SS *Ilorin* sent his promised message from Port Harcourt that all was well with the *Nuneaton* and her prizes, and in the afternoon the *Nuneaton* met with the SS *Ajassa*.

The *Vulcan* and the *Duchessa d'Aosta* finally received an escort from two Navy motor launches as they approached Lagos. On Wednesday, 21 January, after a total journey of seven days from Santa Isabel, they entered Lagos harbour at about 1800 hrs – in fact arriving before the *Nuneaton*, since she was now stranded without the use of her engines awaiting a tug. The *Duchessa d'Aosta* made an impressive and triumphant entry, towed by the *Vulcan* and escorted by the two motor launches, together with another Royal Navy corvette. The Lagos harbour pilot, Mr D. Lewis-Jones, came on board the *Vulcan* at the bar at the entrance to the harbour, took the *Duchessa* in, turned her round and backed her on to her buoy with considerable skill. A great welcome awaited her. The Governor, Sir Bernard Bourdillon, stood whisky in hand on the landing stage to cheer her in, together with a very much relieved Major Victor Laversuch and all of his SOE team. Even General Giffard turned out to welcome the *Duchessa d'Aosta* to Lagos. To the annoyance of some, Giffard, having made life as difficult for Operation Postmaster as he possibly could, now congratulated 'his' forces on their wonderfully successful operation. The Royal Navy, who in reality had imperilled the success of the SOE operation by the late arrival of HMS *Violet*, now took control of the ships in what Agent W30, Desmond Longe, described as 'a most aggressive and domineering manner; the Old Service feeling against the original thought and irregular warfare made itself felt with a vengeance'.

However, a series of congratulatory telegrams arrived from London for Operation Postmaster, sent by M at 64 Baker Street, by Foreign Minister

Anthony Eden, and by the War Cabinet. A message also arrived from the Prime Minister himself. For the members of the Nigerian Marine, and the civilians of the Colonial Service, a night of relaxed but private celebration followed on land. The commandos of the Maid Honor Force, however, remained on board ship. Their presence could not be acknowledged in any way. They remained the most secret of agents.

Thus on the evening of 21 January 1942, all of the five ships finally rested safely in Lagos harbour. The operation, despite all the problems it had faced, had been a complete success. M's Secret Service had pulled off a magnificent coup, and March-Phillipps and the men of his Maid Honor Force had proved themselves to be outstanding Commando Secret Agents. They had not needed to utilize their 'licence to kill', although they had been armed and ready to do so. Anders Lassen, in particular, probably regretted that he had still to wet the blade of his knife with enemy blood.

For Ian Fleming, the performance of the Maid Honor Force, which he himself had in part enabled through his work with M, was clearly inspirational. He stored it away in his mind and eventually used these men to create James Bond, the perfect Secret Agent. True, no individual member of Maid Honor Force could be said to be perfect, but Fleming rolled March-Phillipps, Appleyard, Hayes and Lassen into one, and the result was as near a perfect Secret Agent as was possible. Ironically for Fleming, the only weak link in Operation Postmaster had been the Royal Navy. The failure of HMS *Violet* to arrive at the rendezvous on time had exposed the operation to substantial unnecessary danger, which happily they had survived.

When eventually Victor Laversuch submitted his full report to M, he included in it a poem written by an anonymous poet (possibly Leonard Guise) from amongst the men of Operation Postmaster. It cannot have been the work of Gus March-Phillipps since it lacks the refinement of his verse.

ADDIO A FERNANDO
I had an affaire with a Duchess,
To the north of Fernando Po,
First she hated to be in my clutches
But she had not the heart to say No!
Her husband was down with the fishes[1]
Where the Duce's argosies go,
So I had an affaire with the Duchess
To the north of Fernando Po.

[1] The *Duke of Aosta* had previously been sunk in the Mediterranean

ESCAPE

She was proud and haughty and handsome
(as Italian Duchesses go)
And when I looked over her transom
I whispered softly and low
'T'amo molto bene ma duchessa'
Come with me where the sea winds blow'
She answered softly 'Oh yessir!'
Anywhere, to leave Fernando Po.'

She was tired of the Dons of Espana
And spaghetti a l'Italiano.
So she promised to make it manana
And I said I would be her true beau;
She said life for her was too boring,
The tempo of things was too slow
So I eased her away from her moorings
With the aid of some fuse and some 'dough.'[2]

'I'm tired of the Bay of Isabella
Where the weeds and the barnacles grow
Of bad brandy, cheap fags, sarsparilla,
So please won't you take me in tow.'
So we hitched up together in the gloaming
Neath the Southern Cross hanging low
And, hand in hand, we went roaming
Far away from Fernando Po.

Though the method at first seemed too drastic,
I had to persuade her to go;
With a quarter of good standard plastic
And Caramba! we kneaded it so![3]
Each seaman and fireman and stoker
Made sure that we got a good blow
And eyre longe[4], Grace a dieu and old Coker
We persuaded the Duchess to go.

---

[2] Plastic explosive
[3] A reference to shaping the plastic explosives used to break the cables
[4] A deliberate pun on the names of Major John Eyre and Captain Desmond Longe

And we sailed to the break of the morning
Where the sunshine started to glow,
As I leant on her breast in the dawning
She said: 'Though you may think me slow
My heart is just aching for kindness
And my bottom is foul down below
Thank God for the night and its blindness
So Fernando Po! Addio!'

The high spirits of the men of Postmaster after the operation had been completed are obvious from the poem. It had been a very difficult operation indeed, and yet against all odds and in a very old-fashioned British way, with their amateur civilian volunteers recruited at the last minute, they had won through. On 31 January Laversuch sent his full report to London and attached a note to Caesar, paying tribute to Governor Bourdillon and the men of the Nigerian Colonial Service: 'I must confess that at times we had our bad moments, especially when the intercepting vessel went ashore and we received news that the smaller towing craft had broken down. . . You will note that I have been insistent in my praise of H.E. Governor Nigeria and his splendid men, and I confirm this to you personally, as without their aid I cannot visualise that the Postmaster would have been a success.'

But in fact the operation was not truly over. The final and most vital part was to ensure that the truth of what had happened should remain a secret. Nobody should ever know for certain how the three enemy ships had come to leave the harbour of Santa Isabel.

CHAPTER 23

The International Cover-up

No doubt enormous relief was felt in all British quarters when the five ships finally reached Lagos harbour on 21 January. The days between 15 and 21 January had been very difficult ones. As soon as the ships disappeared from Santa Isabel harbour the Spanish press had begun howling in protest, no doubt egged on by Italy and Germany, and initially it had been impossible for the Admiralty to issue any response at all. They simply did not know what to say, and no creative writing by Ian Fleming was able to help them. From the morning of 15 January, Fleming and his Admiralty team were under considerable pressure to answer the allegations being made against the British Government and the Admiralty, but without knowing what had really happened, and whether the men and ships of Operation Postmaster had got away, they could not commit themselves to any official reply.

However, Reuters, the international Press Agency, reported from Spain on 17 January: 'The Falangist newspaper "Arriba" says that a Free French Destroyer entered the harbour of Santa Isabel on the Spanish Island of Fernando Po and seized three Axis merchant ships. . . there entered the bay off Santa Isabel de Fernando Po a destroyer flying a flag already well known in the annals of filibustering, and after dropping depth charges to break the moorings of three enemy merchantmen there, it seized them and towed them from the port. . . the plot was planned with the most revolting perfidy and embraced every form of cowardice and cruelty. It seems that all members of the crews, who were in the port of Santa Isabel in accordance with their absolute right, were assassinated.'

In Berlin a similar story was circulating that the attack had been by a Free French Destroyer, adding: 'The raid was carried out at a moment when the ship's officers were ashore. Members of the crew who remained on board are reported to have been shot.'

In neutral (but pro-German) Sweden, also on 17 January, came a report that: 'The British Fleet, completely disregarding Spain's neutral status, entered the port of Saint Isabel, Fernando Po Island, off the Cameroons, and attacked

Axis ships anchored in the port according to a despatch picked up here. Spanish Government and public are highly indignant over this British action.'

The confusion was gratifying, as was the allegation against the Free French, but the allegation that the crew of the captured ships had been shot caused obvious concern. However, with the true fate of the ships still unknown by the third day after the raid (all due of course to the failure of HMS *Violet* to make the rendezvous), Britain's hands remained tied. The Lords of the Admiralty had approved a final draft of the intended communiqué, which read as follows:

> Information has been received that the Italian SS *Duchessa d'Aosta* and the German tug *Likomba* have been intercepted off the west coast of Africa by one of our patrols. It appears that these ships were endeavouring to reach the Vichy port of Cotonou to take on sufficient fuel to enable them to continue on their voyage to a port in German-occupied France.

The communiqué could only be released, however, once all five ships were safely in the hands of the Royal Navy. Admiral Willis was instructed on 17 January to inform the Admiralty as soon as the ships had been seized. There was still no sign of them.

Further Spanish claims quickly followed, saying that casualties had been suffered amongst the crews during the raid, and the press in Spain claimed to be outraged. Ambassador Sir Samuel Hoare cabled from the British Embassy in Madrid that article after article in the Spanish press was complaining bitterly at the inexcusable violation of Spanish territorial waters. He quoted as an example, 'the repugnant outrage of Fernando Po has put an end to meddling and to tolerant courtesies. Spain engages herself solemnly before the world to shed the last drop of her blood in order to prevent similar aggressions being carried out with impunity. We declare plainly that in the event of any fresh attempt against Spanish non-belligerency, our guns will fire in defence of Spain's inescapable obligations.'

There had, however, as yet been no formal protest by the Spanish government against Great Britain. The Spanish were obviously still far from certain as to what had actually happened. Nonetheless, Ambassador Hoare in Madrid reported on the evening of 17 January that use was being made of the newspaper reports of the incident to stir up feeling against Great Britain as being ultimately responsible. There were demonstrations in Madrid against the British, and Hoare repeatedly asked if the allegations were in fact true.

Finally good news arrived on 19 January, when a cable from Lieutenant

Nicholas on HMS *Violet* reached Admiral Willis. It was in the following terms: 'Have intercepted *Duchessa d'Aosta* in 003 degs 53' North 02' East steering westwards. Have placed prize crew on board without opposition. Escorting to Lagos unless otherwise ordered.'

Enormous relief swept through Baker Street and the War Cabinet upon receipt of this official confirmation that the *Duchessa d'Aosta*, at least, was now in safe hands. On the same day, understandably feeling the pressure, Hoare in Madrid cabled again: 'Could you inform me most urgently whether the incident did take place, and if so, what happened? If de Gaulle's did make a cutting out expedition, His Majesty's Government will be held responsible on the ground that the ships were under our control. Anxiety is widespread amongst our friends and I am naturally most anxious to reassure them as soon as possible.'

The *Duchessa d'Aosta* was not yet safely in port and the whereabouts of the *Nuneaton* and her two prizes was unknown. However, the Admiralty and the British Government now felt sufficiently confident to issue a 'holding communiqué', and on the evening of 19 January, no doubt with Fleming's assistance as he had promised, a communiqué was released:

> In view of the German allegations that Allied naval forces have executed a cutting out operation against Axis ships in the Spanish port of Santa Isabel, Fernando Po, the British Admiralty consider it necessary to state that no British or Allied warship was in the vicinity of Fernando Po at the time of the alleged incident. As a result, however, of the information obtained from the German broadcasts, the British Commander in Chief despatched reconnaissance patrols to cover the area. A report has now been received that a large unidentified vessel has been sighted, and British naval vessels are proceeding to the spot to make investigations.

This imaginative and mainly untrue communiqué, once issued, became and had to remain an official part of His Majesty's Government's account of the Fernando Po incident. The Government knew they now had the *Duchessa d'Aosta*, but until she was safely in Lagos harbour and they had been fully briefed, they continued to hedge their bets, and were not prepared to say more. Sir Samuel Hoare confirmed from Madrid on the evening of 19 January that the Spanish were still uncertain as to what had actually happened.

The Admiralty, and SOE, remained understandably nervous and Fleming's work was far from finished. The following day Admiral Willis, Commander in Chief South Atlantic, received a cable from London (approved by the First

Lord of the Admiralty) saying: 'It is of the utmost importance that nothing shall transpire to connect HMG with this operation. Consequently, it is suggested that:- (a) the presence of the Colonial Tug [i.e.the *Vulcan*] should be explained as having been diverted to provide assistance for HMS *Violet*, (b) Raiding party must be taken off captured ships and Colonial tug before, repetition before, arrival at Lagos, (c) crew of *Violet* must be silenced and greatest care taken to ensure that no leakage occurs through crew of Colonial Tug, (d) steps should be taken to see that all the members of the raiding party including natives [black Africans] are prevented from returning to Lagos until after all official inquiries or other resulting proceedings have been completed, (e) All members of enemy crews should be kept under closest guard. Vessel should not be placed in prize pending instructions.'

On 20 January Willis received another cable, stating the obvious – namely that HMS *Violet* must not be sighted from Fernando Po. He was able to reply on the same morning to the effect that *Violet* had now reported that the *Nuneaton*, with the *Likomba* and the *Bibundi* in tow, had apparently broken down a mere ten miles from Fernando Po, and that *Violet* was searching for her, but was under strict instructions not to be visible from Fernando Po. No doubt this did little to calm the strained nerves in London. Also on 20 January, the Foreign Office finally cabled Sir Samuel Hoare in Madrid to explain the truth behind the 19 January communiqué, saying: 'For your own information, although no British or allied warship was concerned, the operation was carried out by SOE with our approval. Every precaution has been taken and it seems reasonably certain that no evidence can be traced of our participation in the affair. One of the ships concerned carries an extremely valuable cargo and is herself a valuable modern liner. If you receive a protest or enquiries from the Spanish Government you should confine yourself to drawing attention to the Admiralty communiqué and to saying that you are reporting the matter to His Majesty's Government. Please burn this telegram after perusal.'

Secrecy remained paramount. Caesar cabled W4 in Lagos: 'Grand show, warm congratulations, well done everybody. All that is required now to put finishing touch on fine job is observance of the utmost secrecy.' A further cable from London to W4 suggested that, once back, the Maid Honor Force and the Colonial Government personnel might be sent off on an 'extended cruise' to keep them out of the way.

In Madrid, the Falangists were organizing noisy demonstrations outside the British Embassy and various other British premises, including the Ambassador's residence.

On 22 January the news that London had been waiting for finally arrived. A cable from Willis, sent the previous day, arrived at the Admiralty: 'Likomba and Bibundi have been intercepted and boarded south of Lagos (Nigeria) today January 21, and are being sent into Lagos under armed guard.' A second telegram arrived from Willis saying: 'Duchess d'Aosta, Likomba and Bibundi all arrived Lagos between 16.00 and 18.00 21 January. It appears that their wish was to reach Vichy territory when intercepted.'

No doubt there was much cheering and relief in Whitehall on 22 January as there had been upon the arrival of the five ships in Lagos on the previous day. But the cover story had to be maintained. Even within Willis's official 'War Diary of Commander in Chief, South Atlantic' the truth could not be told. The relevant entry reads: 'On 18 January "Violet" who had been sent to patrol the Gulf of Guinea as the result of a broadcast stating that Axis shipping at Fernando Po had been seized by the Free French Warships, intercepted and took in prize the Italian ship "Duchessa d'Aosta", which was taken to Lagos.'

Meanwhile, from Madrid the British Naval Attaché reported that the Spanish Navy at present thought the raid had been carried out by the Free French without orders. Ambassador Hoare, however, remained exceptionally nervous. He undertook to 'take his stand' with the Spanish solely upon the basis of the 19 January communiqué, but demanded that he be consulted about all SOE activities affecting Spanish territory in future, because he feared serious repercussions.

The formal Spanish protest was prepared on 22 January. Hoare notified the Foreign Office that he had been told of a draft note that the Duke of Alba, Spain's Ambassador in London, proposed to deliver shortly to His Majesty's Government. The Duke of Alba had told him, however, that it was based on hypothesis. He also told Hoare that after the explosion of the 'depth charges', English had been heard on board the *Duchessa d'Aosta*, and that they knew that the ship had now been taken to Lagos.

In response, Fleming at the Admiralty drafted a second communiqué. This was sent on 22 January to Hoare, asking for his comments. The communiqué was again succinct, and simply announced the interception and capture of the *Duchessa d'Aosta* on the high seas. It claimed that the ship had been in difficulties and had been taken to a British port. Although now ready in draft form, the communiqué was not to be officially released until 24 January.

Also on 22 January Caesar could not resist sending a telegram to W, Louis Franck, one of the original architects of Operation Postmaster, who was now in Long Island, New York, visiting his family and advising the US Office for

Strategic Services (the OSS), which after the war evolved into the CIA. Sending the telegram in plain English (and a little French), without official code, and under his real name and address, Caesar said simply: 'Grand old fellow Directeur de Poste [i.e. Postmaster]. Everybody delighted his success on which our sincerest personal congratulations.'

Prime Minister Winston Churchill and the relevant members of the War Cabinet had been kept aware of the progress of the operation, and once the ships were safely 'home', Hugh Dalton, the Minister of Economic Warfare, wrote on 23 January to Churchill to update him, sending copies of his letter to, amongst others, Clement Attlee and Anthony Eden. He said:

> During the night of January 14/15, a tug and a launch, manned by picked crews selected from SOE personnel in that part of the world, entered the harbour of Santa Isabel, boarded two vessels, severed their cables by means of small explosive charges, and took them in tow. Progress towards Lagos was slow, since Duchessa d'Aosta could only be towed at three knots, but a telegram received today from our party on arrival in that port, says: 'Casualties our party absolutely nil. Casualties enemy nil, except for a few sore heads. Prisoners: Germans nil, Italians: men 27, women 1, natives 1.' The same telegram reports that the two ships arrived at Lagos 8.00pm yesterday.
>
> There is reason to suppose that the Spanish authorities are aware that a large tug of unknown origin entered the harbour and took the vessels out; but that is probably all that they know. We do not believe that they will be able to prove that the tug was British, and the greatest precautions have been taken to see that no information leaks out at Lagos. Thus, all the SOE personnel engaged have now been dispersed and are safely out of the reach of any interrogation; while the crew of the two seized vessels have been sent to an internment camp one hundred and fifty miles inland. Although, as you probably know, the incident has given rise to a violent press campaign in Spain, it is not yet certain that the Spanish Government will protest officially. Even if they do, I should imagine that we should not have very great difficulty in denying responsibility. Further, I have a shrewd suspicion that, though they may protest, neutral governments are not unimpressed by such suspected manifestations of force, which they tend to interpret as meaning that His Majesty's Government feels strong enough to disregard legal formalities in the prosecution of total war.
>
> The Duchessa d'Aosta (which you know was duly intercepted by the Navy) carried a cargo. . . This haul must be placed on the credit

> side in estimating the success of the operation. On the debit side, undoubtedly, lie any difficulties which we may experience with the Government of Spain; but, as I have said above, I should myself judge that these would not weigh very heavily in the balance.
>
> I should like to express my high appreciation of the attitude of the Foreign Secretary [Anthony Eden] in allowing the operation to proceed in spite of the political risks involved, and my gratitude to the Admiralty and to the Governor of Nigeria for their invaluable assistance. Great credit, I think, also attaches to SOE West Africa, who planned the operation in minute detail and successfully carried it out.

Thus the highest level of the British Government was fully informed as to what had really happened in Fernando Po. The operation had been a great success, it was to be denied, and hopefully the Spanish could be persuaded not to pursue the matter further.

Another telegram was received in the early morning of 24 January from Hoare in Madrid, reporting that the Spanish Government had concluded its early enquiry into the affair, and had now delivered a note of protest saying that 'all the facts and, even more than the facts, deductions which may reasonably be admitted, force it to believe that the act of aggression was carried out by ships and elements in the service of British interest or of direct collaborators with the British forces operating on the west coast of Africa' and making 'a most energetic protest against this act of aggression carried out in her sovereign waters, unquestionably the most serious of all those carried out since the beginning of the war.'

The good news to be gleaned from this was that the Spanish still clearly did not actually know who had carried out the raid. No evidence had apparently yet emerged to prove that the operation had been mounted by British Forces. It therefore remained deniable. On the evening of 24 January, the Admiralty released its second communiqué. This one read:

> With reference to their previous statement concerning the Axis ships reported by the Germans to have sailed from Fernando Po, the Admiralty announces that the British warships despatched to make investigations have intercepted and captured the 8,000 ton Italian ship Duchessa d'Aosta. The Italian ship, which was in difficulties, has been taken into a British port.

This second communiqué, again little more than pure fiction, became the second foundation stone of the official British position. As the days passed, it remained clear that M's Secret Agents had done their job exceptionally well. The Spanish genuinely did not know who had taken the ships. The obvious inference was that it was Great Britain and her allies, but there were enough other possibilities to keep the matter open to doubt.

On the afternoon of 28 January the Foreign Secretary, Anthony Eden, had a meeting with the Duke of Alba, the Spanish Ambassador to London, at which the Spanish note of protest was discussed. He later reported what had happened in a memorandum to Hoare, the British Ambassador in Madrid. Eden's memorandum reads:

> During our conversation this afternoon, the Spanish Ambassador raised the incident at Fernando Po, which he said had considerably puzzled him. He asked me whether I could tell him anything about it. I replied that I was as puzzled as his Excellency; that I knew no more than the Admiralty communiques, and that the whole story was most confused and bewildering. The Ambassador agreed that it was, and said that he would greatly like it if we were able to pin the guilt upon the Germans. I agreed with him that this would be most satisfactory, and added that I had asked the Admiralty if at any time they got any information to let me know, in which event I would of course be glad to pass it on to his Excellency. Meanwhile we had received a note from the Spanish Government, to which I would return an answer in due course.

The file copy of this memorandum carries a number of endorsements by those at the highest level who read it. One says, 'Excellent'. Hugh Dalton's note perhaps says it all. He wrote simply, 'Yes!'

That same afternoon, 28 January, a cable arrived from Ambassador Hoare dated the previous day. It recounted two rumours then current in Madrid. One was that 'Spanish Reds' had seized the ships, the other was that the Free French had bought the ships from the Italians, and had taken them to Libreville. Officially therefore, the most important aspect of Operation Postmaster could now be declared a success – its deniability. So brilliantly had the operation been conducted that nobody seemed able to pin it on the British, and the British were quite happy to deny all knowledge of it, even at the highest level.

However, unknown to Whitehall, there remained one very real danger that everything might yet fall apart. The Secret Agent to whom much of the credit for the success of the operation was due, Richard Lippett, was still stuck on Fernando Po. Until he was safely back in British territory the British Government's lies about Operation Postmaster, and their connivance at a breach of international law, might yet be exposed.

CHAPTER 24

Richard Lippett

The immediate aftermath in Santa Isabel had been one of confusion. Peter Lake commented later that initially the Spaniards and Africans alike were highly amused by the incident, judging by the laughter and excited chatter that came from the plaza below the consulate. A number of visitors came to the British Consulate to gossip about what had happened, including Collinson, the British agent for the Ambas Bay Trading Company, and a man called Adolfo Jones, who shared accommodation with Zorilla.

The Germans and Italians were furious. Captain Specht, of the *Likomba*, had no doubt as to who was responsible. At 0130 hrs on 15 January, still very drunk as a result of the dinner party, he went round to the British Consulate and burst in, marching through the pantry towards the sitting room, where he was intercepted by Agent Lake. Specht, swearing and cursing, shouted, 'Where is my ship?' Lake told him to get out, whereupon Specht lost all control and hit Lake in the face. This gave young Peter Lake the excuse that he was hoping for, and he and Godden, who had arrived on the scene, then 'knocked the stuffing' out of Specht. Lippett's report describes the detail:

> Godden rushed to the affray and put some heavy North of Scotland stuff on Specht and literally knocking the s—-t out of him. When Specht saw Godden's revolver he collapsed in a heap, split his pants and emptied his bowels on the floor.

Specht was restrained, the police were called, and Specht was handed over to them in 'rather a dilapidated state'. He was arrested and taken into the custody of the Spanish authorities. An armed guard was then placed around the British Consulate, nominally for its protection from further attack. A significant guard remained in place for at least ten days, comprising six African police by day, and between four and eight European NCOs by night. Specht was released by the Spanish authorities later that day, but a report came to the Consulate from African sources in the town that Specht was threatening to kill both Lake and Godden.

Peter Lake, the new Assistant Consul, wrote a formal letter of protest about Specht's behaviour to the Spanish Governor, expressing the Consulate's concern over what constituted a breach not only of civil, but of international law, since diplomatic premises under the protection of Spain had been violated. Bearing in mind the breach of international law that the British themselves had just committed in the harbour, the opportunity to write such a letter must have given Lake much pleasure. Lake asked for the continued police protection of the Consulate, and that the only other British subjects on the island, Mr and Mrs Collinson of the Ambas Bay Trading Company and Mr Lippett of Messrs John Holt, also be given protection. Lake hoped to use Specht's intemperate conduct as a means of gaining Spanish police protection for SOE's key agent, Richard Lippett.

Lake signed off with the words, 'Pray accept the assurance of my highest respect and esteem'. He did not need to add, 'but remember, Governor, we know all about your lady in the bath!' His Excellency the Governor General of the Spanish Territories of Spanish Guinea, F. L. Soraluce, replied in writing on 17 January. He informed the Consulate that he had called the German Consul and Captain Specht in for an interview, and that they had given assurances that no such incident would occur again. However, the police protection of the Consulate would be continued, to avoid another incident 'at all costs'. Soraluce concluded by expressing his regret that such a thing had occurred, signing off with, 'Please accept, Señor Consul, the assurance of my most distinguished consideration'.

There is no doubt that by behaving in the way that he did, Specht had played right into British hands. It is also likely that his reaction was not unexpected. Specht was known to be rather a difficult man, who took considerable pride in his ship the *Likomba*. Either he or his second in command normally slept on board each and every night. He had not attended the first party and had only been persuaded to attend the second by the entreaties of Frau Luhr. At the party, he had been continuously plied with drink. It was entirely predictable, therefore, that when he realized that his ship had been stolen he would explode, and that his anger would be directed at the British (all the more reason, incidentally, for the impressive Richard Lippett to be tucked up in bed at Montilla's Hotel at the time). It was predictable also that Specht would march round to the British Consulate and misbehave.

When Lake commented later that Specht's attack on him had given them 'the excuse that they wanted', he was speaking on two levels. No doubt Lake, a relatively young man, enjoyed getting the better of Specht physically, but more importantly Specht's invasion of the Consulate and assault on Lake gave the British the opportunity to play the aggrieved party under international law at a time when otherwise every finger might be pointed against them. Just as Heinrich Luhr was unknowingly manipulated into 'fronting' the parties, Specht may well have been manipulated into behaving in a way that gave the British the opportunity to go onto the 'front foot' at a vital moment.

The Governor's letter was undoubtedly sympathetic, and makes no suggestion that the British themselves were suspected of a far more serious breach of international law by 'stealing' the *Duchessa d'Aosta* and the *Likomba*. But of course, by their 'honey pot operation', SOE had already assured the sympathy of the Governor. Looked at by historians with the benefit of hindsight, the preparations by M's Secret Agents for Operation Postmaster on Fernando Po can only be described as brilliant.

Lake reported that the day following the raid Santa Isabel was full of rumours. Responsibility for the raid was placed variously at the doors of the Free French, Vichy France, the USA (who had only very recently joined the war), the British, and even anti-Falangist Spanish 'pirates'. Heinrich Luhr was reported as suggesting that Germans might have taken the *Duchessa d'Aosta*, and that if they had those responsible would be honoured with the Iron Cross. Many of the local Spaniards openly expressed their admiration and amusement at the way the operation had been timed and carried out. The *Duchessa d'Aosta* had been a nuisance and they were glad she was gone.

However, the mood changed in Santa Isabel when the inevitable, and vigorous, investigation into what had happened to the ships began. Unfortunately, the investigation was to be handled by the Falangist party, through the Captain of the Colonial Guard, Captain Binea. When the arrests and interviews started, Lake and Godden found that the invitations they extended to various locals to attend at the Consulate for drinks were being refused. Gradually they found themselves cold-shouldered and ostracized. But whilst those in the Consulate were relatively safe, Lippett, the key agent, remained very exposed. He was officially just a British engineer working in a Spanish state. He had always been the most vulnerable of the SOE agents on Fernando Po and yet had been the most heavily involved. Lippett's intention was to sit out the initial storm, tidy up his work at John Holt's and then to leave the island on 23 January.

Initially, all went well for Lippett. On 15 January he was woken at half past five by Señora Montilla, one of the owners of the hotel, and in the relative cool of the early morning went to play badminton as usual with a group of Spanish friends on a piece of ground behind the British Consulate. He found that the Consulate was surrounded by soldiers who forbade them to play. The soldiers told him that the *Duchessa d'Aosta* and the *Likomba* had been taken from the harbour by a fleet of battleships. Not yet knowing of the incident with Specht, Lippett no doubt feared that the British Consulate was under guard because Great Britain was thought to have been responsible for the previous night's raid.

He and Señora Montilla walked to the front overlooking the bay, and observed that the ships were indeed gone. Señora Montilla had absolutely no doubt who was responsible and commented, 'Well done. The English are very smart.' Lippett issued the first of many denials, saying, 'No, the English would never do a thing like that, especially in a Spanish port.' Señora Montilla's response was simply to say, 'Just wait and we shall see, it is a good thing that they are away, I did not like either of them.'

The wild rumours about the possible fate of the ships were rife all that day. Zorilla's mysterious absence was soon noted and the finger of suspicion was pointed firmly at him. His business partner, Señor Moras, was amongst the first to be arrested and interviewed. One rumour had it that Zorilla had been seen slipping the mooring ropes from the *Duchessa d'Aosta*, and that he had then left Santa Isabel on board the ship. Another had it that Zorilla had filled those at the dinner party so full of drink that when the incident occurred they could do nothing, and indeed could hardly walk. Lippett, a consummate actor, remained silent and maintained an attitude of astonishment about what had happened.

On that day and the next, 16 January, the Falangists made wholesale arrests. Suspicion quickly fell on the dinner party and the obvious fact that it had taken the officers away from their ships. Those who had been present and who were known to be friends of Zorilla (apart of course from the ships' officers) were all arrested, including Adolfo Jones who shared his house with Zorilla. The absence of Zorilla was taken by Captain Binea to confirm his complicity in the affair. Dr Sola, who had been at both dinner parties, and the pilot, Alacon, who had been away from Santa Isabel on the night of 14/15 January but had been involved in the giving of the first dinner party, became the prime suspects. When Pilot Alacon flew back to Santa Isabel from nearby Moka, soldiers rushed on to the airfield and arrested him before he even had time to alight from the plane. Great activity was observed in the Falangist party HQ, which was a part of the Government Office building. All those arrested were taken there, and were grilled in Gestapo-like conditions, though there is no evidence of any physical torture having been used.

At 1610 hrs on 16 January Agent W51, Godden, cabled Lagos. He reported that although many Spanish citizens had been interrogated, there was as yet no suspicion of Lippett. The general impression was one of satisfaction at the departure of the three ships, and acceptance of the efficiency of the operation, which had been a complete surprise. Godden reported there were many rumours flying around Santa Isabel, including the suggestion that he, Godden, and Lippett were fully aware of the operation. Godden emphasized that he did not consider the latter to be a serious threat. The cable also reported the conduct of Specht, and that the Fernando Po Chief of Police (Llompert) appeared friendly and had given the Consulate a 24-hour guard. Finally, said Godden, 'We are watching developments.'

Lippett found himself under enormous pressure, but maintained his façade of innocence and surprise. He quietly carried on with his work for John Holt's, observing the well-known maxim, 'Keep Calm and Carry On.' Had all gone as planned with Operation Postmaster, the British cover story would have come into play on 15, or at the latest 16 January. However, because of the difficulties that HMS *Violet* was experiencing, the British remained silent as the days passed. This enormously increased the pressure on everyone connected with Postmaster on Fernando Po, including inevitably Lippett himself.

During the first two confused days, Lippett's local friends remained warm towards him, but by 17 January, the third day after the ships had disappeared, the British had emerged as the most likely suspects. Word of the unpleasant interrogations going on at Falangist HQ had spread, and this was something that everybody wanted to avoid. Most of Lippett's friends became fearful that their relationship with him might be misinterpreted, so they began to avoid him. Lippett rapidly became publicly ostracized.

The reaction of his friend the bank manager, Señor Ruiz, was typical. On 17 January Ruiz asked Lippett to call upon him, which Lippett did. Once in private, Ruiz asked Lippett point blank whether he had had anything to do with 'the ship business'. Lippett assured him, on his honour, that he had not. Ruiz then held out his hand and said, 'Ricardo, I believe you.' He explained, however, that he could not openly remain Lippett's friend, because of the views of his Falangist government. He went on to say he had been asked by Lippett's other Spanish friends to explain the position to him, that although they too always wished to be friends with him, they could not go against their government.

All of Lippett's Spanish friends then deserted him except the Montillas, who ran the hotel where he lived. At the same time, the local German and

Italian communities made clear their resentment of him. One morning, a large number of Germans and Italians came to Montilla's Hotel, and pressurized Lippett over a period of about two hours with menacing looks. The Montillas, showing that they remained true friends, sat beside him in the lounge of the hotel throughout and then took him off to lunch with them.

All this while, the Maid Honor Force and the five ships in their small convoy remained missing somewhere in the South Atlantic, and no announcement was forthcoming from the Admiralty or the British press to help Lippett, or the British diplomatic mission on Fernando Po.

On the afternoon of 17 January, Richard Lippett finished work at John Holt's around four o'clock and returned to his room at the hotel. He was tired but so far, despite the unpleasantness and defection of his Spanish friends, all had gone reasonably well. However, he feared that he was living on borrowed time and eventually Captain Binea's enquiries must involve him. He had prepared the story that he was going to tell. At 1730 hrs that evening, just after he had finished his bath, a knock came on the door. Lippett opened it to find a visitor whose arrival he had been dreading on the doorstep. The Secretary of Police required Lippett to accompany him, then and there, to the Falangist party HQ. Lippett had no choice but to comply; he dressed, and left with the Secretary.

Lippett describes the Falangist HQ as a Fascist-like place, where no defence lawyers were allowed. He was taken to a small upstairs room, where Captain Binea awaited him. Lippett describes Binea as a fearsome looking man, with a long nose and deep sunken eyes hidden behind glasses. The Chief of Police, Miguel Llompert, with whom Lippett had always been on courteous terms, was there too, but Binea was clearly in charge. Nonetheless, Llompert greeted Lippett pleasantly enough and shook hands, which Lippett took as an encouraging sign.

Binea simply told Lippett to sit down. A light was adjusted to shine in his eyes in order to make him feel uncomfortable, to increase the pressure and to make it difficult for him to see the expressions on the faces of his interrogators. Lippett was then required to swear an oath on the bible that he would tell the truth, as was customary in an interrogation. He duly took the oath. He continued to do his best to present an entirely calm exterior.

Binea began with a threat that if he lied, he would be deported to mainland Spain and would be sentenced to serve a long sentence there in a prison fortress. Lippett replied firmly that although it had long been his wish to visit Spain, he had no desire to be locked up in a fortress, that he did not anyway like lies, and that he would not now, at the age of forty-five, start to tell them.

Binea smiled. Lippett then proceeded to lie almost constantly, and with considerable expertise, over the next four hours.

Binea was an aggressive but not very good interrogator. He had been working on the enquiry for three days, but at this time only two of the Spanish suspects remained in custody, the pilot Alacon and Dr Sola. Zorilla was believed to have played a significant part, but he had disappeared and was thought now to be far away from Fernando Po. Binea had concluded, accurately, that the dinner party had been a planned distraction to take the officers away from their ships before the raid took place. He did not know who was behind the raid, but believed, rightly, that if he could identify who had organized the dinner parties that would lead him to the culprits.

Binea's enquiries led him to believe that Lippett had in December paid 2,000 pesetas to Alacon, which he believed that Alacon had used to pay for the first party, and that Lippett had given an expensive gold bracelet to Dr Sola, the other prime suspect. Binea also knew that Lippett had been to Lagos in December. Lippett, of course, did not yet know how much Binea knew, but he had long since worked out what his own story would be.

The threat of imprisonment in Spain having had no apparent effect, Binea began his interrogation in dramatic style. Thrusting out his arm directly at Lippett, so that his fingers almost touched Lippett's face, he demanded:

> 'How much money have you spent on the officers and men of the *Duchessa d'Aosta*?'
> Lippett: 'No money whatsoever!'
> Binea: 'What are you doing on this island?'
> Lippett: 'I thought everybody knew that –I am here on behalf of John Holt's.'
> Binea: 'Why have you stayed here six months?'
> Lippett: 'Because the work justified my remaining.'
> Binea: 'Why did you go to Lagos on 27 November?'
> Lippett: 'Because I was called for a conference.'
> Binea: 'No other purpose?'
> Lippett: 'No.'
> Binea: 'Do you mean to tell me that you did not spend any money on the Italians?'
> Lippett: 'No, we are at war with them, and I never did like them. If I had money to spend, I would spend it on Spaniards, who I like very much.'

Chief of Police Llompert intervened at this point to confirm that Lippett was very partial towards Spaniards.

Binea then moved to the question of the gifts that Lippett had brought back with him from Lagos, asking:

> 'Why did you not accept payment for the presents that you brought from Lagos?'
> Lippett: 'Because it was near Christmas and they were Christmas presents. One does not usually accept money for presents.'
> Binea: 'You appear to have a lot of money?'
> Lippett: 'Yes, I have £125 a month and certain entertaining allowances.'
> Binea: 'You appear to spend money freely?'
> Lippett: 'Yes, always, and I reserve the right to do what I like with my money.'

The questioning continued. After a time, there was a break, probably for Binea's benefit rather than Lippett's. Glasses of water were brought and Lippett, who was clearly feeling confident, made a point of sniffing his, partly to check whether it had been 'spiked' with something, but rather more to annoy Binea. Before the questioning resumed, Lippett asked how long it was all going to take, since he was expected for dinner at the British Consulate that night. Binea's reply was ominous: 'As you are suspected, we may keep you here until we are satisfied, which might take days.'

Lippett, now that it was confirmed that he was a suspect in the affair (as had been the obvious inference from Binea's questioning), asked to consult with his Consul. Binea responded by simply saying, 'I do not care for your Consul.' With perfect timing, a message was at this point brought into the room to the effect that one of the British Consular servants was outside with refreshment for Richard Lippett. Godden and Lake had obviously learned of Lippett's interrogation quite quickly, probably from the Montillas, and this was a way of making clear to Binea that the Britsh Consulate knew what was going on – and also of reassuring Lippett that his fellow agents Godden and Lake knew his whereabouts.

On receipt of the message the light was turned away from Lippett's face and the servant was allowed to come in. In true British style, he had brought a whisky and soda, together with some food. Lippett wisely rejected the whisky, and asked for some plain sodas. He could not risk his wits being befuddled to any degree by alcohol. The servant left to fetch some, but in fact did not, or was not allowed, to return. Lippett ate the food that had been sent in.

After this interlude, the light was turned back on to Lippett's face, and the interrogation continued. During the break, Binea had clearly decided that he would now move to the heart of the matter, and he began by asking rather dramatically: 'So you deny that you gave the pilot Alacon 2,000 pesetas?'

Lippett: 'No, I gave it to him.'
Binea: 'Why?'
Lippett: 'Because it was given to me to give to him.'
Binea: 'Who by?'
Lippett: 'Zorilla.'

With that, Binea left the room for a few minutes. In his absence Llompert said, apparently sincerely, to Lippett: 'Don Ricardo, I am sorry you have been mixed up in this.'

Lippett, keeping up his act, replied rather angrily: 'Yes, this is the curse of having too big a heart, and, furthermore, of liking Spaniards.'

Binea returned with a case, which he slowly opened and withdrew from it a newspaper parcel. This was clearly done for effect and Lippett wondered what Binea had got. As the newspaper was unwrapped, he saw that it contained the gold bracelet that Lippett had brought back from Lagos and had given to Dr Sola. He waited for the inevitable dramatic question from Binea.

'I suppose you do not know anything about this?'
Lippett: 'Oh yes, I gave this to Dr Sola to give to his wife.'

Binea looked astonished at the admission, and asked:

'Why did you give it to Dr Sola?'
Lippett: 'Because I was asked to.'
Binea: 'Who asked you?'
Lippett: 'Zorilla.'

Richard Lippett believed that if you wanted to deceive anyone, you should never deviate from the truth further than was necessary. Thus, it was true that he had given the 2,000 pesetas to Alacon and the bracelet to Dr Sola, though untrue that he had done so at Zorilla's bidding. He had prepared for the expected interrogation with care, and on the basis that Zorilla must by now be safe in Nigeria and could therefore be made the scapegoat. Using as many half truths as possible, he had crafted an account that he hoped would defeat all possible lines of enquiry.

As the interrogation continued, Lippett developed his story. He explained that he had been friendly with Zorilla, who spoke good English, and had seemed to be a very nice fellow. Before he went to Lagos on 27 November Zorilla had asked him to purchase a gift on his behalf, either a watch or a bracelet, since he, Zorilla, wanted to give someone on Fernando Po a present. Zorilla had given Lippett 1,250 pesetas with which to buy the present. Lippett said that he had purchased a bracelet (the one that Binea had showed him) in Lagos for twelve pounds and eighteen shillings, which, at the exchange rate of 100 pesetas to the pound, left him a few shillings out of pocket. Being a generous man, and having exceeded his instructions, he was happy to absorb the loss. He returned to Santa Isabel with the bracelet and gave it to Zorilla.

Lippett said that some days later Zorilla had asked for his help in arranging two dinner parties for the officers of the *Duchessa d'Aosta*. Zorilla appeared to be in a bit of a quandary over how to go about it. Lippett had met the Captain of the *Duchessa d'Aosta* several times, and he didn't see why they should not all have a good time at Christmas. Zorilla had told him he was given the money to hold the parties from a source that he was not permitted to disclose, and that he wanted to enlist the services of Pilot Alacon and Dr Sola, both of whom were friendly with Richard Lippett. Lippett told Zorilla that he did not mind helping him, but on condition that his part in the affair was kept confidential and did not leak out to his Consul.

Lippett explained that the matter had been duly arranged, that he had given 2,000 pesetas each to Dr Sola and to Pilot Alacon on Zorilla's behalf, so they could pay for the parties, and had given Dr Sola the bracelet. Lippett had later suggested to Dr Sola that he should give the bracelet to his wife since it was Christmas.

The explanation seemed, for the time being at least, to satisfy Binea. Lippett was told that he must put his account into written form, and that if he refused he would not be allowed to leave. He duly signed a witness statement confirming his account, and was eventually allowed to leave the Falangist HQ at 2130 hrs, after an interrogation of about four hours.

Binea shook hands as he left, and said good night. He told Lippett to continue his life as normal, but not to talk about the matter. Llompert seemed keen to make amends, saying to Lippett, 'What a pity, Ricardo, that this has happened. I really have a great regard for you, but you understand that I have to do my duty.' Lippett thanked him for being gentlemanly about it and Llompert then asked him to come to his house for a drink. Lippett, believing that his nerves had suffered enough for the night, politely declined. Lippett went to the Consulate for his dinner. He asked Godden and Lake not to press him about the details of his interrogation. He had been ordered by Binea not to discuss it but, more importantly, felt it best to keep the matter to himself on a strict 'need to know' basis.

Lippett believed that his acting had been good enough to convince Binea and Llompert of his innocence. However, though Zorilla was gone, Dr Sola and Pilot Alacon remained in custody and were therefore a potential danger to him. Lippett hoped his own lies, together with his skilful use of Zorilla during the arrangements for the party, would be enough to protect him. Sola and Alacon had known absolutely nothing about the raid itself. They were both innocent men: each was saying he had been duped into helping with the party, which of course was true. Lippett intended that Binea should believe it had been Zorilla who duped them, not he himself.

As the third day after the raid came to its close in Santa Isabel, it still seemed as though the Spanish authorities had no positive evidence of British involvement. So far so good, even though the Maid Honor Force was still missing on the high seas. The following day was Sunday, 18 January, and Lippett attended the Mission Church and read the lesson as usual. He tried to maintain an outward appearance that life was normal. It was a tense day, but it passed quietly enough. Lippett hoped that it would only be a few days now before he would be able to leave Santa Isabel. He did not know it, but matters outside Fernando Po improved considerably that Sunday, since the *Vulcan* and the *Duchessa d'Aosta* finally liaised with HMS *Violet* and came, at last, into official British custody.

On Monday, 19 January, Lippett went to work again at John Holt's and tidied up his affairs, paying the men off. The renovation work had been completed and, subject to Binea's consent, he was now free to leave. Lippett had booked a ticket to leave the island by steamer for Douala on 23 January. He returned to his hotel after work and tried to relax.

However, at 1800 hrs once again a knock came on his door. When Lippett answered it, the Secretary of Police awaited him, with a fresh summons to attend the Falangist HQ at once. This time, when Lippett arrived, he sensed a different atmosphere. The initial dramatics were repeated and the light was again shone in his face, but Binea greeted Lippett by shaking hands, the strain of the investigation was clearly showing on Binea's face, and he seemed demoralized. Unknown to Lippett, a significant discrepancy had emerged between his own account and the account given by the pilot, Alacon, as to how the 2,000 pesetas for the party had been paid across.

Binea sat for a time with his head in his hands, and then with a big effort said: 'I have asked you to call here to reconsider the question of your giving the pilot 2,000 pesetas. Did you do so or not?'

Lippett said that he had, adding: 'You asked me why I did so, and I gave you the reason.'

Binea then warned Lippett that he would confront him with Alacon, who was saying something very different. Lippett was worried, but felt he had no option but to stick to his guns. What Lippett was saying was true, he had given Alacon the 2,000 pesetas, and a lot more besides. However, it was logical that Alacon, under arrest and under interrogation, might have preferred to say that he had got the money from a Spaniard, particularly one who had now fled, rather than an Englishman (or more precisely, a Welshman).

Pilot Alacon was then brought into the same room as Lippett, and was asked to tell Lippett who had paid him the money. Alacon said it had been Zorilla, not Lippett. Binea then asked Lippett to reconsider his own account but Lippett stuck to his story, saying that he had paid Alacon, albeit at Zorilla's request. Alacon again denied this, and indeed denied ever receiving any money from Lippett, apart from an occasion when Lippett had paid him 350 pesetas for some cigars. Neither man mentioned the fact that Lippett had also given Alacon fifty pounds in sterling (the equivalent of a further 5,000 pesetas), in payment for Vice Consul Michie's trips in the Governor's aeroplane with his camera over Santa Isabel harbour.

Rather quaintly, to bring the session to a close, Binea then had it put in writing that the two men gave different versions about the 2,000 pesetas, and asked Lippett and Alacon each to sign the document to this effect.

Binea then took Lippett to another room and asked him point blank again whether it was true that he had given Alacon the 2,000 pesetas. Lippett again said yes. That finally seemed to convince Binea of Lippett's innocence. He put a hand on Lippett's shoulder, and said, 'If you ever meet Zorilla in Nigeria or anywhere else, will you kill him for me?'

Lippett promised Binea that in that unlikely event he would certainly make life hot for Zorilla, complaining that Zorilla had 'used him as he would use an old shoe'. Binea then grasped Lippett very firmly by the hand, shook it, and allowed him to leave. On this occasion the interrogation had lasted two and a half hours. At least for the time being Lippett felt he had convinced Binea that he was telling the truth. Later, he would discover that he had done too well.

Godden had been watching the situation carefully. Lippett was indeed apparently a free man at the end of the second interrogation, nonetheless Godden appreciated the importance of getting him off the island and out of Spanish hands as a matter of urgency. On the next day, 20 January, Godden cabled Lagos asking for a launch to be sent to take off Lippett, and also Lake, as soon as possible. He gave them no reason, although in truth Lake was leaving so that he could give SOE an up to date report on recent developments.

Now it became evident that Lippett had done rather too well under interrogation. Binea decided that he wanted to call Lippett as a witness at what was to be a trial (or court martial) of Dr Sola and Pilot Alacon. Lippett was still booked to leave the island by steamer for Douala on 23 January, and he had cancelled his rooms at Montilla's Hotel from that date. However, when he submitted his passport through the British Consulate for his exit visa, it was refused by the Fernando Po authorities. Binea had decided that Lippett was not to be allowed to leave Fernando Po until after he had given evidence at the trial. Godden, from the Consulate, submitted a protest on Lippett's behalf but to no avail.

Lake duly left Santa Isabel on 23 January. As a diplomat his exit could not be blocked and he was travelling to Free French Douala, where he would report back in detail on Operation Postmaster and the aftermath in Fernando Po. Lippett therefore, when he lost his rooms at Montilla's Hotel, was at least able to move into the quarters that Lake had left vacant at the Consulate without rousing undue suspicion. There Godden could keep an eye on him, though he could do little to help.

On 27 January a report came from Lake in Douala to London, saying that following his interrogation by the military tribunal (Captain Binea), Lippett was not allowed to leave Fernando Po. The protest by Godden had elicited the response from the Governor of Spanish Guinea that although Lippett was not considered implicated in the affair, he could not be granted an exit permit until authorization was received from Madrid.

From Lagos Agent W4, Laversuch, wrote to Caesar in London on 31 January 1942 to bring him up to date: 'I am still a little worried about W25 [Lippett] but I cannot see how the Spanish Government can prove that he had a finger in the pie, as the man who threw the party is now in Lagos, and W25 himself was not at the party.'

As the days went by, the strain began to tell on Lippett. He was not a young man and he had been almost continuously in the field for six months. He had pulled off a magnificent coup by arranging the dinner party distraction, and had survived two gruelling interrogations, convincing both the Head of the Colonial Guard and the Chief of Police that his lies were the truth. Godden became worried that Lippett might finally crack, particularly when in late January Lippett became seriously ill with malaria.

Lippett himself was worried about the pressures of giving evidence against Dr Sola and Pilot Alacon, both of whom had been his friends and had, at least in part, been duped by him. He also worried that, given enough time, the Spanish authorities might find out rather more about his covert activities and some of the bribes he had paid for information to various people (including black Africans) on the island.

SOE were of the view that it was desirable to get Lippett out, but preferred that he should leave through proper channels. There was a quandary. If Lippett stayed, despite his resolute performance so far he might eventually crack. However, if formal protest at his detention on the island were made at too high a level it might cause eyebrows to be raised, and could suggest his involvement in some way in the raid. Lippett was officially just an engineer employed by John Holt's and of no particular importance. If he left illegally, as Zorilla had done, that also would seem suspicious and be taken to support those who accused the British of carrying out the raid.

Finally, the decision was taken that protest should be made at a level relative to his supposed position as a British engineer working in a neutral country, and no more. Therefore, the formal letter of protest already written by Godden from the local Consulate in Santa Isabel was backed up by one from John Holt's, who claimed that Mr Lippett was urgently required by them for work elsewhere. The protests were useless. The question of the trial was apparently now being handled from Madrid, and any 'special relationship' between the Governor in Santa Isabel and the British Consulate could have no effect. There was no point in bringing covert pressure upon Governor Soraluce, because he was no longer in effective control.

The situation worsened when Lippett was told by one of his contacts that a Spanish gunboat was on its way to Fernando Po, carrying a general who would preside over the court martial. There were rumours that interrogations by the general would make Binea's efforts pale into insignificance. January turned into February, Lippett fell very ill with malaria for over a week, and during that time there was no question of him doing anything. When he had recovered sufficiently, he found that he was still not allowed to leave. While Lippett was ill, on 4 February, Godden reported to Lagos that although he thought it unlikely that the authorities had any proof of his complicity, it was dangerous for Lippett to remain on Fernando Po.

At 1515 hrs on 6 February 1942 Lippett himself cabled to Lagos telling Agent W4, Laversuch, that he was still being refused permission to leave Fernando Po. He said that he believed telegrams were now being deliberately mutilated and/or held up, that his early departure would appear to be imperative because he didn't like the situation at all, and that he had been ill and under the doctor for eight days. As a result W4 cabled London, saying again that while the Spanish apparently had no proof of Lippett's complicity he was worried that they might later use 'third degree' methods, which could prove dangerous. W4 stated that he believed it to be necessary for Lippett to leave before the court martial, and asked: 'Would you approve Lippett leaving Fernando Po without, repeat without, an exit permit?'

Three days later, on 9 February, Laversuch was even more worried about Lippett, who was still far from well. He cabled London again, this time saying, 'he is losing his nerve and it would be better from every point of view if his departure could be hastened'. Lippett was later to dispute this, saying in his own report later that he was 'not nervous personally, but for the cause only'.

In truth everybody was becoming increasingly worried about Lippett, including, obviously, Lippett himself. He was a key man, who, if the Spanish managed to break him, knew enough, even on the 'need to know' basis under which he had operated, to satisfy them that the British had been responsible for the raid. He was in reality a prisoner on the island, he was far from well, and there was an obvious danger that he might finally crack up. The enormous pressure Lippett had been under before, on, and most certainly after the night of 14/15 January 1942 is illustrated by the concluding paragraph of his final report to SOE, written in late February 1942 on Fernando Po. It reads: 'There are many more things I would have liked to have said and told you, but one has to be most careful. This report has been written under difficult circumstances, behind closed doors, and in great heat, so I trust you will forgive mistakes.' He also commented that he was thankful that no younger man had had to go through what he had gone through at the Falangist HQ, as they might have broken a younger man down.

As Lippett became increasingly worried about his prospects, he consulted with Godden about the possibility of leaving the island by irregular means, as Zorilla had before him. Godden, weighing up the situation, concluded that it was no longer safe for Lippett to stay and agreed he should get off the island as soon as possible, by whatever means he could. Lippett was in effect a hostage to fortune whilst he remained on the island, and for the British the stakes remained extremely high. Godden knew that exposure of the truth of Operation Postmaster at this stage would do significant international damage to his country, since by now, His Majesty's Government had formally adopted the position that the *Duchessa d'Aosta*, the *Likomba* and the *Bibundi* had been discovered and seized on the high seas by HMS *Violet*. At the highest possible level, Foreign Secretary Anthony Eden (who in fact knew exactly what had happened) had denied any knowledge of British involvement in the Santa Isabel raid.

On 20 February, Godden asked SOE to send a launch to take Lippett off the island covertly. They declined to do so. Now Richard Lippett took his own decision: he would leave the island of Fernando Po secretly, whatever his bosses in SOE might say. It was more easily said than done. He was still suffering from intermittent bouts of fever, and he faced the difficulty that he was now under regular surveillance. Some suspicion of his complicity in the raid itself had again surfaced and, more importantly perhaps, the Spanish authorities were now well aware that Lippett was very eager to leave Fernando Po and to return to Nigeria. Lippett knew that to try to escape covertly was a desperate throw of the dice. If he was caught, he would be in very much greater trouble than he was already.

Godden entirely agreed with Lippett's decision and offered to help him in his attempt to escape, but Lippett turned him down. If it all went horribly wrong, Lippett did not want the Consulate to be embroiled in the mess that inevitably would follow. The fact that he was currently living in the Consulate would create enough problems even if he succeeded in his escape.

Lippett had long cultivated contacts amongst the black African population of Fernando Po, many of whom were pro-British Nigerians. They had proved valuable as a means of obtaining intelligence, and now Lippett decided to use them to facilitate his escape. He had played no direct part in Zorilla's departure, but he knew how it had been done. First, Lippett had to evade the surveillance that was in place on him. This he did without great difficulty, and made his way apparently unnoticed to an African fishing village. There he made arrangements for a native canoe and its crew to come and pick him up, to take him to the mainland. He sheltered in the hut of a friendly fisherman while waiting for the boat to arrive. Something then went wrong.

Lippett had been on the loose for more than twenty hours when either he was betrayed, or he was simply unlucky. It may have been that he had been spotted by unsympathetic eyes on his journey to the village. In any event, the boat that he was waiting for did not arrive, but the Spanish police did. Lippett, not a small man, was hidden under the floor of his host's hut whilst the police searched the village. After two hours, believing that the police had gone, the fisherman summoned Lippett out from his hiding place. The boat that he had arranged for had still not arrived, and Lippett presumed now that it was not coming. The 'hue and cry' was obviously on and it would only be a matter of time before he was caught unless he could leave the island. The consequences of capture would be dire.

Lippett decided to try to make a break for it. His very simple plan, born of desperation, was to steal one of the small native dugout canoes from the seashore in front of the village, and to paddle for the Nigerian mainland.

Leaving the cover of the hut, Lippett began to make his way quietly and carefully towards the canoes. Suddenly, he found himself confronted by a policeman. The fisherman had been wrong, not all of the Spanish police had gone. Happily, Lippett, despite his weakened state, had not lost his old skills as a heavyweight boxing champion. He laid the policeman out with his fists before he could effect any form of arrest. There was no possibility of going back now – Lippett had just added assault to the list of his many other crimes against the colony of Spanish Guinea. As he headed towards the beach he encountered a second policeman, and treated him in similar fashion to the first. Unfortunately, in one or other of these confrontations he broke one of his thumbs, which was to cause him very great pain during the voyage that followed.

Having dealt with the 'opposition', Lippett successfully launched one of the small dugout canoes from the beach and set off out to sea. To propel the dugout Lippett had to use a paddle, which with a broken thumb was extremely painful. The journey to mainland Nigeria was about forty miles, across a perilous and ever changing sea. Every stroke hurt him, but he did not give up. At this point Richard Lippett had run out of options, he had to go on. It took him fifteen hours to complete the journey. Finally, on 26 February 1942, Lippett landed on the Nigerian shore. Exhausted and in considerable pain he was nevertheless a free man again, and the secret of Operation Postmaster was secure.

Having rested, Lippett reached Lagos on Sunday, 1 March, and submitted his detailed written report, which he had carried with him on his journey. His condition upon arrival in Lagos was officially described as consisting of a broken thumb, recurrent fever, and 'cracked nerves' as a result of severe cross-examination and nervous tension. Richard Lippett had served his country well, but he was now totally exhausted. In accordance with the general policy of dispersing all those who knew the real story of Operation Postmaster as quickly as possible, Lippett immediately received orders to return home to Britain. He embarked from Lagos on 5 March 1942 on the SS *Mary Slessor*, bound for England.

Lippett's report was forwarded to M in London. W4 attached a covering note as follows:

> Careful reading of this report will, I think, make it clear to you that Lippett was in a highly nervous state when he left Fernando Po, and

> we are of the opinion that, taking this into consideration, it is wise that he is no longer there. It is our opinion that if he had remained for the Court Martial, under pressure of cross examination he would most likely have confessed completely his complicity in the affair. . . The Governor's Pilot and the Doctor appear to be in a serious situation. . . the least they can hope for is several years imprisonment, with a distinct possibility of being executed. . . Taking everything into consideration, we think that Lippett has fully accomplished the work which he went to do, and whilst it is unfortunate that two Spaniards have to stand their trial by court martial, this, the present time, is one of war and they, presumably, fully realized the risk they were running when the party was organized.

In the light of what became known later about Lippett's achievements, that covering letter from Laversuch is faint praise. There is no doubt that Lippett carried out his work in Santa Isabel to the highest possible standard. His role was a vital one in the plot, and the successful ruse to lure the officers away from the two target ships was of substantial importance to the success of the raid. Lippett survived what were undoubtedly two very difficult interrogations and successfully arranged his own escape to Lagos. His courage and resourcefulness was of a different character to that of the Commando Agents of the Maid Honor Force, but was in equal measure to theirs, and of equal importance to the success of the mission.

Godden, still the Acting Consul in Santa Isabel, reported on 11 March that he had expressed his official regrets for Lippett's unauthorized departure to the Spanish Government, but that the matter seemed quickly to have died down. The key witness having disappeared it seems that both Dr Sola and Pilot Alacon, if ever in fact tried, were acquitted. Much later, as Lippett had always wished, the finger of suspicion in Santa Isabel moved in the direction of the Nazi, Herr Heinrich Luhr, apparently the host at both dinner parties, and the German was accused of being a British spy.

In the shorter term events proved that Richard Lippett was undoubtedly right to have left when he did. Three weeks later, on March 18, substantial military reinforcements numbering 17 officers and 18 sergeants, all Europeans, together with 419 other ranks, landed at Santa Isabel, thus doubling the size of the garrison. By May, the Governor had also been changed and a Lieutenant Colonel Mariano Alonso Alonso was in post.

CHAPTER 25

Dispersal, Recognition, Reward

Upon their arrival in Lagos the men of Operation Postmaster had been rapidly dispersed. All the commando agents of Maid Honor Force were ordered to make their way back to England by a variety of routes. They were not allowed to sail home together in the *Maid Honor* herself. The risk of capture and interrogation was now unacceptable, and in any event there were questions about the seaworthiness of the *Maid* to make the long journey home, since she was increasingly suffering from attack by worm. Agents W.01, March-Phillipps, and W.02, Appleyard, were required to return home immediately, since a diplomatic storm was still brewing and London wanted the fullest briefing. They were found berths on the first suitable ship bound for Britain by the shorter route. On arrival in London in February they were debriefed by M and by the Admiralty. M's diary records meetings with March-Phillipps on the evening of Thursday, 12 February and again on the following Monday, 16 February. Both March-Phillipps and Appleyard had already submitted their detailed and highly confidential written reports, and it appears that the debriefing in London was deliberately done by word of mouth only. No doubt, Ian Fleming had already read the written reports in his role as assistant to Admiral Godfrey. Now he had the opportunity to hear all that March-Phillipps and Appleyard had to say about the operation in person. A little later M and SOE held a discreet party in their honour, which Fleming is bound to have attended.

When interviewed many years later about the source of his inspiration for James Bond, Fleming was to say that 90 per cent of it came from what he had learned during his intelligence career. Fleming was a very imaginative and creative writer, and the James Bond plots took his Secret Service agent all over the world of the 1950s and 1960s. The true inspiration for the James Bond character, however, can only have come from the real M's real Secret Service, and from the men of Maid Honor Force and their exploits. Fleming was a deskbound warrior – as Godfrey's assistant he knew too much to be risked in the front line. He never went into action himself, except once as an observer from a safe distance. He was an ideas man and a bon viveur, who would certainly have been won over by the romance and flair, the courage and achievements of Gus March-Phillipps and the Maid Honor Force. Fleming had many interests in common with March-Phillipps and Geoffrey Appleyard, but they were the achievers, he merely the observer. James Bond was in due course to fight fictional battles against powerful and evil international forces such as SPECTRE, SMERSH and Ernst Blofeld. March-Phillipps, Appleyard, Hayes, Lassen and their colleagues fought their real battles against the ultimate and only too real evil force, Adolf Hitler.

Whilst Fleming and others in London were admiring the success of Operation Postmaster, Gus March-Phillipps was already planning for the next stage of his war against the Germans. As early as 17 February 1942, the day after his second debrief meeting with M, March-Phillipps submitted a plan for the formation of a new covert unit, the Small Scale Raiding Force. This was to be a commando intelligence unit that would strike across the channel to seize German prisoners and other sources of intelligence from selected targets. With M's support, March-Phillipps put the proposal to a meeting at the Combined Operations HQ on 18 March 1942 and it was agreed in principle. March-Phillipps then set the unit up at Anderson Manor in Dorset. The men of his Maid Honor Force all joined him there, and he began recruiting other suitable personnel.

It is very interesting to note that just two days after March-Phillipps had gone before the Combined Operations committee and obtained approval for his project, on 20 March 1942 Ian Fleming (now styling himself on internal correspondence simply as 'F') put forward a very similar project to his boss, Admiral Godfrey – one for which historians have subsequently given Fleming great credit. Fleming proposed a 'Naval Intelligence Commando Unit', that would accompany forward troops attacking enemy naval installations, proceeding with the second or third wave of the attack, and would make straight for any buildings where intelligence documents might be found, seize them, and return directly with whatever they found. This idea was adopted by Naval Intelligence, and led to the setting up of what became known as 30 Assault Unit.

The only logical explanation for the timing of Fleming's proposal is that March-Phillipps had discussed his idea for the Small Scale Raiding Force with Fleming in the weeks after his return to England, and that Fleming had decided to borrow the idea to use within the context of his own work in Naval Intelligence. The similarity between the two proposals is too striking for it to be coincidence. No doubt March-Phillipps would have had no objection to this (if Fleming told him), in the cause of fighting a common enemy.

For Gus March-Phillipps, his return to London in February 1942 brought a happy development. At M's offices in Baker Street, he met the beautiful young Marjorie Frances Esclamonde Stewart, an actress who had enlisted in SOE in August the previous year. They fell in love, and were married after a whirlwind romance. When he first began chatting to her, she told him that she was the lift attendant – even inside the SOE building, you didn't discuss what you really did with anybody. In truth, she was initially a secretary in the Polish and Czechoslovak section of SOE, and later became a Conducting Officer, responsible for the care of female SOE agents who were undergoing training before being sent abroad.

Marjorie Stewart became one of the first women to master the art of parachuting. Before meeting Gus March-Phillipps, she had heard of his exploits. She recalled many years later how, when she was first working at SOE, she never asked unnecessary questions but listened with great interest to all that was being discussed around her. One lady who was very regularly mentioned was 'May Donna', and Marjorie Stewart wondered for many weeks who May Donna might be. It was only later that she realized the female everybody was talking about was in fact her future husband's ship, the *Maid Honor*. Gus and Marjorie were married two months after their first meeting, on 18 April 1942, at the Church of Our Lady of the Assumption in Warwick Street, London W1. M was a guest at their wedding, as were a number of the men of the Small Scale Raiding Force.

Anders Lassen also found himself a prospective wife in the weeks after Operation Postmaster. In the interests of security, the remainder of Maid Honor Force had been split up and sent home at a more leisurely pace. A number of them went via Cape Town, where they enjoyed two weeks of leave, others stayed in Nigeria either on board ship or up country. Lassen was one of those who remained in Nigeria. He and Desgranges were sent up country to assist at Agent W39, Dismore's training school for black African guerrillas at Olokomeji. Lassen enjoyed his training role, but was distracted by a very attractive young African girl who lived in the neighbourhood. He later wrote home, 'Unfortunately, I left Africa just when I was completing negotiations to buy an exceedingly pretty wife. At first the father wanted the shocking price of £15 and I was only going to pay £10. He had agreed that I could have her on trial, and if she was any good I was to pay £10 and two bottles of Trade Gin: if not, the deal was to be called off except for the gin. A great pity for that and other reasons that I was recalled.' It being Anders Lassen, the hunter, who tells the story, it might well be true – and James

Bond, whose attitude to women was very much the same, might well have negotiated such a deal.

All of the men of Maid Honor Force eventually reached home safely, where they were reunited under March-Phillipps' command as a part of the new Small Scale Raiding Force. As recounted earlier, Richard Lippett, when he successfully reached Lagos in early March was sent straight home to England. Señor Zorilla was given a passage to the USA, where he was found a good job 'somewhere in the American continents'.

The other SOE men, Agent W4, Laversuch, Agent W10, Guise and the others who had been on the *Vulcan* and the *Nuneaton*, settled back down to their usual roles in West Africa. Desmond Longe was sent back to England for an operation on his hands. He travelled by air, together with another Postmaster 'veteran' Police Superintendent John Harris, the head of Lagos CID, via New York, where he reported to W, his old boss, on the details of Operation Postmaster. When Longe arrived back in London, he underwent an operation at St Thomas' Hospital. The damage to his hands was obviously severe, since he records that he remained in St Thomas' for three months.

The four men of the Nigerian Marine returned to their normal duties, all sworn to secrecy so far as Operation Postmaster was concerned, as did those in the know on HMS *Violet*. The volunteers from the Colonial Service went back to their desks. Their position was perhaps the most difficult of all – like the others they were sworn to secrecy, and were allowed to tell no one of their remarkable adventure. They could receive no medals and no public recognition for what they had done.

The unfortunate Italian prisoners, once they arrived at Lagos, were also in the unhappy position of knowing too much. It was to be a long time before they saw the sea again. They were kept segregated from other prisoners of war and taken to a prison camp at Imuahia in the Nigerian interior, where they remained apart from all other prisoners until after the Italian Armistice in September of the following year.

His Majesty's Government stuck to its cover story during the months and years that followed. The affair dragged on and eventually, in late 1943, prize court proceedings were quietly commenced in the English High Court in relation to the *Duchessa d'Aosta* and her cargo. When the Spanish government sought to play a part in these, Foreign Minister Anthony Eden wrote to the Spanish Ambassador in London on 22 December 1943, concluding his letter once more with the official lie: 'As the Spanish Government were informed. . . the *Violet* had been despatched to the area in question in consequence of information obtained from German broadcasts.

It is clear therefore that the interception of the vessel on the high seas by HMS *Violet* cannot justify representations from the Spanish Government in respect of her capture.'

The *Maid Honor* had to be left behind in Lagos, much to the sadness of her crew. It is said that she returned to her original life as a fishing boat, and in due course plied the coast between Lagos and Freetown, before finally succumbing to the persistent attentions of the sea worms.

When attempts were made to get the *Duchessa d'Aosta* ready for sea, not surprisingly she was found to have significant problems with her engines. These were eventually fixed. A small fire broke out on board on 31 January 1942, whilst she was moored in Lagos, but happily it was quickly contained and extinguished and did not do any substantial damage. A Royal Navy prize crew sailed her back to Greenock, Scotland, where she eventually arrived in early July 1942. She was handed over to the Canadian Pacific line, and her name was changed to the *Empire Yukon*. She was used as a troop transport ship until the end of the war. She was valued for requisitioning purposes at £98,000. The greater part of her cargo was sold, and realized £188,706.

The *Likomba*'s name was changed to the *Malakal*, and the *Bibundi* became the *Kalomo*. Both ships remained in West Africa and were put to work. Neither became a part of the British prize proceedings.

Congratulations on the success of the operation poured in from every quarter. Even General Giffard wrote to congratulate Laversuch and the Maid Honor Force, though by late March of 1942 he was again recording that he was 'unhappy and seriously disturbed about the activities of SOE', suggesting that they be disbanded or placed under his command, because as things stood, they were 'a menace to the safety of the colony'.

There could be no public recognition of the Postmaster raid, because of course it had never officially happened. Further, as was said in one memorandum, it would be hardly tactful for His Majesty's Government publicly to award decorations for a breach of neutrality. Thus, medals and promotions could be awarded to the military personnel and to the men of the Nigerian Marine, but only if the true reason for them was not disclosed, and provided that the public entries for the awards in the *London Gazette* were sufficiently obscure. The true citations were never published.

March-Phillipps wrote on 23 January to the Director of Marine, Lagos. He said:

> I wish to thank you for your co-operation and for the loan of the tug 'Vulcan'.
>
> I wish also to state my appreciation of the excellent services

> rendered by Mr Coker, Mr Oldland, Mr Duffy and Mr Goodman. I have no hesitation in saying that the success of the project was very largely due to the work of these four men. They worked almost without sleep for a whole week, under difficult and dangerous conditions with the utmost cheerfulness and disregard of themselves.
>
> I would particularly recommend to your notice Mr Coker, the tugmaster, for his handling of the tug during the operations, and on her entry into Lagos harbour. I consider Mr Coker to be a brilliant seaman at all times, and at times an inspired one.
>
> I would also like to commend to your notice the fine seamanship of Mr Goodman, who with Mr Hayes, my second officer, brought the Likomba and Bibundi to Lagos under the most difficult conditions with an engine that was constantly breaking down; and that of Mr Jones, the Senior Pilot, in bringing the Duchessa to her moorings against the flood tide and without the use of the steamer's helm.
>
> I would like to thank you once again most sincerely and to express my admiration to the Nigerian Marine, Lagos, to whom I owe much.

March-Phillipps did not forget young Buzz Perkins, now just eighteen, and still in Nigeria. He wrote to Perkins' mother to reassure her of her son's well-being:

> I have been meaning to write to you for some time to give you news of Buzz. I must say that he is very well and should be enjoying himself at the moment seeing Nigeria with some very good friends he has made in the Colonial Service. He is on leave and has elected to spend it in that way.
>
> Some months ago I recommended him personally for his excellent services under very difficult conditions and I have since had further cause to congratulate him. He has been a great help to me during the past year, and I can honestly say that I have always found him more than ready and willing. Nor has he been any trouble, in spite of his youth and spirits.
>
> You have no need to worry about him. He is having, perhaps, the best training and the best life a boy of his age could have – perhaps could even imagine. I hope when you see him, which may be quite soon, you will find him a great credit to you.

March-Phillipps was not, of course, at liberty to tell Mrs Perkins what her son had been up to. For a young man of just eighteen, he had already enjoyed a remarkable career as a secret agent, having sailed with the *Maid Honor* from Poole to Freetown, served on her during four voyages along the West African coast, and taken part in Operation Postmaster. March-Phillipps had been forced to leave the *Maid Honor* behind in Lagos, but he had brought home her log, which he later presented to Buzz Perkins as a souvenir.

March-Phillipps also wrote to M in London on 26 February 1942 to make certain recommendations and commendations regarding others involved in Operation Postmaster:

> I wish to recommend Anders Lassen for a commission in the 'Maid Honor' force. His work was the most outstanding in the operation on the Duchessa. I wish to recommend Lieutenant Hayes for promotion to Captain. He is a most accomplished all round fighting soldier and took charge of the operation of cutting out the Likomba and Bibundi with outstanding success. I should like to draw your attention to the work performed by Captain Appleyard on board the Duchessa. He was the only member of the cable cutting party to succeed in jumping from the tug to the liner over a gap of at least six feet, as the tug at the time was receding owing to a slight shock when she actually came alongside. When one of the forward cables did not blow, he placed and blew the charge in a matter of thirty seconds. He proved himself a most efficient officer with a great gift for organization and command.
>
> I should also like to commend Major Eyre and Mr Longe who cut the stern cables with phenomenal speed and were a great stand by during the ten days which it took to complete the operation.

Upon those recommendations, Private Anders Lassen was duly commissioned as a Second Lieutenant. He attended no officers' training course. The pips were simply sewn on to his uniform. Graham Hayes also got his promotion to Captain. As March-Phillipps' letter makes clear, Appleyard had already received promotion to Captain by the time the letter was written. Gus March-Phillipps himself was promoted to Major.

André Desgranges, since he was on loan from the Free French Forces, could only be given an honorary promotion by the British. He became 'Second Lieutenant' Desgranges, was allowed to wear a Second Lieutenant's uniform, and thereafter received a junior officer's pay.

Caesar suggested that Agent W10, Lieutenant C. A. L. Guise, be promoted to Captain, and he was.

M personally signed the recommendations for awards to Agents W.01 (March-Phillipps), W.02 (Appleyard), W.03 (Hayes) and W10 (Guise). All were approved.

Gus March-Phillipps, Agent W.01, was awarded the Distinguished Service Order.

Geoffrey Appleyard, Agent W.02, was awarded a Bar to his Military Cross.

Graham Hayes, Agent W.03 was awarded the Military Cross.

C. A. L. Guise, Agent W10, was awarded an MBE.

Victor Laversuch, Agent W4, was awarded an OBE.

Richard Lippett, Agent W25, was awarded the MBE. The award seems relatively modest when bearing in mind the very significant role that he had played, but, in truth, the full extent and difficulty of what he had achieved was not appreciated until much later.

C. W. Michie, the Vice Consul of Fernando Po, Nigerian Civil Service, was awarded an OBE.

Mr T. Coker, Tugmaster of H. M. Nigerian Marine, was awarded an OBE.

Lieutenant J. Goodman, H. M. Nigerian Marine was awarded an MBE.

Coker and Goodman thoroughly deserved their awards, but they were not allowed for a long time to wear the medals or the medal ribbons, lest they excite comment in the small community that was European West Africa. Indeed, they were not initially gazetted at all in the appropriate publication, the *Nigeria Gazette*. It was not until two and a half years later that this changed. A memorandum to W (by now Louis Franck's successor) on 13 June 1944, emphasized the enduring security concerns: 'The time has not yet come when Goodman or Coker can disclose how they won their decorations, if, indeed, that time ever comes. I see no reason why, after this lapse of time, they should not wear those decorations. After all, these particular decorations are frequently given for good service or gallant conduct over a period of time. . . I would suggest that a notice in the Gazette attributes no date to the service – viz: is merely an announcement of the award of the OBE to Coker, Tugmaster Nigerian Marine, and of the MBE to Goodman, Marine Officer, for services rendered in West Africa. It is perhaps rather unfortunate that we have just missed the King's Birthday, or we might have sandwiched the announcement in with all the others.'

There remained the volunteers from the Colonial Service, who had played such a vital part in the operation. Agent W4, Laversuch, hoped that at least some small souvenir might be given to them as a memento of the raid. In a letter to Caesar on 31 January 1942, he wrote: 'There is another point I would like to mention to you, and that is would it be possible to present each member of the party, including the Headquarters staff at Lagos, with a souvenir? After all, excluding salaries, I do not suppose that the total cost of the whole operation will amount to much more than five or six thousand pounds including the charges, and if you can in any way put this suggestion forward I shall be most grateful. I would suggest a small silver model of a ship or, if this is not possible, a silver cigarette box, not a case, with the simple inscription: "Midnight – 14th January 1942".'

It seemed at first that London was sympathetic to W4's suggestion, and it reached the ears of some of the Government officials in Lagos that a souvenir would be forthcoming. However, the necessary formal permission was never given. W4 did not give up. He was still in Lagos in January 1943, and arranged that a dinner to mark the anniversary of the Postmaster raid should take place on 14 January, to which he invited the personnel involved. Shortly before the dinner, on 12 January 1943, he sent a polite memorandum to SOE London, reminding them that nothing had as yet been received, adding, 'Will it be possible for you to modify my suggestion and send out, say, twenty-five cigarette cases of an approximate value of £5 each so that Government officials (not SOE personnel) would have some small souvenir of the date and some slight recognition of the invaluable services they rendered. If it is felt that public funds cannot be utilised for this purpose, I am sure that the former W [Franck] would be willing to go halves with myself in paying for a souvenir of this kind, and therefore if you cannot see your way clear to fall in line with this suggestion would you please place on order for my account twenty-five cigarette cases inscribed simply with the date 14th January 1942. On receipt of your advices I will send you my cheque for the amount involved.' Sadly, even this modest request fell on stony ground. The enduring concerns that the secrecy of the operation should be maintained effectively killed off the proposal.

As the second anniversary approached, two further reminders reached London. This time one came from Agent W39, Major Dizzy Dismore, now back in England, who although playing a subordinate role had been one of the most senior ranking officers on the raid. In a letter dated 8 January 1944, he pleaded: 'As my ways are now directed into sedentary paths, it would be gratifying to possess such a reminder. . . although it was all in the line of duty, it did involve, you will recall, possible consequences of which the recollection even now evokes a slight constriction of the larynx.'

Agent W4, Laversuch, also now back in England, wrote again on 10 January 1944 reminding SOE that 'the government officials were all volunteers, and indeed, until on the high seas, knew nothing of the job for which they had volunteered'.

Unhappily, still for reasons of security, the matter remained closed.

However, in August 1948, the seventeen civilian volunteers who had joined Maid Honor Force were quietly awarded the Defence Medal. They undoubtedly deserved far more.

Agent W4, Victor Laversuch, had suffered from his extended period of duty in West Africa. He had arrived in Lagos in December 1940 as a part of the original Franck Mission and was confirmed as Head of Mission in June 1942. He stayed until April 1943, by which time his health had been seriously affected by the climate. On his way home, he stopped in Capetown, where he was diagnosed as suffering from a form of malarial infection that necessitated the removal of all his teeth.

Finally and bizarrely, the question arose as to what should happen to the ship's bell from the *Duchessa d'Aosta*. This had for some reason been taken from the ship before she left West Africa, and left behind when she sailed. It was, of course, by then no longer a secret that the *Duchessa d'Aosta* had fallen into British hands. The bell was unmarked, it did not carry the name of the *Duchessa d'Aosta*. It was still apparently languishing in West Africa in June 1944, when somebody there noticed it and enquired as to what its fate should be. Two suggestions were forthcoming in the correspondence between Lagos and London – the first that it should be donated to a local church tower, the second that it should be presented to Major (now Lieutenant Colonel) Laversuch as a memento of Operation Postmaster. The answer eventually came from London that there were enough noisy church bell towers in Nigeria already, and that the bell should be presented to Laversuch (who was now stationed in London).

Operation Postmaster remained a diplomatic hot potato for the remainder of the war and for a very long time afterwards. However, it was not forgotten by those who had taken part in it. In 1948 Tugmaster Coker, who in the *Vulcan* had towed the *Duchessa d'Aosta* all the way back to Lagos, stirred things up by making an application for a reward of prize money in relation to the *Duchessa* and her cargo, which was perfectly acceptable naval practice. A number of others who had been concerned in the seizure of the ships then joined in with him.

Apart from its sensitivity, the situation was unusual due to the irregular means by which the ship had been seized and the irregular Force that had seized it. The Lords of the Admiralty, however, viewed the enterprise as a fine effort and worthy of reward. After much discussion, they finally decided to make monetary awards to all of those who had sailed to Fernando Po with the Operation Postmaster Force. This included the black Africans on both ships, the Colonial Service civilians, the SOE officers and the commandos of Maid Honor Force. The sums to be paid were graded in accordance with the seniority of the personnel and army ranks were translated into the equivalent naval rank.

A detailed and lengthy investigation followed as to the whereabouts of all of the personnel involved or, if deceased, their next of kin. There was also some argument as to who exactly had been a part of the raiding party and who was entitled to a share in the prize money. Richard Lippett, who had done so much to ensure the successful seizure of the ships, was denied a share since he had not been a member of the raiding party itself.

Finally, in early 1950 payments were made. The ship and its cargo had been valued and sold at a total of £286,706. By comparison, the awards were extremely modest, ranging from between £40 to £50 for the senior officers down to £12 12s for the other ranks and black African seamen. The Colonial Civil Servants were paid as though they held the rank of Lieutenant RN, and got £40 19s each. Agent W10, Lieutenant Guise, by now promoted Lieutenant Colonel, did best. Ranked in error on the list of payouts as having been a Lieutenant Colonel at the time of the raid, he received the sum of £47 5s.

The British Government remained extremely sensitive about Operation Postmaster. In 1948 when M, urged on by Ian Fleming, wanted to write an official history of his Secret Service and to do justice to the many heroes within it, he was refused permission. Fleming then invented his fictional agent James Bond in 1952, the tenth anniversary of Operation Postmaster, and the first book came out a year later. However, Fleming remained subject to the Official Secrets Act until his death in 1964 and the embargo on telling the truth of Operation Postmaster and its cover-up far outlived him. At the end of 1969, Henrietta March-Phillipps, who had been conceived only shortly before her father's death and who had never known him, was making plans to broadcast a radio programme about his wartime exploits. M was informed of her plans, and wrote to her mother, his ex-agent Marjorie Stewart, now Lady Marling, saying: 'Operation Postmaster is still a very, very hot potato indeed. From tactful enquiries I have made, no mention of it would receive prior clearance, and mention without prior clearance would be against the Official Secrets Act.' He asked Lady Marling to pass this on to her daughter, and to warn Henrietta not to speak about Operation Postmaster to any foreign journalists.

A row developed between the Foreign and Commonwealth Office (Anthony Eden's old department) and the BBC, which dragged on for three years. Gubbins was allowed to make certain recorded comments for the programme, but only in accordance with careful Foreign Office editing.

Henrietta March-Phillipps and the BBC were determined to continue with the programme, and the Foreign and Commonwealth Office was equally determined that if broadcast, it should contain nothing that would reveal the secrets of Operation Postmaster. On 2 March 1972, over thirty years after Postmaster had been so successfully completed, and with Edward Heath's Conservative Government in power, Dame Barbara Salt, once another of M's agents in SOE and now a high-ranking Civil Servant, wrote to M from the Foreign and Commonwealth Office:

> As you know, the Postmaster discussion with the BBC Radio 4 intention [sic] has long been (and alas still is) dragging on and on. But the present position is that there is a very remote chance the whole programme may yet be dropped. But we cannot count on this, and must therefore assume that it will be broadcast in its unamended form, of which we have the text. . . we cannot, and indeed do not wish, to press them further. But apparently, someone else does! What success they may or may not have we have no idea, and have only made it perfectly clear that the pressure . . . was not inspired by anyone in the Foreign and Commonwealth Office [perfectly true] although we do now know of it and remain neutral in the affair; although naturally in view of what we have already frankly said to them, we would not be displeased were it to succeed.
>
> In fact, we do not think the programme will attract much informed publicity and it would by now, I personally believe, take the long arm of mischance indeed for it to get back to Madrid via any Spaniard who happened to hear and realize its significance in this country.

The letter demonstrates that there was still concern in government circles as to what effect allowing the true story of Operation Postmaster to be told would have. Dame Barbara Salt only hints at the source of the pressure then being put on the BBC not to go ahead with the programme. There were many politicians and Senior Civil servants still alive who had been involved and of course General Franco, Spain's dictator, was still in power. In the event, the programme was broadcast, and the world did not fall in on Whitehall or the British Government. Although as the years went by the veil of secrecy over Operation Postmaster increasingly slipped, the Government embargo on it remained in place until after the collapse of the Soviet Union. Ian Fleming had no chance to tell the full story, and it has been left to a modern historian to do so.

APPENDIX 1

Full list of personnel engaged on Operation Postmaster

This list is compiled from the contemporaneous report submitted by Major Victor Laversuch in January 1942, from the Admiralty's investigations during the prize proceedings after the war, and from the later recollections of those actually involved. All the official lists seem to suffer from error. Lieutenant Duff is missed off Laversuch's list, but undoubtedly took part. Borge Franck is included on the later Admiralty list, but the evidence makes clear that he did not actually take part in the operation. The presumption must be that he was absent sick. In the list of Maid Honor Force personnel, the numbers 01–03 come directly from the contemporaneous reports still available, the numbers 04–011 are in order of rank and then alphabetical order, but do not appear on the written lists.

No record appears to survive as to who the 'three friendly Spaniards' actually were.

Maid Honor Force

W.01 Captain Gustavus H. March-Phillipps
02 Lieutenant J. Geoffrey Appleyard
03 Lieutenant Graham Hayes
04 Lieutenant Leslie E. Prout
05 CSM Tom W. Winter
06 Maître André J. M. Desgranges
07 Private Ernest F. Evison – the unit's cook
08 (Private Borge Franck – absent sick)
09 Private Anders F. E. V. S. Lassen
010 Private Frank C. 'Buzz' Perkins
011 Private W. M. 'Jock' 'Haggis' Taylor, March-Phillipps' batman
012 Private Dennis F. G. Tottenham (ex-Sub Lieutenant RNVR)
013 Unidentified, believed to be Danish

SOE (Lagos)

W10 Lieutenant C.A.L. Guise
W30 Captain D. E. Longe MC
W39 Major L. H. Dismore
Major John Crosthwaite Eyre
W18 Lieutenant R. A. McKenny
W36 Second Lieutenant H. A. Schoofs (Dutch)

Nigerian Marine

(a) ST *Vulcan*
Tugmaster (Chief Warrant Officer) T. C. T. Coker
Lieutenant Duff
Lieutenant Commander J. A. K. Oldland – Chief Engineer
Lieutenant Commander J. O. C. Duffy – Second Engineer
M. G. Hammond – Junior Assistant Fire Superintendent, Grade II

L. Gbadamosi – Junior Assistant Fire Superintendent Grade II
T. Gansallo – Fitter
S. Bassey – Donkeyman
J. Chukuma – Greaser
Peter Ebu – Fireman
MacKintosh – Fireman
New Year – Fireman
T. Obata II – Fireman
J. Ofuokowu – Fireman
M. Borugu – Fireman
A. Anudu – Fireman
D. Atagama – Fireman

(b) MT *Nuneaton*
Lieutenant K. H. Goodman
O. Hanson –Driver, Messrs Elder Dempster Shipping Co. Ltd
Olu David – Second Driver, Messrs Elder Dempster Shipping Co. Ltd

Colonial Service Civilian Volunteers
R. G. Henderson – Senior Assistant Superintendent of Police
H. John Harris – Superintendent of Police, Head of CID, Lagos
D. S. Fountain – Assistant Superintendent of Police
A. Cooper – Assistant Superintendent of Police
V. B. V. Powell – Education Officer
W. T. Mackell – Senior Education Officer
H. H. Jeffers – Acting Principal, Kings College, Lagos
E. R. Ward – District Officer
A. F. Abell – District Officer
W. F. H. Newington – District Officer, Ilaro, later Captain of Bicycle Patrols
E. le Mare – Senior Accountant, Treasury Department
J. W. W. Hallam – Water Mains Superintendent, Public Works Department
D. H. Lawson – Executive Engineer, Grade I
J. W. Tallentine - Executive Engineer, Grade I
F. W. Bailey – Storekeeper, Public Works Department
E. G. Fitt – Legal Assistant, Land and Survey Department
Dr J. G. MacGregor – Specialist, Medical Department

Three 'friendly' Spaniards (names unknown)

In Santa Isabel
W25 Richard Lippett
W51 B. Godden
W53 Peter Ivan Lake
Abelino Zorilla
Vice Consul Alan Michie (until December 1941)

In Lagos
W4 Major Victor Laversuch
W26 G. Sweetman
Mrs Broadbent, Secretary
Mrs Hughes, Cipher Department.

APPENDIX 2

The citations

Captain Gustavus Henry March-Phillipps, MBE, Royal Artillery was awarded the Distinguished Service Order.

Captain March-Phillipps was in command of the operation for the cutting-out of the 10,000 ton Italian liner 'Duchessa', and the smaller German vessels, 'Likomba' and 'Bibundi', which were lying in the neutral harbour of Fernando Po. The Operation took place on the night of 14–15 January 1942.

The operation was of a most delicate and difficult nature, owing to the over-riding necessity of ensuring that no direct evidence of complicity on the part of the British Government or participation by British Forces would be secured by the Spanish or Axis Governments. It was known, moreover, that the 'Duchessa d'Aosta' with her deep draught, was lying in a very narrow channel, any divergence from which would run her aground.

The nucleus of the cutting out party was formed by the crew of the SOE ship, 'Maid Honor', a Brixham trawler of some 60 odd tons which sailed out to West Africa from Poole in September 1941, under the command of Captain March-Phillipps. The crew consisted of five army officers and other ranks, and this successful voyage in a time of war was in itself a considerable feat.

On the night of the operation, when the harbour of Fernando Po had been safely entered, Captain March-Phillipps according to his plan detached Lieutenant G. Hayes and party in one tug to secure the German vessels, while himself in another tug proceeded towards the 'Duchessa d'Aosta.'

Leading the boarding party himself, he leapt on board as soon as the tug had approached sufficiently close, followed by the demolition parties whose task was to blow the holding cables with specifically prepared explosive charges.

All opposition was quickly quelled and the 28 Italians put under guard, while the cables were blown, and the tug's hawser made fast, and the 'Duchessa d'Aosta' got under way. Captain March-Phillipps himself took command from her bridge of navigating her in the dark along a narrow channel. This was successfully accomplished and by daylight the convoy was below the horizon, and after a difficult passage reached Lagos safely.

Captain March-Phillipps displayed military qualities of very high order in his successful execution of this very difficult task, which secured for the British Government a 10,000 ton liner carrying a cargo valued at several hundreds of thousands of pounds, in addition to two smaller but valuable vessels. By his leadership and by his skill in training, planning and navigation, the operation was completed without any effective opposition from the enemy, or any trace of its origin becoming known.

Captain J. G. Appleyard MC, RASC, was awarded a Bar to his Military Cross.

Captain Appleyard was second in command of the operation for the cutting out of the Italian liner Duchessa d'Aosta and the German vessels Likomba and Bibundi at Fernando Po. The operation took place on the night of 14/15 January 1942.

Captain Appleyard led the party which was to blow the forward anchor chains, boarding the liner from the tug which carried his party. Owing to a slight recoil as the tug made contact with the liner in the dark, Captain Appleyard was faced with a rapidly widening gap between the steamer and the tug, and he was the only member of the party to attempt the jump, gaining the steamer's side over a good eight feet of water. He then dealt single-handed with the forward cables until the rest of his party came up. One of the charges failed to explode on the prearranged signal and Captain Appleyard, without waiting to see if the fuse was still burning, laid and blew another charge in less than a minute, thus ensuring the freeing of the liner which was a matter of vital importance. These operations were performed with complete disregard of his own personal safety, and the cutting out of the liner was ensured.

Captain Appleyard then assumed the position of second in command of the captured liner and throughout the voyage of one week displayed initiative and ability to command under circumstances of great difficulty of a very high order indeed.

Lieutenant Graham Hayes, The Border Regiment, was awarded the Military Cross.
For the operation of cutting out the Italian and German ships at Fernando Po on the night of 14/15 January 1942, Lieutenant Graham Hayes was in command of the tug and boarding party to deal with the German vessels Likomba and Bibundi. Lieutenant Hayes led a boarding party of four men in two Folbot canoes across the harbour in the dark and was the first to swarm up the steamer's sides, carrying explosive for the blowing of the cables and armed with an automatic pistol. On being challenged, Lieutenant Hayes made a non-committal answer which gave him time to gain the steamer's deck when the watchmen and crew took flight by diving over the side. With the help of his sergeant, Sergeant Winter, Lieutenant Hayes then laid his charges and blew the forward and after cables, searched and secured the ship and conned her out of the harbour behind the tug to open sea.

Throughout the voyage to Lagos the small tug was constantly breaking down and Lieutenant Hayes on many occasions performed feats of great physical endurance, swimming between the tug and the captured ships and working with heavy five inch hawsers in waters where sharks are very numerous.

Throughout the voyage home, he displayed complete disregard for his personal safety and bodily fatigue.

Lieutenant C. A. L. Guise, General List, was awarded an MBE.
Prior to the seizure of the Italian and German ships lying at Santa Isabel on the night of 14/15 January 1942, Lieutenant Guise was employed as a Foreign Office Courier. He travelled to and from the island of Fernando Po in native craft in all weathers, sometimes in considerable personal danger. In the course of his visits to the island he made a series of extremely valuable personal reconnaissances whose complete accuracy was confirmed subsequently.

He took part in the actual operation. With personal knowledge of the anchorage, he was pilot of the leading tug when the cutting-out vessels entered the harbour. He then ensured the successful approach of the tug Nuneaton manned by Lieutenant Hayes and his boarding party.

Throughout the period of preparation and in the operation itself, Lieutenant Guise did invaluable work. The operation could hardly have been carried out successfully without his most skilful and accurate preliminary reconnaissances.

APPENDIX 2

Captain R. A. J. Lippett, Royal Engineers, was awarded an MBE.
Captain R. A. J. Lippett, R.E., was sent to Fernando Po in the capacity of a Civil Engineer charged with the repair of Messrs. John Holt's buildings. Over a period of months he maintained his cover while making extremely valuable reconnaissances.

His share in the operation was to ensure that as many as possible of the officers and crew of the ships were on shore. In this he was very successful.

It was on him that Spanish suspicion fell. He was refused permission to leave the island and subjected to intensive grilling by police who, however, failed to extract any information from him. Subsequently on his own initiative he took the decision to leave the mainland. After eluding the police supervision for twenty-four hours he had to knock out two policemen in making good his escape. After a dangerous journey of some fifteen hours duration in a small native canoe, he reached the mainland.

His escape to the mainland prevented further enquiry in his direction and relieved a very embarrassing situation.

Major V. Laversuch, Intelligence Corps, was awarded an OBE.
Major Laversuch was largely responsible for the preliminary work and for planning the operation.

In the actual operation he was called upon to accept the disappointing decision that he must stay behind in Lagos in order to co-ordinate its various phases. He was not present therefore to see the plans carried out that he had been responsible for drawing up.

The success of the whole operation, however, was very largely due to his skill, judgement and balance of mind in the preparation.

The operation came as the culminating point of fourteen months service on the coast distinguished by loyalty to the Chief of Mission, and by close co-operation in establishing and organizing two Missions on the West Coast of Africa.

C. W. Michie Esq, Nigerian Civil Service, was awarded an OBE.
Mr Michie was stationed at Santa Isabel as Consul. In the months of intensive preparation for the operation, he was engaged extensively in collecting the information on which plans were based. He was responsible for much careful and thorough preparatory work. In the discussions which preceded the operation he displayed a keen mind and sound judgement.

Although he had been withdrawn from Santa Isabel prior to Postmaster, it was largely due to his cool handling of a difficult situation and to his foresight in the preparatory stages, that the operation was successful.

Mr T. Coker, Tugmaster, H. M. Nigerian Marine was awarded an OBE.
Mr Coker was in charge of the tug, *Vulcan*, as tugmaster and as such conned and manoeuvred his ship throughout the operation. He displayed skill and courage of a very high order indeed, bringing out a ten thousand ton ship through a narrow rock strewn channel and never once displaying the slightest trace of anxiety. Mr Coker contributed very largely to the success of the operation and it is not exaggerating in any way to say that his seamanship was inspired on that occasion and a great credit to the Nigerian Marine Service of which he is a member.

Lieutenant J. Goodman, H. M. Nigerian Marine was awarded an MBE.
Lieutenant Goodman, Nigerian Marine, was in charge of the tug Nuneaton with Captain

Hayes, and conned and manoeuvred his ship throughout the operation. He displayed great skill and courage in performing a very difficult piece of seamanship, and on the week's voyage home, which was one of great hardship for the crew of the small tug, he co-operated most ably with Captain Hayes and was largely responsible for the safe return of his ship and the two German vessels, after constant breakdowns within sight of the Island. Throughout the operation, his coolness, cheerfulness and skill were a constant example to the crew.

APPENDIX 3

Author's note

Ian Fleming's fictional character, James Bond, is now world famous. As a British Secret Agent, licensed to kill, 007 has survived numerous perilous encounters throughout his career, both in the original books and the subsequent films. There has been much speculation as to where Ian Fleming got his original inspiration from for the James Bond character, and a number of books have been published on the subject. It has even been suggested that Bond's M was named after his mother.

When I started my historical researches into the Maid Honor Force and Operation Postmaster, I had no idea that I would stumble across Ian Fleming, the real M, and the inspiration for James Bond. The story of Maid Honor Force is a remarkable one, and forms the first chapter of the history of the Small Scale Raiding Force (SSRF), which Major Gus March-Phillipps went on to found following his return to England in early 1942, after Operation Postmaster had been completed. During my researches, I had the good fortune, unlike many historians before me, of having access to the numerous files held at the National Archives in Kew which record the ramifications of Operation Postmaster, and which are now open to public inspection. I also had the opportunity to inspect a number of collections of documents and photographs donated to the Imperial War Museum after the deaths of Colin Gubbins (M), Gus March-Phillipps, and other persons concerned in Operation Postmaster and the Maid Honor Force.

As I read into those files and collections, I discovered purely by accident the truth about M, Fleming and James Bond. M existed in real life, and ran a real Secret Service (The Special Operations Executive) during the Second World War. Fleming knew all about M's activities, and those of his agents, and worked closely with them. After the war the service was disbanded and by 1952, when Fleming started to write his Bond stories, M and his Secret Service no longer existed (although the ex-M, Major General Sir Colin Gubbins, was still very much alive). Therefore, Fleming obviously felt it safe to borrow the structure and code names of the Special Operations Executive, even though he remained forbidden by the Official Secrets Act to reveal the details of Operation Postmaster itself. When he began to write his Bond stories it was only ten years since Postmaster. Fleming knew that it was still top secret, as it remained until long after his death. In an interview at his Jamaican home Goldeneye, a year or two before his death, Ian Fleming said that 90 per cent of the plots for the stories came from his personal experience and were taken from incidents in the espionage field that had occurred all over the world. He acknowledged, however, that he could not stick too closely to what he had learned in his intelligence work, or else he would be in trouble with the Official Secrets Act.

M's 'good hunting and good luck' telegram to March-Phillipps (W.01), sent on 10 January 1942, still exists within the National Archives in Kew, as does W.01's letter to M of 26 February 1942, after Operation Postmaster had been completed and he had returned to London, recommending Lassen and Hayes for promotion and commending others. A film survives in the Imperial War Museum that shows Agents W.01 and W.02 on board the *Maid Honor* in Poole harbour before their voyage to West Africa.

IAN FLEMING AND SOE'S OPERATION POSTMASTER

Operation Postmaster was carried out from first to last in 'James Bond' style. An anonymous SOE commentator wrote in a report at the time: 'Some day, perhaps, another Froude or better still, another Robert Louis Stevenson, will delight the public with the story of the operation.' Because of the intense secrecy surrounding the operation for many years after the Second World War, that story could not be fully written. Now, it can finally receive the public acclamation that it deserves.

The average James Bond plot can be summarized as: action, intrigue, an exotic location (probably a volcanic island), perhaps a seaborne attack, almost always something being blown up, and a pretty girl or two. Bond is handsome, athletic, physically very tough, an efficient killer with all weapons, an excellent shot, equally at home in the water and on skis, and very patriotic. He is also a great survivor. Bond is willing to regularly put his life at risk for his country – he is cool and resourceful, but has a quiet contempt for authority or the use of 'proper channels'. His personal tastes are for fast cars and the good things in life, in particular dry martinis, bourbon and women, not necessarily in that order. The story of Maid Honor Force, and later the Small Scale Raiding Force, includes all of the elements that Ian Fleming used for his James Bond. Although licensed to kill, during their time in West Africa, and in the carrying out of Operation Postmaster, Maid Honor Force did not need to do so. After their return to Great Britain, that changed, as they took their part in Churchill's 'butcher and bolt' campaign with the Small Scale Raiding Force, proving how effective they were as killers (see the sequel to this book).

Successful characters in fiction that seek to emulate real life dramas are often an amalgam of several real individuals. Those of us who were practising at the Old Bailey in the 1970s could easily recognize amongst our colleagues those whose personality and foibles had been joined together to make up the delightful character of John Mortimer's 'Rumpole of the Bailey'. My personal view is that James Bond was an amalgam of the dashing but fiery March-Phillipps, the cool and controlled Geoffrey Appleyard, the aquatic Graham Hayes and the expert hunter and ladies' man Anders Lassen. Perhaps a dash of the spy Richard Lippett was also thrown into the equation. Each possessed qualities that go to make up Fleming's perfect secret agent, James Bond.

One advantage for Fleming, when he lifted from the story of Maid Honor Force the essential elements of his 'Licenced to Kill' Secret Agent and the organization, headed by M, that was to give Bond his orders and to support him, was of course that nobody would publicly complain. Further, the four particular Secret Agents upon whom I suggest that James Bond was founded were all long dead by the time that Fleming started the books. All had been killed before the end of the Second World War, so nothing he wrote could expose them to danger.

Providing that Fleming stopped short of naming those involved in SOE or Maid Honor Force, and providing that he did not write about the events of Operation Postmaster itself, there was nothing to stop him using SOE's secret commando agents and their boss, Sir Colin Gubbins, as material to model his James Bond and M characters.

It is important to bear in mind certain aspects of Fleming's own character, particularly since he conceded that there was a portion of himself in Bond, and that Bond's dislikes were his dislikes. Fleming was a suave and charismatic womanizer, who enjoyed the good things in life. He liked cards and casinos. He had been a good athlete in his schooldays at Eton, but became a heavy drinker and smoker, both of which undoubtedly shortened his life. He died at the relatively young age of fifty-six. He passed some of his vices on to James Bond. In modern health-conscious times, a reader may conclude that Bond drinks far too much alcohol, and smokes a lot more than is good for him, yet somehow it never affects his performance. This no doubt reflects Fleming's personal input into his perfect Secret Agent.

After his six wartime years in the world of intelligence, there is no doubt that Fleming loved playing with codes and clues. He leaves numerous clues in his Bond stories for those in the know or for later historians to find. Further, there was a streak of cruelty in Fleming's nature, and he enjoyed unkindly teasing a friend. One of his close friends was fellow old Etonian, Anthony Eden, the wartime Foreign Secretary. Eden had, of course, been prominently involved in the international cover-up after Operation Postmaster, and had advanced the 'official lies' contained in the cover story to the Spanish, in order to conceal the breach of international law. Although Fleming had long left Naval Intelligence and turned to journalism by the time he came to write the Bond stories, Anthony Eden had remained in politics. Following a period in opposition during the Labour Government of Clement Attlee, when the Conservatives returned to power in 1951 under Winston Churchill, Eden became a member of the Churchill government. And in April 1955, following Churchill's resignation, Anthony Eden became Prime Minister.

Fleming knew all about Eden's role in the Postmaster cover-up – in effect he had written Eden's script at the time. He knew the potential damage that the story could still do to Eden in the 1950s if it came out. Franco, the Spanish Dictator, was still in power and would be for many years to come. In the year Eden became Prime Minister, Fleming published his third Bond story, *Moonraker*. At the end of the book, M talks to Bond about the cover-up that is being put in place for the operation just completed.

M says, 'Naturally it is going to be a risky business. The big lie always is. But what is the alternative? Trouble with Germany? War with Russia?'

Bond asks dubiously if the press will 'wear the story' and M shrugs his shoulders and says, 'The Prime Minister saw the editors this morning. . . I gather he's got away with it so far. If the rumours get bad later on, he'll probably have to see them again and tell them some of the truth.'

Clearly, Fleming was being rather cruel here. Eden had been in exactly the same position with the real agents, the real M and the Santa Isabel raid in 1942, and the last thing Eden would have wanted now was for that story to come out, exposing him as a liar on the international stage. Fleming may well have seen it as a private joke, but one is bound to wonder whether Eden appreciated it. Of course, Fleming was not breaching the Official Secrets Act by writing his fictional account and involving a fictitious British Prime Minister telling 'the big lie', but was simply discomfiting one friend and no doubt amusing others. If it was a joke at Eden's expense, their friendship survived it. When Eden fell ill the following year, under the strain of the Suez crisis that eventually led him to resign, Fleming lent him his house in Jamaica in which to recuperate. 'In-joke' or not, the *Moonraker* passage demonstrates the way Fleming was drawing upon Operation Postmaster for his Bond material.

Ian Fleming gave James Bond the rank of Commander in the Royal Navy. None of the four men who formed the basis for Bond was a commander, or indeed any sort of official member of the Navy. However, SOE was free with its ranks and promotions, and one is bound to say that had it seemed useful to M to give anyone a particular naval rank, he would have done so. SOE embraced all the Services (they were the Inter Service Research Bureau), and Naval officers worked alongside Army officers and those from the RAF. One of SOE's very successful agents was Commander Gerry Holdsworth. The members of Maid Honor Force were treated in West Africa as members of the Navy, and received supplies and considerable assistance from them. Appleyard, in one of his letters home from Freetown, describes them as being at that stage to all intents and purposes Navy, as indeed they were. They were M's Secret Navy.

Fleming eventually gave his M the rank of Vice Admiral, in *On Her Majesty's Secret Service* (1963), the eleventh Bond book. He also gave M a last ship, HMS *Repulse*, and he makes clear that he only took up the post as M after retiring from the Royal Navy. In *The Man With The Golden Gun*, book number thirteen out of fourteen, published in 1965 after his death, Fleming gave M the name of Sir Miles Messervy. By this time James Bond had become world famous, three films had been made, and a Bond cult existed. Fleming could really write whaetever he liked, short of naming those involved in the real Secret Service – SOE. What he did in his fiction was to continue the existence of SOE after the war, so his M held the post in the 1950s and 1960s. The wartime M had been Sir Colin Gubbins and Fleming clearly could not use his name, but for a successor he could easily appoint a Vice Admiral to replace a Major General. Perhaps it was simply loyalty to his own Senior Service, or perhaps a piece of self-indulgence that led Fleming to make his agent a Royal Naval Commander like himself, and M also ex-Navy.

It has been argued that the prototype for 'M' was Fleming's old boss during his early years in Naval Intelligence, Rear Admiral Godfrey. But Godfrey never used the code name M, and was moved from his job at the end of 1942. Gubbins did use the code name M, ran a Secret Service that contained agents who were licensed to kill, and remained in post throughout the war. It was to Colin Gubbins that Fleming wrote in 1949 urging him to publish 'these great adventure stories'.

After ten years of his fictional life, James Bond announces in *On Her Majesty's Secret Service* in 1963, that he is half Scottish and half Swiss, and that Scotland is 'where I come from'. Yet Bond had started his fictional life as an Englishman. In *Casino Royale* his good friend Mathis describes Bond to others and to his face as an Englishman, and Bond does not protest. However, when the first Bond film came out in 1962, he was played by the Scot, Sean Connery, whom Ian Fleming liked and approved of. The Bond films were commercially successful from the start and Fleming, by giving Bond some Scottish blood in 1963, was simply giving Sean Connery a helping hand and making the films more convincing. Ian Fleming was quite happy to change his plots where he thought it was sensible to do so – they were fiction after all, however real the source of inspiration.

An interesting example of such a change of storyline is in relation to James Bond's first long-term personal weapon, a .25 Beretta. The Beretta appears in *Casino Royale*, when Bond carries it in a light chamois leather holster. In *Dr No* (1958), Bond tells M, 'I've used a Beretta for fifteen years.' When M insists that Bond change his weapon, Bond claims that the Beretta is his preferred weapon for close-up work and concealment, and is reluctant to give it up. M insists, and Bond is given a Walther PPK 7.65mm, which he carries thereafter and which 'packs a bigger punch'.

Fleming himself clearly did not know very much about the .25 Beretta. Why therefore choose it as Bond's personal gun? The answer can only be because Anders Lassen, the supreme hunter/killer of Maid Honor Force, carried a Beretta. Lassen would kill with any weapon, including knives and the longbow. He would customarily carry an arsenal of weapons on his person when going on a mission. Apart from any pistols holstered at his waist, he would carry a Beretta secreted in the waistband of his trousers, in the small of his back. It was his secret pistol of choice. Lassen had no scruples that prevented him from killing at close range, or when in physical contact with his victim. Fleming's use of the Beretta for James Bond suggests that he must have known this, even though he obviously didn't know enough about the pistol itself to know it was a 'last resort' weapon, and that Lassen carried it for that purpose.

Having armed Bond with the Beretta in his first book, Fleming attracted the criticism of a real-life firearms expert, Geoffrey Boothroyd. Boothroyd wrote to Fleming that in his professional view the .25 Beretta was a ladies' gun, and did not carry sufficient stopping power for a secret agent to carry as his only personal weapon. He recommended that in future books, Bond should carry the heavier hitting Walther PPK. Fleming duly adopted the suggestion, and also abandoned Bond's chamois leather holster, which Boothroyd told him was not appropriate, due to the danger that the gun might catch on the material when being drawn. In *Dr No*, when Bond changed to a Walther PPK, Fleming paid Boothroyd the compliment of including him in the plot, naming him as 'Major Boothroyd, the greatest small arms expert in the world'.

Ian Fleming is no longer with us, and the speculation about his M and James Bond will no doubt continue into the future. However, the remarkable story of the Maid Honor Force and Operation Postmaster is entirely true and Fleming played a significant part in it. He met the men of Maid Honor Force, and visited them and their ship in Poole harbour. He played a vital part in helping M to obtain permission from the Admiralty for the Maid Honor Force to go to West Africa and in November 1941 helped M to obtain clearance for Operation Postmaster itself from the Admiralty. In January 1942, he wrote the cover story that was to be used at Government level.

Gus March-Phillipps, owner of a splendid Bond-style car, the Velox 30/98 Tourer, had much in common with Ian Fleming, and was an inspirational 'action man'. Most interestingly perhaps, March-Phillipps had himself created a perfect Bond-style hero in John Sprake, in a novel called *Ace High*. Can there be any doubt that March-Phillipps, the established novelist, would have gone on to write more 'James Bond' stories had he survived the war? In tribute to him, I have included *Ace High* as the first of the Bond books listed in Appendix 4.

Where else did Fleming need to look for the inspiration behind his James Bond?

APPENDIX 4

The James Bond stories

The Books
Ace High by Gus March-Phillipps (1939), published by MacMillan & Co Ltd, London
Casino Royale (1953)
Live and Let Die (1954)
Moonraker (1955)
Diamonds are Forever (1956)
From Russia with Love (1957)
Dr No (1958)
Goldfinger (1959)
For Your Eyes Only (1960)
Thunderball (1961)
The Spy Who Loved Me (1962)
On Her Majesty's Secret Service (1963)
You Only Live Twice (1964)
The Man with the Golden Gun (1965)
Octopussy/The Living Daylights (1966)

The Bond Films made during Fleming's lifetime:
Dr No (1962)
From Russia with Love (1963)
Goldfinger (1964)

APPENDIX 5

Source material

(A) Files held at the National Archives

There are numerous files now open at the National Archives, Kew, that touch upon Maid Honor Force and Operation Postmaster. The individual contents of the files are rarely indexed, but simply run in chronological order. The author sets out below what are, in his view, the most important of the files, and summarizes the relevant topic or topics that each deals with. This list is not exhaustive, but will provide a researcher with all of the core information. A number of obviously relevant files (particularly SOE personnel files) still remain closed.

ADM 116/5736	The Prize Court Proceedings/Salvage file for the *Duchessa d'Aosta*, material re *Likomba* (*Malakal*), *Bibundi* (*Kalomo*), crew of *Duchessa* etc, Coker's report on Operation Postmaster
ADM 199/653	Admiral Willis's War Diary, January 1942
ADM 223/257	Ian Fleming's role in Naval Intelligence
ADM 223/480	A description of the *Maid Honor* and her armaments, Royal Naval approval for her transfer to West Africa, suggestion that she returns home 14/10/41, and references to Fleming and Goldeneye
ADM 223/481	Ian Fleming liaising with SOE
ADM 223/500	30 Assault Unit, and Ian Fleming's involvement with it
AIR 8/897	Operation Savannah
AVIA 22/1588	SOE's special gadgets department
CAB 121/522	Giffard instructed to look at possibility of invading Fernando Po.
CO 323/1800/1	Information on Germans who went to Fernando Po from Tiko at the outbreak of war, *Bibundi* and *Likomba* were the names of plantations
CO 537/4286	Grant of defence medals to civilians on Postmaster in 1948
CO 967/117	Governor Bourdillon's views of General Giffard
DEFE 2/1093:	Anthony Eden re the fate of the *Duchessa*
FO 369/2711:	Lake and Michie, Lake's appointment to Fernando Po, and his CV
FO 371/1171	The arrival of a new Governor of Fernando Po to replace Soraluce, and Spanish reinforcements in 1942 after Postmaster
FO 371/26922	Michie's weekly reports, German invasion of Consulate
HS 3/72	Franck, his arrival in Lagos, etc.
HS 3/73	The setting up of SOE Nigeria, NEUCOLS/FRAWEST, includes a report on Operation Postmaster.
HS 3/74	General Giffard describes SOE as a 'menace to the safety of the colony on 23/3/42
HS 3/77	Useful maps, and late 1942 report on Fenando Po
HS 3/86–93	Contain the essential information about the planning and carrying out of Operation Postmaster: HS 3/87 includes M's 'good hunting' cable; HS 3/89 includes the specifications of the *Duchessa*

	d'Aosta; HS 3/91 and 92 contain detailed reports on the operation from a number of those involved.
HS 3/96	Includes a report on the arrival of Operation Postmaster in Lagos
HS 6/345	Operation Savannah
HS 7/22	Contains a further report on Operation Postmaster
HS 7/27	Full history of SOE's gadgets department under Newitt, and many of their inventions, and reports on their work in progress.
HS 7/47	SOE's catalogue of special devices
HS 7/210	SOE's instructions on how to fake illnesses and deal with the doctor's questions
HS 8/115	SOE/OSS liaison
HS 8/218	HQ progress reports on the Maid Honor, what employment for the *Duchessa d'Aosta* once in British hands? Lobbito raid abandoned.
HS 8/244	General Giffard abandons plan for raid on Fernando Po 7/2/43
HS 8/946	Fernando Po did not want to fall out with the British because they relied very heavily on Nigerian labour.
HS 9/48/1	Appleyard's personnel file
HS 9/426/8	Desgranges' personnel file
HS 9/434/5	Dismore's personnel file
HS 9/518/5	Peter Fleming's personnel file
HS 9/538/2	Franck's personnel file
HS 9/630/8	Gubbins personnel file
HS 9/652/2	Hannau's personnel file
HS 9/680/5	Hayes' personnel file
HS 9/877/5	Lake's personnel file
HS 9/888/2	Lassen's personnel file
HS 9/895/3	Laversuch's personnel file
HS 9/937/8	Longe's personnel file
HS 9/1183/2	March-Phillipps' personnel file
KV 4/309	Lagos paid scant attention to black-outs
WO 106/5201	Order to General Giffard to cooperate with SOE
WO 193/1003	Franck Mission (W Section)

(B) The Imperial War Museum

Documents:

12618 Gubbins Collection	Box 04/29/8
12792 Major D. E. Longe Collection	Box 03/54/1
15029 Lieutenant Colonel D. J. Keswick Collection	Box 06/22/1
14857 Major March-Phillipps Collection	Box 06/103/2
14319 F. C. Perkins Collection	

Film and Video Archive:
MGH 4321

The L. H. Dismore Collection 9106-01

Audio Recordings: Lady Marjorie Marling: 12306
David John Coleman: 8673
Henrietta March-Phillipps *et al.*: 8321

(C) Bibliography

Appleyard, J. E. (1946) *'Geoffrey'*, Blandford Press
Beevor, J. G. (1981) *SOE Recollections and Reflections*, Bodley Head
Boyce, F. and Everett, D. H. (2009) *SOE – The Scientific Secrets*, Sutton Publishing
Butler, E. (1963) *Amateur Agent*, George Harrap
Fairbairn, W. E. (1942) *All-In Fighting,* republished by the Naval and Military Press
Fournier, G. and Heintz, A. (2006) *If I must die*, Orep
Kemp, Peter, (1958) *No Colours or Crest*, Cassell
Langley, Mike (1988) *Anders Lassen V.C., M.C., of the SAS*, New English Library
Lassen, Suzanne (1965) *Anders Lassen VC*, English edition. Frederick Muller
March-Phillipps, Gus (1939) *Ace High*, Macmillan and Co. Ltd
Messenger, Charles (1985) *The Commandos*, Kimber
Rankin, Nicholas (2011) *Ian Fleming's Commandos*, Faber and Faber
Warwicker, John (2008) *Churchill's Underground Army*, Frontline Books
Wilkinson, Peter and Astley, Joan Bright (1993) *Gubbins and SOE*, Leo Cooper

Index

Tracing Your Family History?

Read

Your Family HISTORY

ESSENTIAL ADVICE FROM THE EXPERTS

FREE COPY

Your Family History is the only magazine that is put together by exper genealogists. Our editorial team, led by Dr Nick Barratt, is passionate about family history, and our networks of specialists are here to give essential advice, helping readers to find their ancestors and solve thos difficult questions.

In each issue we feature a **Beginner's Guide** covering the basics for those just getting started, a **How To** … section to help you to dig deeper into your family tree and the opportunity to **Ask The Experts** about your tricky research problems. We also include a **Spotlight** on different county each month and a **What's On** guide to the best fam history courses and events, plus much more.

Receive a free copy of *Your Family History* magazine and gain essential advice and all the latest news. To request a free copy of a recent back issue, simply e-mail your name and address to marketing@your-familyhistory.com or call 01226 734302*.

Your Family History is in all good newsagents and also available on subscription for six or twelve issues. Fo more details on how to take out a subscription, call 01778 392013 or visit **www.your-familyhistory.co.uk**.

Alternatively read issue 31 online completely free using this QR code

*Free copy is restricted to one per household and available while stocks last.

www.your-familyhistory.com